DIVERTIKA

Dedicated to Leonard Dietz, Brian Kent, Alan MacKay
& Joseph Francis.

And to all heroes of diversity.

DIVERTIKA

Edited by Steve McLeod and Gerry North

D

Published in 1995 by City Media Production Services
122 Bourke Street Wooloomooloo NSW 2011 Australia
PO Box 1494 Potts Point NSW 2011
Telephone (02) 368 1462

Cover Illustration by Nigel Buchanan

Publisher's note: Some of the selections are works of fiction.
Names, characters, places and incidents are either product's of
the author's imagination, or are used fictitiously, and any
resemblance to actual persons, living or dead, events or
locales is entirely coincidental.

Printed by Southwood Press Pty Ltd, Marrickville, NSW.
Typesetting & layout by Write Design. Tel: (02) 569 4782.

ISBN 0 646 20748 2

ACKNOWLEDGEMENTS

Special thanks to the readers: Ruth Dewsbury & Craig Hassall and photographer Eros Candusso, for works especially undertaken for Divertika.

This publication was proudly supported and made possible with the assistance of:

Sydney Gay & Lesbian Mardi Gras

The Sydney Star Observer

Campaign Magazine

Queensland Pride

Brother/Sister – Melbourne

Adelaide GT

West Side Observer

Xtra West – Vancouver

Pink Paper – London

Boyz – London

OUT – New York

CONTENTS

MOUSTACHE

Richard Gohl

M R. AND MRS. BAKER LIVED IN A
rural outpost in the middle of South Australia. They had spent their nine years of
married life in an old but spacious government home. Thirty other people lived in
the district which existed purely because of the railway line that dissected it and Mr.
Baker worked in the railway office from nine to five. Mrs. Baker occasionally
worked behind the bar at the local pub and sometimes prepared sandwiches for the
railway workers but aside from these chores she mainly kept herself busy running
the house, which she did very well. Her other main interest was her garden, which
considering the climate, was wonderfully fertile and produced a most succulent
array of vegetables which supplemented their and the district's otherwise bland diet.

Mrs. Baker was now well into her forties, just how well it is perhaps unnecessary
to say but she had, in the last ten years, begun to notice a certain thickening of the
hair above her upper lip. Like most people, she had always been rather hairy and
Mrs. Baker was also very dark, thus whatever hair she did have tended to register its
presence all the more strongly. Had she heard snickering remarks behind hands as

*Richard Gohl lives in Adelaide with a lovely view of the hills and a charming bitumised road. Preferring to live
on his own, he feels the dirty dishes from Coco Pops and two minute noodles are nobody's business but his. He
has had 'smatterings' of written work accepted in various Adelaide publications. He is a writer, musician and a
sometime childcare worker. He believes in diversity; total freedom of expression in artistic and practical senses.
"If its okay for the U.N., it is okay by me. The greater the wealth of experience and expression 'spread' before the
world, the greater the world."*

she worked behind the bar at the hotel ? It is difficult to say, as Mrs. Baker was not a vain woman and she therefore would never have suspected such attention. However for some reason, one morning, she began studying her face in the bathroom mirror, as people sometimes do, and the darkness and abundance of her facial hair suddenly struck her as being unacceptable. With little more ado she reached for her husband's razor in the cabinet, lathered up some cream on her face, and began shaving. The fine, long hairs slipped off very easily and she found that she had to rinse the razor four of five times in order to unclog the twin blades of the virgin whiskers. To her surprise and joy the skin underneath was beautifully smooth and white. She rinsed with warm water and then padded her face dry. The skin felt as though it was new and was so soft and sensitive that she couldn't help trying it with her fingers for the rest of the day.

Her husband arrived home that night at the usual time and to Mrs. Baker's surprise he didn't say anything about the absence of her moustache at all. He ate his meal and as usual went off to the hotel for several beers before returning at nine-thirty to watch television and smoke his pipe, until he fell asleep by ten-thirty. Mrs. Baker gave him a shove and he awoke with his usual grunt and shuffled off to bed.

After Mr. Baker left for work the next morning Mrs. Baker went into the bathroom to check on her beautiful new flesh. However as she ran her index finger slowly across the thin piece of skin below her nose she noticed a faint shadow where the whiteness had been. She made small brushing movements upwards with her finger and the tiny whiskers made a sandy, scratchy sound. Once again Mrs. Baker took her husband's razor and carefully shaved away the shadow. She then went into her bedroom and, removing her night gown, began to dress for the day. She began looking through her husbands draws and removed a pair of his clean and pressed 'Y' fronts. She loved the feel of the cotton and especially the soft thickness of the material. She put them on. She had never done this before and said to herself that they seemed more practical then her own, "..warmer or something," she thought. Indeed they fitted snugly enough, and putting on an old dress over the top, she wore them as she went about her work for the rest of the day.

That evening when Mr. Baker arrived home from work he began eating his dinner and as he looked up at his wife sitting across the table from him he spluttered out some mashed potato and said "What have you done !"

"What?" said Mrs. Baker, swallowing a piece of schnitzel.

"Here," he said sucking in his top lip and pointing below his nose. "I shaved," she said.

"You used my razor?" he asked.

"Yes."

"Oh." he replied. He stared at it for a while and then started nodding slowly as if in approval. They finished the rest of their meal in silence.

The next morning Mr. Baker seemed to have forgotten about his wife's recent hairlessness and hurried off to work with his lunchbox and briefcase. After cleaning away the breakfast dishes, Mrs. Baker again looked at her face in the bathroom mirror. What had yesterday been a shadow was today a thin rough line of whiskers. She was intrigued by the rapid change. "I'm alive," she thought, "my face is growing." Her thumb and forefinger moved in and out from opposite sides of her moustache, much in the way that she had often observed her husband doing when attempting to give the impression that he was deep in thought. Mrs. Baker decided not to shave her moustache and going into the bedroom selected some of her husband's overalls. She put them on and spent several hours working out in the garden.

At about one o'clock that day Mrs. Baker came inside for her customary 'light lunch' and after showering she went into her bedroom to change. Going through her clothes she found none of them satisfactory, especially after noticing an old brown pin-striped suit of her husband's. She immediately unhooked it off the rack and began putting it on. The pants initially seemed slightly oversized but after some adjustment and a pair of braces they fitted like a charm. A lovely paisley waistcoat went on over a white shirt and Mrs. Baker then selected a diagonally striped tie which, after slipping on the rather cumbersomely cut jacket, set off the outfit perfectly. Finally, she put on a pair of thin black socks and some shoes of her husbands which had originally been brown but had been so highly polished that they now appeared red. Mrs. Baker was not one to skimp on fine detail and selected the more appropriate of her husband's two hats.

As Mrs. Baker began to stroll around the house she decided that it was the tight waistcoat and shoes that were making her walk differently. The broad souls and heels were making her lean back more than she usually did when she walked and as she slipped both her hands into the coat pocket this somehow balanced her out more evenly and she achieved a very stylish gait up the hallway and around the house. She strode straight out the back door and into the garden and swaggered around there for ten minutes, enjoying the rhythm of her new walk until she heard a car pull up out in the street. She realised that this was probably her husband being dropped off from work, so she ran inside throwing all her clothes off and onto coat hangers in the cupboard.

As Mr. Baker entered their bedroom he saw his wife, as he hadn't seen her for some time, standing naked in front of the mirror apparently selecting something to wear.

"Put some clothes on love," said Mr. Baker.

"Oh hello dear. How was your day?"

"Are you going somewhere?"

"No I just stepped out of the shower. I've been out in the garden all day."

Mr. Baker sat on the bed and removed his shoes.

"Are you going to come and watch the big game tonight, down at the pub?"

"I don't think I'll have time dear. I was going to make all that apricot jam tonight."

"Oh right. Well don't worry about tea for me. I'll have a counter meal down the pub. Love. What are you doing? Put some clothes on ey?"

"Oh I don't know what to put on anymore, my clothes are all so old and drab."

"What's wrong with them?"

"I'm just fed up with them that's all." Mrs. Baker turned on the bedroom light and suddenly her husband exclaimed, "What the hell...I thought you'd taken care of that hair lip thing!"

"No it just keeps growing back. I think I'll leave it alone from now on."

"Well you can't just leave it like that. It's more pronounced than mine!"

Mrs. Baker looked contemplatively at herself in the mirror. "You think so?" she asked.

"Well it's getting bloody close. If people see you out in the backyard like that they'll think your brother Ian's come up from Adelaide. You're starting to look more and more like him every day with that thing."

"Well he is my brother..."

"Or are you his brother, it's getting bloody hard to tell."

Mrs. Baker just looked at her reflection in the mirror while Mr. Baker pulled on a jacket and said "Well I'm off, back about ten."

Mrs. Baker slept well that night and didn't even hear her husband arrive home from the pub. It was just as well, as the next day was a busy one. Mrs. Baker was rostered to make twenty sandwiches for the hotel by around midday for some rail workers who were coming through the station. She got this done early and delivered them to the hotel, leaving the package on the bar. As she turned to go, Mrs. Baker saw Vera, the bar manager, who said to her, "Bakes darling, what on earth are you cultivating there?" Mrs. Baker became slightly embarassed but then more annoyed at the nosey publican. Vera continued, "Listen love why don't you come around and have that waxed. I'll do it for free."

"Waxed?" replied Mrs. Baker.

"Yes, I'll pull them all out, won't take a minute."

"Thanks, Vera, but I can look after my own face."

"Only trying to help."

After she arrived home, Mrs. Baker went straight into the bathroom to look in the cabinet mirror at what had caused Vera to say something about which she had never said anything before. Indeed her moustache was more pronounced than ever. She noticed the other hairs on her cheeks and chin. There were some fine, black and quite long hairs there. Mrs. Baker much preferred the shorter, darker whiskers and proceeded to shave her fine cheek bones and rather pointed chin. The flesh looked younger without this down and the chin much firmer without the straggly hairs. She left the moustache, which was growing wonderfully well in two thin lines leading away from each nostril and slightly raised at each end. She gave her right jaw line, just below the ear where she'd missed a spot, an extra going over. Accidentally, she turned the head of the razor slightly, the skin buckled under the blade and she felt a sting. Rinsing the blade, she saw a small smudge of blood and realised she had cut herself. She washed the cut clean and looked on in shock as the blood seaped out again even faster, like a puddle of red ink. Making sure the water was cold she wet a cotton ball and pressed firmly on her jaw bone. She held it there for a minute and wiped it away clean. The blood was gone and she could see the tiniest little gash. It winked at her and squeezed out a tear of blood. "Shit !" said Mrs. Baker, as it started running again. She ripped off a small piece of toilet paper, as she had noticed on her husband's face before, and placed it over the cut. The blood spread in a small circle and then stopped. Mrs. Baker waved air onto it with her hand in an attempt to dry out the cut once and for all. After flapping her hand over it for a while she slowly, slowly began peeling the little piece of tie - dye toilet paper from her face. With a gentle tug it was off and immediately it began bleeding again. Mrs. Baker groaned. Then she ran into her bedroom and got her hair dryer. She wiped away the blood and turned it on, furiously blowing hot air onto the cut. This did not work at all and only spread the blood back towards her ear. "Right!" she said and wiped the blood away again, padded it dry with a towel and started squirting fine jets of talcum powder over it. This blocked the hole for a moment but it soon came oozing out in a gluggy mix. "AHHH!" she yelled. Finally, washing her face again, she put on another piece of toilet paper and promptly forgot about it.

Mrs. Baker made a cup of tea and went outside to water her garden. Half an hour later she got some water from the hose and sprinkled it on her face and rolled the toilet paper off with her finger. "Hooray," she thought.

Mrs. Baker soon went back inside to check her wound. It now looked nothing more than a scratch. It was a scratch. Why then did it bleed so much, she wondered.

One of the many mysteries of the face, she supposed. Along with the moustache, she thought, there's another one. Mrs. Baker looked at the untidy wisps of black hair on her head with disdain. She pulled it back in a bun. Letting it all hang out again, she grabbed an old jar of hair mousse from the cupboard and began applying it liberally. She massaged it into her hair and then ran a comb through it, slicking it back tightly against her scalp. Moving back into her bedroom, she again removed from the cupboard her husband's hat, suit and shoes and put them on. She strolled around the house and went into the lounge to see how she looked in front of the large wall mirror. "I suppose I do look a bit like Ian," she thought, "but unfortunately I'm too much myself to really look like anyone else." Mrs. Baker was not worried by what she perceived as 'her plainness,' and was in fact quite content with her new look. So much so she headed off to the general store to pick up some groceries, a paper for her husband and some cigarettes, as she had decided to take up smoking again.

The several people she saw as she walked to the shop were not sure who she was and tried to stare inconspicuously as they attempted to work it out. Undeterred Mrs. Baker did her shopping and spoke only to the manager, Mrs. Wilson, at the checkout counter. "Going to some sort of fancy dress are we. It's all very effective. I wasn't sure who you were there for a minute."

"How are you?" asked Mrs. Baker.

"Oh very well thanks. Is there something on tonight I don't know about?"

"No I don't think so."

"Oh," replied the confused shopkeeper.

"How much is all that?"

"Er, that all comes to eighteen dollars." The money changed hands and Mrs. Baker picked up her shopping and said, "thanks, bye."

Once home Mrs. Baker made herself a cup of tea and decided to read the paper from cover to cover. She couldn't think why she wanted to do this but started reading anyway. She lit a cigarette and put her feet up on the table, trying to get comfortable. "These cigarettes are horrid," she thought, taking an extra draw to be sure. Instead Mrs. Baker decided to smoke something she was a little more familiar with and took her husband's pipe and tobacco from the lounge room into the kitchen, sat down with her red shoes on the table again, and started puffing away while she read. She became so engrossed in the world news section that she did not hear her husband arriving home from work. As he walked in, he paused for a moment then yelled:

"Ian! Why don't you make yourself at home mate?" he said, putting down his bag and laughing. "We were just talking about you last night, how are you mate?

This is uncanny. What brings you out here?"

Mrs. Baker was stunned and thought, "My husband cannot act! He really thinks..."

"Just passing through," she said in a deeper voice, playing along.

"Where's my wife, have you any idea?" said Mr. Baker, sidling up to her.

"Out I expect."

"Well I guess that doesn't leave us much time."

Mr. Baker grabbed her head in his hands and began moving his tongue around in her mouth in a way that she had not known him to do in a very long time. He then pulled his wife up out of her seat and gently pushed her back forcing her to sit on the kitchen table. He knelt down and began undoing the fly of her pants. He reached inside but suddenly, as though he had received an electric shock, whipped his hand out and flung his head back to look into his wife's eyes. Mr. Baker looked shocked and as he slowly got to his feet he said, "Ian?"

"Yes?" said Mrs. Baker.

Photo: Lisa Zanderigo

Photo: Eros Candusso

DINNER PARTY NO. 1
The Pragmatic Approach to Elizabeth Taylor

David Dakar

I have a very pragmatic approach toward Elizabeth Taylor. It's cost me a few friends, but I have no intention of revising my position. What Liz does well, she does very well. But while in, say, 'The VIPs,' when Orson Welles dons a one – dimensional caricature, he still acts circles around the Taylor school of trauma drama. Nevertheless, who else but Taylor could don an organic-looking Givenchy mink hat, as though at the touch of something barbaric Liz would retract inward and leave just the mushroom cap fur perched on her shoulders? Who else but Givenchy could design something so uncomplimentary to the female form and who else but Ms Taylor could carry it off?

I want to make it clear that I don't hate Elizabeth Taylor; neither do I hate the British for colonising about seven–tenths of the globe. They are both elements of my capitalist cultural heritage, but there are residual effects of both which can't be ignored. Let's take Elizabeth's breasts. How many well–endowed actresses survive a

David Dakar lives in Vancouver, Canada, with his lover. He travelled the globe for many years until the lure of hot water, electricity and clusters of literate queers in urban areas enticed him back to his place of origin.

According to David, his relationship shows no signs of deteriorating or otherwise waning, save for the threat of ill-health. Provided he buys his lover a constant stream of china, he lets him write which according to David is an act of love in itself.

David has previously been published with a recent inclusion in Dennis Denisoff's anthology 'Queeries,' Arsenal Pulp Press, 1993.

"I feel privileged to be included in 'Divertika,' not just because having my fiction published is good news, but because Australia means (meant) so much to me. I've always thought leaving was a mistake and that I should have stayed illegally when my visa ran out. Hindsight is 20/20, memories have little discretion, and all that."

lifetime in Hollywood? It just doesn't happen; breasts have an inversely negative relationship with career survival. The larger your breasts, the more prone you are to suicide, decapitation, role extinction. Do I need to supply examples? The movies do not sustain endowed females. Similarly, all that divide and conquer, indirect rule and mercantilist trade spread thin dealt Britain a crushing blow in the Twentieth Century. But Britain survived. And Liz survives. It's what I believe characterises this survival that gets me into hot water at cocktail parties.

As with any good political ideology, Liz is a force to be reckoned with, read about, talked about and taken seriously. Consequently, persons of dissimilar intellectual persuasions have adored her with varying degrees of political acumen. Some argue that she represents a cogent use of self–promotion to further a nationalist rationale. Others, such as myself, note what a fine example of classic liberalism she makes:

a) she is a jetsetter who travels the globe as a free and equal individual encapsulating a theoretical world absent of political boundaries and social constraints;

b) she exploits economic returns through contract negotiations, multiple marriages and, in later life, overcoming marginal opportunity cost with economic expansion into perfume;

c) and her movies offer aggregate social benefit; she is, perhaps, the archetypal individual able to maximise return from scarce resources (which is a fancy way of saying that 'Butterfield 8' was a really silly movie, yet she still took home an Oscar).

It must be said, too, there is an element of Marxism in Liz, and any objective critique should include it – although I personally don't adhere to Marx (and this has repeatedly cost me the opportunity to engage in radical sex with tortured, tempting agitprop pros or simply sustain friendships with elegant near–fascist designer queens. The spread between Marx and Mussolini is not as great as most imagine).

Here are the basic left–wing assumptions: Liz's production and distribution of wealth is at the centre of her public and political life. It's true, and not unfair to say, that at her zenith she may have overproduced particular types of goods (say, numerous mediocre film performances). And, although by public accounts her net capital wealth hasn't deteriorated, if there was ever a falling rate of anything in her public persona it was a lack of good roles and then her screen absence for many years. I have no idea whether Liz saved – the tabloid press would have us believe she spent wildly – but she certainly invested and accumulated. And it must also be said that if competition forced Liz to increase her efficiency at the risk of extinction, she took every measure, from scrubbing floors at the Betty Ford to surgical upgrades, simply to maintain her marketability. And maintain she has.

For many Taylor aficionados their blind idolatry of the lady had led them down the Marxist path. Some Marxist–Lizabeths act as though they are a supreme holy tribunal on all things Liz. "To hell with positivists, relativists, pragmatists and their ilk," I hear them state. "A star is at stake." It's here that I part company with many adoring fans. The transformation of Liz from film star to international superstar to living legend was, it's true, an example of enormous exportation – the media ensured that her image preceded her wherever she went – and this led to a process of uneven growth. While I can't dispute her uneven output, I take a more realistic outlook towards the cause. There was simply conflict between any number of rising and declining stars, and as all these players sought to improve or maintain their relative positions in the international superstar hierarchy Liz was a victim of the tendency for unevenness. It may be unpopular in academic circles to say something so forward and obviously un–left, but I feel the leftist view is too attached to a Liz that doesn't really exist; the left has tended to fabricate Liz to meet any number of personal agendas. (Of course we all know about the power of the agenda setter.) The left also claims that as Liz became an international celeb there was a correspondent increase in personal insecurity and interrelationship conflict. They cite Eddie Fisher right alongside 'The Egyptian': This is just leftist hokum. A distinction must be drawn between Taylor the person and Taylor the commodity. A Marxist will mistakenly tell you that a superstar can neither reform nor eliminate her worst features. But take the 1980s. Liz, the ultimate liberal legend, increased her productivity, modified her disproportionality and increased consumer demand – all without starring in a general release movie! This is my pragmatic view of Elizabeth Taylor. Catch me later for trickle–down Taylor economics...

As I said, this pragmatic view has cost me a few friends. The first friend it cost me was Percy. He was an elegant queen, when I met him, in his twenties, of the sort that tended to mature top down; that is, unlike a beer in which the froth settles after a time, Percy increased in forth and decreased in substance. I had seen Percy in nightclubs, at a distance, and caught his cologne as he'd breezed by me in malls. I always liked his fashion sense, so I made the rash judgment that I would like him, too. I picked him up in a bar, he introduced me to numerous other elegant hommes, then it petered out.

At the height of the relationship, after a week of getting to know each other better, of getting to know each other too well, we attended a private function. The host's name was Max; he owned a Gehry cardboard dining suite. It was also apparent that at one time Max had owned Percy. We three and four others [flight attendants] were the group, all affecting a very relaxed disposition in a sunny room with the doors open to the balcony and the fall air sailing in and urban birds cawing in their loud and irritating way and the smell of freesias wafting though the apartment along with a haze of smoke that came illegally to Canada as diplomatic cargo and Ute Lemper singing lesser–known show tunes on a Bang and Olufson stereo. No sooner were we seated, acquainted, and all initially assessed as future sexual partners, when Liz came up. She's popular in conversation.

Our host told us that he had managed to get a pirate copy of the original 'Reflections in a Golden Eye,' which was, so he said, released in gauzy sepia tones, before being re–released in standard colour. This immediately started animated group chat about Brando playing a repressed homo, and Max mimicking Marlon applying cold cream. Then we talked about sexy male actors of the fifties –Marlon Brando, Paul Newman, Montgomery Clift, Rock Hudson, John Gavin...

Percy got little disagreement when he noted that "It's hard to choose whether Clift and Taylor, in 'A Place in the Sun,' are better looking than Taylor and Newman in, 'Cat on a Hot Tin Roof,' and although most people choose Cat, because of the glorious Technicolour, Clift was really the best looking actor for about twenty post–war years." Even I have a hard time trying to pry apart the early Clift from the early Newman on a scale of sexiness and charisma. But by the time, 'Raintree County,' rolled by, with Clift half handsome/half disfigured, well Newman starts to come out ahead. But since I was new to these young well–to–do queers, I attempted to keep my abrasive self to a minimum, and agreed with the group.

We all began making good–natured remarks about how much we hated, 'A Place in the Sun,' but couldn't get enough of it. I made an embarrassingly disparaging remark about Liz's performance, which didn't go down well. During the ensuing pregnant pause, Max poured more drinks. As he did so, skillfully drawing attention away from me, I ignorantly added that, 'A Place in the Sun,' is the movie Halliwell said was so clearly intended to be a great film it couldn't be boring, which Percy, already on the defensive over my previous comment, took to be a slight against Taylor, rather than a humorous addendum, and then despite what Max did the sparks began to fly.

"Well Halliwell was a jerk and what right did he have to go saying anything about anyone?" Percy was perched on the edge of his seat, anticipating a public feud.

It's true, I thought. I tried to rationalise: What right did Halliwell have to deliberately leave out from his guide modern movies that didn't suit his palate, like great Russ Meyer flicks or mammoth cult successes like 'Rocky Horror'? How could he forget Josephine Baker in his companion and how, in the same book, could he put, 'The Trouble With Harry,' in italics, and not, 'Vertigo,' – and then go and give, 'Vertigo,' only two stars in his guide? And what nerve to quote The Christian Science Monitor in his entry for 'Valley of the Dolls,' ("a skillfully deceptive imitation of a real drama..." which might as well be a description of my social life,) and to never include a quote by Kenneth Anger for any movie (whose films he spitefully calls "short, inscrutable and Freudian"). I mean who did Halliwell think would be reading his books? If this was indeed the argument Percy was putting forward, then I was on the side of consensus.

But that wasn't the point. Percy thought that since Halliwell selected, described and rated movies according to his own particular ideas, and these ideas weren't universally shared, he had no right going about compiling film guides. Percy put Halliwell and Rushdie in the same boat. Now that is an inscrutable point. Which brings me to a whole lot of personal things about Percy which drove me crazy and explain why our relationship lasted nine days. Is nine days a relationship? Yes, why not. We moved in together on the third day. We were telling intimate stories of our abusive past lives on the fourth, arguing about tidiness on the fifth, and dividing up a box of Godiva chocolates on the sixth. Day eight we fondled the Gehry chairs. Day nine we cancelled plans to spend Halloween in Paris.

How the honest relationship with Percy soured: He decided to divest all our internal honesty − externally. Surrounded by his friends, he took the opportunity to maximise my embarrassment, and therefore to ensure the rapid spread of gossip and character innuendo throughout the local gay community.

Someone said their favourite Elizabeth Taylor movie was, 'The White Cliffs of Dover,' which most of us had never seen, and in which "Roddy McDowall and Taylor are childhood lovers, then as adults they turn into Peter Lawford and June Lockhart."

"June Lockhart!" we all screamed. "The Lassie lady?"

Another guy shared with us his favourite Taylor lines from 'The Sandpiper.' Both "I've lost all my sense of sin" and "Don't you realise that what happened between us is good?" He said "good" in the over−emphatic Taylor−patented manner, and as we laughed I was sure Percy was no longer angry. We drank and smoked some more. But like an elephant, trade never forgets.

Amidst the laughter there was agreement that "And they were eating him," from Liz's maximum−emotive monologue in, 'Suddenly Last Summer,' was far and away Taylor's most special screen moment. Everyone took turns delivering it, in an almost Katherine Hepburn−like tremble. Max, with a resonance aided by his large round belly, and his multiple appearances as the Lady E herself, won this contest unanimously.

"Her pace in that movie is so slow," I added, "that you just want to stick a finger up her butt to get her going."

To which Percy added, "Speaking of fingers up butts, Russell, I'd hate to tell the story about coming home to an open bottle of lube." Talk about your social graces.

"Actually, Percy's got it wrong. He came home and asked me what I did today and I said I had a wank and stuck a finger up my butt. And he said, 'What were you doing sticking a finger up your butt?' and I said 'cause nothing's been up that butt – this decade.' That's what really happened with my butt today."

The cluster of men was not intrigued by the turn in our tone. I'm sure everyone would have preferred to start in on, 'Virginia Woolf,' but for some reason, only about five minutes later, I found these other words slipping from my lips. "Percy likes me to fuck him and when I'm fucking him he likes me to shove his face into a pillow and yell at him 'take my long hard cock you fuck' and fuck him really hard." This led to an unnerving social silence. Flight attendants are known to have very strong diplomatic cargo.

Percy immediately responded. "That's after I've finally got your cock up my asshole, the location of which still seems to escape you. And if I didn't have you tell me you're fucking me, I might not have the time to figure out I'm being fucked at all." Apt, precise, so very mean. It's funny how people who look so nice can be so mean. That's why I've never collected cute collectibles, like Himmels or the Royal Doulton clown couple. Rather, I collect mean looking tribal masks and sculpture. Mean looking things often have a most amenable demeanour. Percy, like the expensive clown couple, was yet another example of something I wouldn't collect.

Without further insult, we both gave our premature regrets to Max and made to leave. We were helping Percy's friend Arif do Diana Ross that night, and had to go style her wig. Or so Percy lied, and it seemed, at the time, a most plausible lie. While we were getting our coats on I could hear the other guests taking turns saying "I've lost all my sense of sin" and laughing hysterically after each imitation. Over and over and still finding it hysterical. "I've lost all my sense of sin." It was like a mantra, to breathe life back into the conversation which Percy and I had destroyed. A camp mantra.

Shortly afterward (the day afterward), I fell out completely with Percy. We cautiously avoid each other when accidentally in the same vicinity. It's much harder to avoid his many 'in' friends though. They love to converge when they see me and make it painfully obvious that they're talking about me in front of my face. Whenever I see those ElizabethTaylor friends of his they look at me with cynicism, remembering how I called her role in, 'Suddenly Last Summer,' "halfway to a cavity and sharp as a Pekinese bark." I've never been forgiven. I never will be I guess. But that's the thing about these gay flings. That's why you have to be so careful. My advice is: Go for the mean looking ones, and betray your honest self as long as possible.

DINNER PARTY NO. 2
The Chauvinism of Prosperity

A highly recommended pick-up strategy. Ask the guy you're interested in if you could have a look at the label on the collar of his shirt. Pull back the collar, read the label, and proclaim: "Just as I thought. Made in heaven." I've had a lot of success with that line. Unfortunately so many men nowadays are out and about without shirts. As such, I'm often forced to resort to my second most successful pick-up line, which I picked up from a Stephen King short story. Fortunately for me, I'm always picking up guys who don't read. This is how it works: I just walk up to a guy who I've never met in my life and I ask him "What's Goofy?"

If the guy has never read 'The Body' you've scored. Think about it: What was Goofy? Most people say Goofy was a dog – but they're wrong. I've walked up to people in bars and asked them what Goofy was and when they say a dog I say "How could he be a dog when Pluto was a dog?" Pluto didn't talk and Goofy talked. If Goofy talked he couldn't have been a dog. Or else Pluto couldn't have been a dog. And we all know that Pluto was a dog; that's explicit. Mickey used to say, "Here Pluto, here boy" and give him bones to chew on.

Goofy wasn't a cow either; he didn't have an udder and he didn't have horns. Disney cows have horns and udders, which is slightly more than any of their mermaids ever got. Anyway, once you get some trick thinking hard about what Goofy was, the pick-up comes easy. I get little argument from trade when I explain myself with such precise empirical evidence. I usually get a perplexed look. But I often get a blow job too. The other day I got a dinner invitation.

It was at a cabbagetown row house, neatly done up in Architectural Digest inspirations. Kurdish kilims, overstuffed pouffes, Corbusier collectibles, you know. All that expensive taste meant nothing however: there was the exquisite aroma of cabbagetown cookery wafting through the living room. No goat cheese, no tiramisu.

No Philippine Mung Beans in Coconut Milk. We dined, without any guest dissent, on red meat: a marinated flank steak, which had been sitting overnight in Moroccan spices (cumin, coriander, pepper, oil, soy sauce, sherry, garlic, onion—I obtained the host's favour and I would be happy to share with you the recipe at a later date—call me). The steak was then grilled and sliced in thin strips, placed elegantly alongside a salad of baby lettuce greens, leafs of radichio, and a mound of 'peaches and cream' corn, fresh off the cob. Being a one-time strict vegetarian I knew exactly what we were really digesting: a large piece of animal flesh extracted from a region ahead of where top round comes from, below where sirloin is cut, and to the rear of where short ribs make their home. I put aside dietary concerns and allowed my neo-carniverous digestive tract to chart an acceptable social course: I ate the meat. Our superb retail cut was complimented by a gamay beaujolais from California which, although not the best wine for this particular meal, was perfectly suited for the hot summer weather, and which the host had courteously chilled beforehand then decanted fifteen minutes prior to supper. The delicate, almost fragile scent, swirled up our nostrils, and barreled down our throats: if there's one thing gay old age gives us on a plate, it's the gift horse of wine and food. In case you haven't figured it out, it was a dinner party full of gay men. People in neat attire, the sort that I would normally hesitate to call queer without risking retribution in regards to the 'name' debate. After we contentedly finished our main course, discretely leaving one square of foccacio in the bread basket, and contemplated whether to engage in desert promptly, or tardily, the conversation died away, and all eyes turned to my end of the table. I guess everyone finally wanted to know: What was Goofy? I was, after all, the new boy at the table, and I'd scooped up the prize at my side – a brunette who wore base – with the very same pick-up line described above. No doubt he had surreptitiously described my pick-up, in detail, to his cabbagetown friends, the elite of the 'in community queers', and the creme of the Bon Appetit slash bathhouse crowd. It's strange the way we all talk about pick-up lines in the same behind-the-back way we talk about sexual appetites, as though, outside of bars and bedrooms they're both just figments of our imagination. If there's anyone that needs to come out of the closet, it's all those out queers who still can't talk about sex in public. At any rate, one thing that had made it out of the closet was my outrageously loud Versace shirt I'd scooped up at Holt's on Boxing Day. Perhaps, I thought, that's why everyone is looking my way. Later, I was informed that it was the skins of corn that were clinging off my front teeth, which showed up in yellowish glory each time I smiled or sneered. Skins or no, the conversation had to carry on.

If I had a proper gift, such as being able to play the piano or recite the Iliad, I might have been a much more popular dinner guest, much more in demand. As it was, my popularity rested solely on the uncommon depth of my pick-up line. I certainly needed an outrageous story tonight, I certainly wanted to be invited back, I certainly enjoyed a good glass of wine. Nectar from the vineal gods. I took it upon myself to relate a great, if sad and disturbing story, one which would make a great novel but which I couldn't bring myself to write. To write such a long and perverse story as the one that follows would be like immersing yourself in the life and psychology of some really wretched social being. Like compiling a biography on Charles Manson or Ike Turner or Roy Cohn. No, this was just a story for dinner guests or hosts, when slightly drunk–to add good alcoholic shock–but not beyond recall, a digestive aid in lieu of a glacé where, in our modern age, we've shortened four course dinners to two, a story to give hope to our own perilous lives, in that those more fortunate are often worse off, and to reinstate the dysfunctional nature of the 'family' amongst a number of people who'd survived the grim years of heterosexual suburban upbringing intact. Relatively intact.

A story I heard in a bar:

A woman named Moira had a call last year from her parents.

"Moira, the story goes, has been an off-again on-again lesbian for most of her adult life. When she finally decided to dump her boyfriend, take up with trade from the Rose, and be a gay and/or lesbian, her parents stopped speaking to her. One interpretation of their intolerance is this: they rejected lesbianism because they are fundamentalist Christians. My interpretation is, however, that they rejected their daughter because they are assholes. Interpretation, I must remind you, is a very subjective thing. Now it's true that anyone who's sipped more than one martini in a nameless Church street bar has heard, overheard, or been told third hand the story of how Moira was violently attacked and sexually abused, on more than one occasion, by her elder brother, when she was only a child. And when she told her father, a somewhat respectable Halifax lawyer, he didn't believe her – even when her brother admitted to it! Frankly, I'm tired of all the 'sexual assault' stories every unemployed North American wishes to share with us all, on North American cable TV no less, but to be fair to Moira, she was abused and on separate occasions violently beaten by her loving siblings. Despite this gruesome fact, I continue to cynically describe her family as a seven person Maritime household who, with four cars, is one car short. Her father can be best described as a man who, when he doesn't get his way, holds his breath until he passes out. (This is a guaranteed third hand story: why would I bend the facts for cabbagetown queers?) So Moira's father and mother come to visit her, insisting her girlfriend be present–despite the fact that Moira's mother has told her face to face that she will have nothing to do with her sapphic daughter and abhors the idea of meeting her lesbian lover. Come the specified day they all get together. Anyway, sexual tensions aside, the meeting boiled down to the parents telling Moira that she owes them $276,000.00 (Canadian). So Moira asks why? Now, obviously the answer is because she's a lesbian. But Moira wants to know why the 276 grand and how come such an exact figure and her parents, wait for it, her parents produce a ledger — a ledger they kept from birth (one for each of their children) of every single expenditure they incurred on behalf of or as part of raising their sons and daughter. They hand Moira a copy of this ledger and, upon their abrupt exit, inform her that all further correspondence between them will be done through the family law firm. I suppose that if there's a good side to this story it's that the $276 k was in constant, rather than real dollars (i.e. not adjusted for inflation).

"There's no punch line; what I've told you is the truth. There's no camp tangent. And so now that I've told you you're wondering how come I haven't softened in my attitude toward Moira and how come I still avoid her and how come I don't feel sorry for her or tell this story in a lesbi-sympathetic tone. Well let me tell you this little gem — just as a sort of caveat, rather than a punch line.

"Moira had a cat. Had. It was a pretty nice cat, so I heard, as cats go. It was a male cat. And she had it for some time. And after she had had this cat for some time — let's say several months, enough time to really become attached to it — well after this time it started to spray; as male cats are wont to do. Or so I'm told, never having had a cat. Well Moira, unaware that this would happen, was quite upset. So she had the cat put down. Which is pretty horrible in itself, I think, because you really shouldn't enter into a parent/child, owner/pet or any sort of truly responsible relationship without knowing at least the bare facts of care-taking. Obviously, her parents' solution to unanticipated problems was simple responsibility be damned, pull out the ledger and make the children pay. Anyway, the politics of having your pets put down aside, catch this: On the day Moira had the cat put down, (killed actually, I don't know why we say put down as though eventually these animals will get up), yes, so on the day she killed the cat, on this day she knew, to the penny, exactly how much that cat had cost her. To the penny."

I waited for everyone at the dinner table to create their own particular look of disgust and shock, then I added "Moira has since bought an expensive female cat." It worked well. Much discussion on the horrors of parental prudishness broke out around the table as well as many numerous and humorous 'bad cat' stories. I felt relieved knowing I would now enter the good graces of a peripheral gay clique. The host served up a chocolate cappuccino dacquoise from Dufflet's, and plunked down a bottle of Martell. Better still, two other guests at the table later invited me over for drinks that weekend.

And you never know – some day someone else may turn that story into a novel. My company should be considered a public service.

CAN'T SMILE WITHOUT YOU

Dean Raven

M

ARCIA IS DOING HER NAILS. SHE concentrates very hard, making sure that each stroke is perfect. At last she finishes and lifts her hands in triumph.

"Ta-daaaa!"

She swings around and smiles broadly at Scott, who is sitting on the couch. To Marcia, the perfect application of nail-polish is a noteworthy achievement. Marcia rarely achieves anything.

"Well, at last," says Scott peevishly. He has been sitting there for ten minutes and has not been allowed to say anything. Marcia says it breaks her concentration.

"Ah, Scott," she sighs. "I know how much this bores you. But you know how depressed I get if things aren't exactly right. God knows I have to make the most of what limited attractions I have."

Scott rolls his eyes. He knows he should make the obligatory remonstrances but tonight he really doesn't feel in the mood. Anyway, what Marcia says is perfectly

Dean Raven lives in Perth with his partner, Shane, and feline companion Jessica (the two cutest people he knows). He has had one story published in Outrage magazine and two in the 1993 Austrlaian Gay and Lesbian Short Story Anthology.

In 'Cant Smile Without You,' the intertwining of music and prose is a reflection of the importance of both in his everyday life. Another subject that colours a lot of his writing is a loathing of the notion of tolerance. "Tolerance is a ploy by a patriachial society to marginalise and subvert us, to pat us on our collective heads and tell us we are acceptable as long as we look normal and only 'do it' in private. Instead we must continue to embrace and celebrate the diversity of queer culture, to promote the politics of difference and ensure that with growing acceptance and recognition in the wider society, our culture is not decimated by being assimilated into the mainstream."

true - she doesn't have much going for her. If she did she wouldn't have to hang around with him all the time.

"So are we ready now?" he asks with a hint of sarcasm.

"Just a bit longer, Scott. I've got to make sure they dry properly."

She waves her hands in the air, pretending not to notice his exasperated looks. They are already an hour late and will now almost certainly miss the little show the Empress has reportedly thrown together.

"Come on then, Grumblebum," she concedes at last. "But if my hands stick to my skirt, I'm going to throw a wobbly."

*

As with most relationships there was a turning point - an almost definable point in time when the relationship between Scott and Marcia changed from mere acquaintanceship to one of friendship. The transition occurred at a Halloween party in 1988.

Scott was there with John and Terry Turner-Baxter, known to their friends and enemies alike as the 'orgy sisters'. These devoted lovers were busy trying to line up a particularly impressive specimen of young, gay machismo for a coming debauch, leaving Scott to his own devices. Scott had his eyes on a half-naked devil with a perpetual hardon and bad breath who (despite the former and no doubt because of the latter) was failing to turn any of the other guests on. Although Scott had a secret weapon (two packets of Tic Tacs) he was nonetheless failing dismally in his attempts at seduction. He had also found to his chagrin that consumption of half a bottle of gin did nothing to improve either his wittiness or his allure.

Marcia on the other hand was sober. Being attracted to misery in all its many and varied forms, it was not long before she was seated next to Scott, squeezing his hand and listening patiently to his drunken tales of rejections and lost opportunities. Her eyes never left his face. At the end of these tales she enfolded him in her spongy arms and patted his back like a baby.

At first Scott had found Marcia's propensity for physical contact slightly exhilarating. He had never before been close to a woman, and touching Marcia (however platonically) made him feel like a pioneer exploring new territory.

As time passed though, the novelty began to wear off. He found himself getting increasingly aggravated at the liberty with which she treated his body. Even in gay bars she would hold his hand or cling to him like a mollusc, and he began to compensate by staring at any good looking man who walked past, indicating with his eyes how irksome he found this creature.

Eventually he took to standing out of arms reach.

22

Now they only hold hands in the street.

★

The time is now ten-thirty and Scott and Marcia have just arrived at the party. The house is ablaze with colour and music. The first sign of revelry is two beefy men, both with moustaches, who are perched on the stoop kissing frantically. A neighbourhood cat gazes at them, transfixed. Scott reaches down to pat the creature but it registers him at the last minute and scurries away with a strangled meow.

As they squeeze past, Scott smiles indulgently at the men. He turns to Marcia for encouragement. Marcia, however, pretends not to notice them. She has a Mills and Boon approach to life and despite her affinity with anything gay, often ignores things that make her feel uncomfortable. That way a sizeable proportion of the real world does not exist, which suits her just fine.

They are met at the door by their host, Vince. He is already blind drunk. He tells them he has been drinking moselle since ten o'clock in the morning.

"How'sh the party?" he slurs in Scott's face.

"Great," replies Scott, shrugging his shoulders.

Marcia smiles patronisingly. Seeing her for the first time, Vince peers down at her. He squints narrowly.

"Hey man, you make a great woman," he eventually says.

Marcia's smile wilts and drips away. Her face turns a bright purple. Without a word, she grabs Scott's hand and drags him into the house. Vince is left leaning against the door jamb, buffeted by non-existent winds.

Inside, the living room is packed with people. A formless cloud of smoke hangs over everyone, punctured by the thunder of apocalyptic techno music. Garbled conversations rain down on people's heads. There are a few people Scott knows - many more he would like to know - and he smiles salaciously at the prospect of a fruitful night.

Tactfully he acts as if he did not hear what Vince said to Marcia. That way he can avoid shovelling dirt into the grave that Marcia is right now digging for herself. Instead, he points towards a G-string waiter, who is bending over to pick up a glass that someone has super-glued to the floorboards. Marcia glances over. Her eyes boggle.

Suddenly freed from Marcia's attention, Scott glances around the room. In the far corner he spies a Michael Biehn look-alike. Their eyes lock. Instinctively Scott steps away. Marcia, her eyes glued to the waiter's muscular buttocks, does not notice.

A little later, when Marcia absently reaches for Scott's hand, she finds it is no longer there. Startled, she swings around. Scott has gone.

2 3

★

Three months ago they went together to Marcia's cousin's sixteenth birthday party. Clarissa is an undersized version of Marcia, with the same limp blond hair and wide, plump hips. Marcia's parents were there, as was Clarissa's widowed mother. Two other uncles, whose names, like their faces, were obscured by mediocrity, also put in a brief appearance, leaving immediately after gifts and over-dramatised hugs were exchanged.

The only person present of Clarissa's age was a skinny girl with black-rimmed glasses, who sat in the corner for most of the night playing with a giant teddy-bear and watching the action with glazed, owlish eyes. Every so often Clarissa would join her and they would sit in silence together, surveying their surroundings like visitors to a giant aquarium.

The cake was a three-tiered pink and white extravaganza, covered with sprinkles and fat little Jelly Bellies. All evening Clarissa's younger brothers huddled close around the table, jostling each other for the best position. Their red little tongues licked incessantly at the sight of this amazing construction.

This was the first time Scott had met Marcia's family. He swore afterwards it would also be the last.

"So, Marcia," her mother croaked, leering up at Scott like an ageing harlot, "where have you been hiding this handsome young man?"

She was leaning so close that Scott could smell the whiskey on her breath and see the tracks of her wrinkles as they fought to liberate themselves from her impacted make-up. When Scott glanced down, he was startled to see that Marcia was smiling proudly.

Just before this party, Marcia's mother had confronted her with what she had called her, "God-given right as a parent to know."

"Are you a lesbian?" she had asked.

Marcia had almost choked on her sausage roll. Afterwards she had worried continuously that her denials had been too insistent.

Now, it seems, she had finally found an alibi.

Clarissa's party eventually ground to an overdue halt. As the empty plates were being collected, Marcia cornered Scott in the kitchen and immured him in her voluminous arms. Barry Manilow was singing, 'Can't Smile Without You', in the living room, and she sang along discordantly in his ear. Her body swayed to and fro with the music, taking his with it.

"I love you", she suddenly whispered, as if she meant it.

"Yeah, you too," Scott replied flatly.

And just at that moment Marcia's mother walked in, her arms filled with dirty crockery. Seeing the two standing there she came to a sudden halt, and a knowing smile stretched like rubber across her face. She mouthed the word "Sorry" to Scott's burning face, then backed slowly out, her watery eyes blinking spasmodically.

Scott had felt sick. Afterwards he went out to Connections and picked up a ruined businessman, who was as bad in bed as he apparently was in business.

★

An hour has passed. Marcia is talking to an animated skeleton named Clarke, whilst Scott is across the other side of the room, deep in conversation with Michael Biehn. Every so often Marcia looks up to see what Scott is up to. She wonders why he has been talking so much to the one person; she is sure he does not know him. However, she resists the urge to intervene, feeling intuitively that Scott needs some space tonight. Anyway, Clarke works as a sales representative for a perfume company, and she feels that if she gets to know him well enough she might score some free samples.

"So," Clarke is saying, "Franco gave me this little package, wrapped in pink tissue paper of all things, and guess what it was? You'll absolutely die, Marcia."

Marcia looks up at the sound of her name. Her thoughts have been drifting and she realises she has not heard a word Clarke has said for at least the past five minutes. Clarke has his hands clasped in front of him and is leaning over her like a giant praying mantis.

"Huh?" she says.

He hesitates a second for effect. "Old Spice!" he suddenly blurts out. "Wouldn't you just die on the spot? Well at least it wasn't Brut. Anyway, two days later I dumped him. I told him I absolutely refuse to go out with anyone who doesn't agree that Tuscany is the scent of the nineties."

Marcia smiles weakly. At least Clarke enjoyed the story, she thinks.

"Um, Clarke," she ventures, "I think I'd better go see what Scott is doing. He does some silly things when he drinks. He might need rescuing."

"OK, Marcia," pipes Clarke. He leans closer. "I've just seen that bitch Nigel. I think I'll race over and drop some crabs down the back of his neck. Won't his boyfriend just love that?"

He shoots off towards the other side of the room, like a spider which has just snared a fly. Marcia moves towards Scott.

Scott and the stranger are standing very close. They are both smiling, though neither is speaking. Marcia stops in front of them, an arms length away, and the three unwittingly form an isosceles triangle with Marcia as the apex. They do not

2 5

notice her.

"Cough, cough," she says.

They turn simultaneously and glare at her, as if she has intruded on something very personal. Then Scott smiles and exclaims: "Marcia! Where have you been all night?"

"Oh around," she states noncommittally. She feigns weariness, hoping Scott will see the contrast between her boredom and the good time he has been having. She looks significantly at Scott's friend. Scott takes the hint and introduces him. His name is Brett.

"Brett's from Brisbane," Scott explains. "He leaves tomorrow, unfortunately."

They smile at each other and Marcia once again ceases to exist.

"Oh that's too bad," she intervenes, sabotaging their symbiosis.

They peer at her as if she has just beamed down from the USS Enterprise. Marcia eyes Brett suspiciously. She decides she does not like him.

"Scott," she says, "come and meet Clarke." She leans closer and smiles conspiratorially. "He works for a perfume company."

"Uh, maybe later Marcia," Scott replies. "Brett and I were just about to go for a walk. Brett has this thing about smoky rooms – don't you Brett?"

"Oh – um – yeah," replies Brett, unconvincingly.

"He has sinus trouble. You don't mind if we leave you for a little while, do you? We'll only be about ten minutes."

Marcia is caught off guard.

"Oh – OK," she says.

Almost instantly they are gone.

Marcia continues facing the corner, too embarrassed to move. When she eventually turns around she feels as if everyone is laughing at her – at the little fat girl who has once again been outdone in the popularity stakes. She glances at her watch and works out when ten minutes will be up. Then she sits down next to the food table. Feigning nonchalance, she picks up a chocolate eclair and studies it for a while. She glances nervously around the room. Then very quickly, guiltily, she eats it. After a few seconds she picks up another.

*

It's now after midnight. The scene is Vince's bedroom. Brett is lying on his back and Scott is straddling his legs. Their shirts lay tangled at the bottom of the bed.

Scott has just managed to undo Brett's trousers and is now slipping them down over his hips. As turgid flesh is exposed, he gasps.

It's been so long, he thinks. Fuck the foreplay.

He goes down and takes Brett's short, thick cock straight into his mouth. Unfortunately he has not done this for a while, and his teeth scrape painfully across tender flesh. Brett yelps. Scott jumps.

"Shit I'm sorry," he breathes.

"Don't worry about it," Brett laughs. "It didn't hurt . . . much."

"God you're cute," says Scott, kissing the injured member lightly. "It's just my luck to meet someone who lives thousands of miles away."

"Well you can always come and visit," replies Brett, running his rough hands down Scott's arms. Even in the darkness his brilliant white teeth can be seen as he lies there, breathing deeply, his mouth slightly parted.

"Yeah, I'll do that," says Scott, knowing full well that it is out of the question.

He shuffles up and plants his lips firmly over Brett's. Brett's breath is sweet and warm and licking inside his mouth is like tasting ambrosia.

"Scott? Scott, are you in there?"

Scott sits up. It's Marcia's voice. There is a slight tapping at the door and the handle is gently tried. Fortunately, the door is locked.

"Shhh," says Scott, putting a finger to his lips. He places his other hand over Brett's mouth. Brett sticks his tongue between Scott's fingers and Scott giggles softly.

"Don't," he admonishes gently.

"Scott, I know you're in there. Vince's friend told me so. What are you doing?" She taps again with her fingernails.

Still Scott does not answer. He hopes that by staying quiet she will eventually go away.

"Scott, I want to go home. I'm feeling depressed."

A short silence. Then: "Scott, please. I'm getting a really bad headache and I'm bored. Please Scott. I can't stand it here any longer."

Her voice is beginning to sound desperate. She is sniffling quietly, though it can be heard quite clearly through the door. Then, quite unexpectedly, she departs.

Scott continues listening. When he is certain she has gone he removes his hand from Brett's mouth. Brett remains silent.

Scott reclines on the bed and kisses Brett's neck. However, he now feels distracted, expecting at any moment to hear pounding at the door as the crowd demands an explanation for the ill-treatment of his best friend. His imagination works overtime: he pictures Marcia sitting in the bathroom with a giant razor blade poised over her wrist, or stumbling down the middle of the road with tears blinding her eyes and a Mack truck bearing down on her in the darkness.

Brett reaches for Scott's groin and takes the limp member in his hand. He moves the foreskin back and forth for a while but gets no response. Scott's face reddens in the darkness. His embarrassment at not getting aroused only makes it more difficult to do so. Eventually he sits up.

"It's no use," he says. "I can't get into it now. I'll have to go."

He kisses Brett deeply, regretfully, but still fails to get an erection.

Eventually he disengages and gets dressed.

"Here's my card," he says, handing it to Brett. "Ring me sometime, or send me a postcard."

"Yeah, I'll do that."

They say their goodbyes quickly. Scott leaves the room without turning back.

*

Scott and Marcia are in the car on the way home. Although Scott is concentrating on the road ahead, he is aware of Marcia staring at him. He wishes she will stop. She is fidgeting, and it is obvious she is struggling to find something to say. She looks alternately from her hands to Scott's face.

"Oh Scott, I forgot to tell you," she eventually says with false cheer. "Mum rang last night and said to give you her love. And get this: she wants to know when we're getting married." She snorts. "Isn't that a hoot?"

Scott grunts.

Later on, when he senses that Marcia is no longer looking at him, he turns his head slightly and stares at her.

She is slouched in the seat looking straight ahead. A barely perceptible smile is dancing across her parted lips. She appears to be mouthing the words of a song.

And funnily enough she looks radiant. And happier – truly happier – than she has in a long, long time.

DIVINITIES

Alana Valentine

AFTERWARDS ASSUMPTA WENT OUT. She could not go home and sit in her house or stand in her bathroom being unhappy so she went out. She went to the lesbian dance club hoping that there would be some people there she did know and could talk to. And she knew there would be people there she did not know that she could look at with interest and maybe talk to. She knew there might also be people there she did know but did not want to talk to but that would be fine. Assumpta was wearing a short leather vest with four silver buckles down the front. Truth be told it was not leather and the buckles were not silver, of course they were not. Everyone would know the buckles were not silver but none would know the vest was not leather. Most people would look at it and think, 'Ooh, dishy leather'. Only those woman who walked past her and casually stroked her back would know, those women who she did not know but would

---

Alana Valentine is the recipient of a NSW State Literary Award, A Churchill Fellowship and the 1994 ANPC/ New Dramatists Award. She has written a film, 'Mother Love', several stage plays, including 'Shudder' and 'Southern Belle', and three radio plays.
"*I was raised by a gay style queen named Adam Marriot who taught me that my political acumen should be as astute and discerning as my fashion sensibility. Though my mentors have now been taken by HIV/AIDS, their personal rigour continues to inspire me. When I think about diversity, I think about a community unified by a catchy wardrobe and an active brain.*"
The following is an extract from a novel called 'Divinities'. 'Divinities' is about a lesbian who is visited by the Holy Spirit, wearing a tartan skirt, after the death of one of her friends from HIV/AIDS. Assumpta is a common women's name in some European countries, it is based on the Assumption of the Virgin Mary into heaven.

maybe like to get to know her. Only those of her friends who gave her a long lingering stroke on the back would think that it was maybe not leather. There was a lot of casual stroking and lingering stroking on the back that happened when you wore leather out, even when it was not leather, and Assumpta looked forward to it.

The sound of the inside of the club was audible from the outside, even from almost half a block down from outside the inside of the club. They would gradually creep the sound up during the night and that is when Assumpta would leave but first she would dance and sweat and rub her vest and her chest up against the other dancers. She would bump and grind and not mind at all the smiles of women on the floor, the eyes that meet on the floor, the lone women who came up and danced with her and danced around her and didn't say anything at all but gave out tiny almost indiscernible signals that they were now dancing with her. And now they were, they were, they were, they were not, no they were now moving away because they got the message that she was not giving them any tiny almost indiscernible signals back. Into the club went Assumpta flashing her membership card at the dyke on the desk with a big smile of hello and throwing back the two doors at the entrance that came together in middle like some late Twentieth Century saloon.

The club was full and people were drinking beer. Up to the bar went Assumpta and ordered a beer for her queer self. Up behind her came two hands they came up behind her back and grabbed her around the waist. Assumpta turned her head and saw one of the women who had been at the wake, one of the women with filthy, deliberately filthy, blonde hair.

"Hello, you're Assumpta aren't you?"

Was she glad she had come out? She was very glad.

"Were we introduced at the wake?"

"I don't think we were introduced, I'm Syreeta."

Of course you are Syreeta you're not Daphne or Betty or Anne, you are Syreeta and wow I wonder who is here. I wonder who saw you put your arms around me and say hello to me, I hope someone saw you.

"How have you been since the wake?"

"I've been busy. I thought it was a great memorial service."

"It's a beautiful church, he would have liked that."

"I didn't know that you and he were friends. He kept all of us separate," said Syreeta as she ran her hand down the side of her glass and looked under her eyelashes, "I could kill him for that."

Terribly, terribly embarrassed. That's what happens when people die. When people who you loved die you sometimes forget that they are dead and you say things like

"I could kill him." Syreeta looked like fireplace ash.

"Can I buy you another drink?" offered Assumpta.

"No thanks. How about a dance instead?"

How about a dance instead, how about we go to bed, how about I kiss your head, how about I part your legs.

"Love to."

They moved onto the dance floor and Syreeta went to the centre. Assumpta usually danced on the edges of the dance floor, stayed on the edges of communities of political parties of groups of any kind. Assumpta was on the outer edges never getting too entrenched. But Syreeta liked the centre where the sweat flicked at you from a circle of bodies. Syreeta swung her hips and Assumpta smiled at her through the miasma of flashing colours and tossing hair. Everywhere there were bare stomachs and bare shoulders and everywhere there was need. Desire need desire need desire need desire. Love desire hate desire fun desire spite desire stale desire stare desire want want want to the beat. Boom boom boom boom boom boom boom and Assumpta's head shut down and her brain shut down and her body came into centre of the dance floor next to Syreeta, in the club and on a high.

Back in the mass again shrouded in the crowded room standing with Syreeta saying nothing at all. Standing at the back to look at the others at the back of the rack. The talk turns once again to Tony.

"On the memorial table at the wake there were photos of you with Tony in the hospital," said Assumpta.

Syreeta smiled.

"I visited him a couple of times. You could never tell what sort of a mood he would be in," she said, "Sometimes he would be quite glad to see me and once he just stared at me and said who are you? I said I'm Syreeta and he said hello Syreeta, pleased to meet you. Then he held out one of his beautiful hands."

"And what did you do?"

"I took it and told him that he had hands like Lytton Strachey and he looked at me more closely and said do come again."

Assumpta laughed and laughed and without warning started to cry. Not big heaving sobs or anything. Not overstatement, no it was a choking in the back of the throat, a burning sensation in the nose. The eyes were hardly affected until the last but Assumpta could not speak. Syreeta was dabbing her eyes with the back of her hand.

"Let's go outside," she said, "the smoke in here is getting to both of us."

Out in the cool night air.

"Do you know if Tony came from Cairns?" Assumpta asked Syreeta.

"As far as I know he grew up in Sans Souci, why?"

"I just never knew where he grew up, thanks."

"When were you two friends?"

"When I first came to Sydney about nine years ago. He was one of my style mentors."

They walked through the back of the Cross, in a street decked out with bright lights. The street where people meet and let go of themselves and in the street were too many people who had let go of themselves. There were urban tragedies up and down the footpath, not romantic, gutter low life who were poor but happy. There were people who could hardly see, men so drunk with fat dirty stomachs and women without smiles. People who had the gutter come up and slam them in the face every couple of days, who paced with the patter patter of irregular heartbeats. They were dancing out here too, sliding up and down on each others opportunities and peeling off the layers that would leave them with bitter bones, bones eaten away with dreams denied, and shoulders shrugged. Mostly they were tired.

They dragged themselves always on, ever on, the life dripping and dragging out of them, the love renewed and the confessions whispered but the faith draining from their face and their side full of holes. Perhaps they leave themselves to stiffen in some cathedral, some confessional where there is begging for a warm word. There is the same boasting of success, the same longing for reason, the same unrequited love of life that is ever known. Did the Spirit come here and weep? Did the Spirit swirl in an ocean of tears and fears and did the Spirit see it another way, a way that she could not see that Assumpta wanted to see? To see without judging to see without assuming to see without looking down. To see without sentiment, without the restlessness of middle-class improvement, to see without the desire to change.

"I'm going home to have a cold bath."

Syreeta lived close to the club, close to the centre of the scene, close to the middle of the dance floor.

"That sounds nice."

You don't have a spa or a car or a star on your door. You don't have a bar full of drinks or a jar full of chocolates or a far eastern flavour in your decor but you do have a bath and you do like them cold.

"Come and join me"

"It'd be good to get wet."

Assumpta never one for understatement.

Syreeta lived in a free-standing house. There was the sound of no one underneath them, there was the sound of no one above them. There was still the low buzz of traffic from the bathroom window but there was the buzz of traffic everywhere. There was a buzz from the vibrator that Syreeta was using on herself in the bath too. In the bath, in the dark and there was a candle in the corner which was blowing in the breeze from the open window. If you have an open window you are going to have to put up with the buzz of traffic even with the sound of the stereo from the lounge room. In the bath in the dark with Syreeta and Assumpta and a new battery in the vibrator they were using for pleasure. At one end was Assumpta, with her wet arms on the lip of the bath. In the middle of the bath on her knees was Syreeta with the dildo teasing the folds of her behind from behind.

"Will you do it?" she said, and Assumpta turned the buzzing off so that there was only the size and the shape and Assumpta slowly pushed it into Syreeta and there was the size and the shape going in and out and there was the sound of the water lapping and Syreeta breathing and the suck of the sound of the size and the shape and the sound of the traffic and the stereo and the small cries from Syreeta. In the candlelight water glistened on Assumpta's arms and Syreeta's arse. There was a harder and faster sound of breathing and sucking and Syreeta was arched back holding her buttocks and Assumpta was breathing and Syreeta was moaning and the water was lapping and the shape was sucking and the pleasure was coming in waves and waves and waves and waves and again and again and then there was pause.

Syreeta turned around and lay on top of Assumpta in the cold shallow water and told her that she had perfect timing. She stroked Assumpta's hair with her wet hand till it stood up in peaks on the crown of her head. When she got out of the bath Syreeta wrapped a towel around her waist and came back with a hot cup of white tea which Assumpta drank as she stretched her legs along the length of the bath. The candle flickered and flickered and the talk turned once again to Tony. It turned to Tony because he was the only thing they had so far discovered that they had in common. It was so sudden and spontaneous and rather than say do you do this all the time, which would be rude and stupid and denigrate the pleasure, the talk turned to Tony.

"Who was the man at the funeral who sat up the back of the church all by himself?" Assumpta asked this into the air which was still heavy. Syreeta did not look unhappy or saddened or sorry to be reminded of the funeral.

"That might have been Jerry who came down from Foster on the north coast," she replied. "He went up there to live when he found out that he was positive. He used to work with Tony at that clothing store in the strand."

"What did he look like?"

"He was wearing a rainbow coloured crochet cap."

"No, this man was wearing no hat, a blazer, no tie but quite good dressy shoes. He looked very unhappy but a little out of place."

"You must mean Tony's elder brother, Terry."

"Was that Terry?"

"That was the famous Terry, who refused to see him after he contracted the virus?"

"No," said Assumpta, "those two fell out long before that. He wasn't seeing Terry when I knew him. I remember asking him once if he had a brother and he said he did but they weren't particularly close. Then one Christmas he told me that they had had a falling out and didn't even send birthday cards or Christmas cards. What gave you the idea that it was because of the virus?"

"That's what Tony implied. He went out to visit him one day about six months ago and from what I gathered they had a terrible fight. "

Assumpta got out of the bath and looked in the mirror. She dried herself and looked out of the window but there was no sign of the Spirit. Syreeta went to bed and Assumpta sat by herself in the lounge room for a little while hoping the Spirit might appear to her. For the Spirit to appear and put her arms around Assumpta's waist and rest her head on Assumpta's shoulder. The Spirit did not appear but Assumpta felt sure that she was close by. That she would sit in the doorway of the bedroom that she was about to sleep in and watch over her as she slept. Assumpta imagined the Holy Spirit perched above the doorframe in her tartan skirt and she imagined the Spirit's face. This was Assumpta imagining to reassure herself which was not to say the Spirit was not there but that it was not on this occasion appearing to her as it had twice already.

Laying down next to Syreeta she smelt a strong smell of peppermint, which was the scent of the shampoo that Syreeta used. When she was in bed Assumpta wondered about Tony and his brother Terry and for the first time got scared about being all alone with this thing with the Spirit and this thing with Tony. Cuddling closer into Syreeta's back she was glad she was not on her own at home alone with these things. Instead she was breathing in mint and making a dint in her loneliness. Syreeta turned in her sleep and Assumpta lay her cheek close to Syreeta's mouth to feel the hot breath. In the night, in the dark, in a week of worry, in the passage of a plague, there is much comfort to be had from a cold bath and a gentle human breeze.

BARS, FRIENDS AND THINGS

Drew Marchant

WE ARE GOING TO GO, MARK AND I. I'm looking forward to it as I'm bored with staying at home for two nights on my own. Mark laughs when I tell him it is time for a G.N.O. - a girl's night out. We've agreed to meet at the pub at ten-thirty. Something we have done hundreds of times. This pub, that pub and I'm still a little excited about going. I can already taste the first beer and see the crowd of queens when I open the door.

I've got to have a shower, iron a t-shirt, shave for the second time in one day, and maybe not only my face. It will be cold wearing only a t-shirt but the walk to the pub will warm me up. Besides I don't want to hide what little I have to show by wearing a thick shirt. I'll put up with the cold. A small sacrifice.

I hate going out on my own. I hate eating in a restaurant on my own or seeing a movie alone. I feel intimidated by others in company when I do so. I feel less alone when I am at home alone. Tonight is going to be great. Mark will be there.

God, I hope he doesn't go on and on about how fat he is getting, how much he still loves his old boy friend or how the last fuck he had might be his last. Mark, tell me how great your job is, how wonderful it is to be alive, the fabulous film you have

---

Drew Marchant lives in an unpainted terrace house in Newtown with his lesbian sister. He is a part time public servant but would rather be a 'pubic servant,' full time. He is single but remains hopeful someone stupid enough will take him as a partner.

"I wasn't queer until I came in contact with the word. Before that I just liked men and I have since I stepped out of short pants, maybe even berfore that."

This is Drew's first published work, which took one night to write.

just seen and tell me how great I look. Tell me it is a living wonder I don't have a boy friend. Crack a joke. Tell me a story. Laugh at my jokes. Be with me tonight, Mark. Fill me up with the intoxication of your good company. Treat me like an empty vessel. And forgive me when I look over your shoulder while you are telling me something important because I think I've seen Him. We'll get drunk together, Mark. We'll be silly drunks flirting.

Of course I want you to get laid, but not before I've sorted myself out for the rest of the evening. And if someone does take an interest in me just leave us alone. Don't hang around like you normally do. Can't you see when I'm going for it, when I'm in the home straight. And don't dump me after thirty minutes either, if you get lucky. Stay with me. We agreed to go out together, didn't we? I know you will be late, Mark. You always are and I'm always on time. Some things never change. But you will be there, Mark. You always are.

The doorman does what he does and the pub is full. The first sight coming off the street is an onslaught of queen humanity, a little frightening. One minute I'm alone in the street and the next I'm surrounded by a cacophony of cackling queens. I love them. It is like I have just been beamed in from another planet. Get a drink, that's the trick. A drink in the hand makes you look not alone. You now have a purpose for being in the pub - to drink.

Can't see Mark but he will be here. Late bastard. He is always late and when I do challenge him about it he makes me feel bad by saying, only boring people arrive on time. End of story. He's right. I know it.

I've started to pull focus on the crowd now I have that first beer. It is so crowded it's hard to drink it without having it knocked all over me. Where are they all moving to? Where are they all going? It is like the game is over and everyone is leaving. But no one is leaving, they are just doing the rounds. Visions of sheep dogs doing a round-up come to mind.

"Get back, move right back. Bring them in boy."

Got to find a comfortable spot. Not too far in a corner where you can't be seen by anyone. Also not out in the middle of the sea either. Stand alone out there and you really look a loser. Find something to lean against, some part of the structure. There, you now look part of the decor, a fixture not a piece of furniture stuck in the centre of the carpet.

God, it looks, they look, a little dull tonight. Where is Mark? There's someone I haven't said hello to for a while. Only two weeks actually. But he seems to be ignoring me as much as I him.

He's cute but look at those white track shoes. Why do they still wear them?

There's the vanilla leather queen. What a big girl. The barmen look spunky and they stay sober, looking more attractive as the night wears on. They pay you some attention for three dollars. You need them, you have to be nice. It's the only way to get a drink.

Everyone seems to be with someone except me. No, there are a few loners. There is the guy who never talks to anyone, ever. And there is another one. God, I hope I don't end up like them.

Maybe tonight will be the night. It's been five weeks and I'm feeling a little horny , to touch and be touched, to kiss and be kissed and the excitement of being wanted by someone new. All over. I still have no idea after thirty three years why some nights I'm the flavour of the world and others I can leave the pub without even a glance. Same clothes, same mood, same needs, same interests but different outcomes. One night lots of opportunities for sex, others zero. One of the mysteries of my world.

Got to get that look right. Available but nonchalant. Interested but not desperate. Conversation to be non-threatening, easy and relaxed. No gay politics, no world events and definitely no talk of old boy friends. His or mine. Let the eyes roam around the bar in a natural fashion. Don't move them or your head too quickly or you look like a slut. Casual. That's it, take it easy.

And when you find those eyes you like, when you see that spark, when you know it could happen, try to relax. A little smile. Now look away. Feel his glance. Yes, there it is. Look his way and now it is his turn to look away. Wait for it. His eyes are coming back. Yes! Yes! Yes!

Now don't just stride over there. Move to neutral ground, somewhere in the middle and see if he moves towards you. Don't look yet. Now. Shit! A friend, an acquaintance, someone he is more interested in, last week's fuck. It doesn't matter, they are talking and laughing together.

I see him walking towards me smiling. "Hi. No, just got here. Yep, I'll have one. A middy. Ta." So far so good. Mark is in a good mood. We're going to have a great time. I love it here. I really do.

FLEAS AND HASH

Steven J Carter

S OMETIMES I WORRY THAT I'M LOSING my mind. No, not my mind, my memory. It's Saturday morning and I'm tired and I've been up since three, but that's no excuse. I want to recall for you the events that took place between 1am on Wednesday and 9pm on Thursday, but I'm afraid that it will be a trial and much that is important will slip between my fingers, the fingers of my failing memory.

It's a story of fleas and alcohol and hash and gullibility and coincidence and interconnectedness (yes), and we will give it our best stumbling, fumbling shot.

Actually, I'll start before Wednesday. Tuesday is my dole day, the day I drop off my application at the office for Social Security in Newtown for continued funding while I finish my book. They have been unfailingly supportive of my needs now for ten months. They are genuinely good guys. It should probably be established at this juncture that I am one who believes that to have been born an Australian is to have won the most wonderful and important victory in life's lottery. As far as I am concerned, there could be no finer place, heaven on earth. This attitude is unchanging, no matter how I find myself - rich or poor, healthy or sick, straight or gay, friendless or popular. Whichever way I turn I am met with kindness and generosity and humour and fairness.

Steven J Carter was born in Perth and bred in Perth, Melbourne and Sydney. For the moment, he chooses to stay at Sydney's Sebel Townhouse. He is completing a picaresque novel, 'Lost & Found, Sentimental Lies.' He spends his days in a variety of fashions, more often alone than not, more often sober than drunk.

All this, however, could not disguise from me the fact that yet again on this wild and wet Tuesday I had failed to stretch my dole allowance from one payment to the next. I had run out of money and I was hungry and bored, with no stories either to edit or write. There was no avoiding it: I would have to go out and find myself a story. Only problem is, they are much easier to secure with a bit of cash to dispense. Still, I would make do with what I had. I called up a friend and arranged to go over to his place to watch Seinfeld on the telly. I was secretly hoping there would be a meal in it.

I took off down the street early, figuring on scanning a few magazines in Sydney University's library. I rugged up. It was Sydney's first cold and wet day for the year. We were well into June by now and the weather had only just turned.

Halfway down the street I bumped into my old mate Eleanor. I didn't recognise her until she prompted me. She was under an umbrella and dressed elegantly in a blue suit, svelte and collected. Not so me. I was in a gladbag of colours, white, black, brown and red, with a multi-hued wool jacket.

Eleanor and I had been scheduled to meet the previous day at the Blue Cafe. She'd stood me up. Didn't matter. After six months running around Australia crying in quiet corners, I'd lately resolved to accept all that fate served me up with complete equanimity, a smile frozen to my dial.

"I called the cafe to tell you. Five eight, five nine, five ten, something like that, but they couldn't find you. My description was hopeless."

"Well, I'm well under that."

"And I'm busy all week."

When I was a teenager in Perth, Eleanor and I had lived around the corner from each other and shared many a class at City Beach High School. We'd then gone on to do the same course at the West Australian Institute of Technology, both of us majoring in theatre arts. Eleanor was to be an actress, me a playwright, ambitions which both of us have pretty well maintained over a course of sixteen years. Eleanor was in the first play I ever directed, an elegant queen in an elegant frock. We were bosom buddies, sharing my pink Austin Seven as we raced across the freeway to keep our early morning classes. Many a night would find us locked in conversation over a bottle of red. As much as I could in those clumsy days, I loved her. She was a big girl, plump and jolly and Rubenesque and undeniably beautiful. When she was about 21, she'd shed the weight in one easily executed move. At 33, she now had that same body she'd won for herself a decade earlier, and was commonly reckoned a beauty of a high feline order. I, too, had played around with my weight, at 18 rake thin, ballooning disproportionately in my twenties, reasserting myself in my early thirties, and, while no beauty, I was commonly thought of as nice looking.

And now, after much travelling on both our parts, we were again domiciled within easy walking distance of each other, Eleanor living above a shop in Enmore with her husband (a man I would be incapable of identifying on the street), and myself in a room in a boarding house, a room I was slowly learning to treasure in the same way I had treasured my fancier abodes in Melbourne and Perth. Sydney was still taking some getting used to, but weekly meetings with Eleanor in Newtown's Blue Cafe were of enormous assistance in the settling process. And here we were on Enmore Road, chatting, the sky threatening to foreclose on our comfort.

And I was scratching myself.

"What on earth is wrong with you?" Eleanor asked.

"It's a litany of disaster. I sprained my ankle twice in quick succession and then I was in hospital with kidney stones and now I've got this."

"What is it?"

"It's hard to say. I've been to the doctor and he doesn't know. He's given me a cream, but it's not helping much."

It was Eleanor who'd told me that I should take myself to a doctor to get my teeth cleaned. I was also experiencing another bout of gingivitis, and the wisdom tooth which had been threatening now for five years seemed to have finally made up its mind to make an appearance. Yippee yi ay, the joys of the corporeal world! I was certainly one for fleshly pleasures.

"Is it hives?"

"Don't give it a name," I moaned.

"I'm busy all week working and promoting a play. Let's get together early next week."

"Whatever."

We said our goodbyes and I scooted off, scratching away.

I hadn't been exactly truthful. I had been to the doctor and he'd given me a cream and an anti-histamine injection (which had knocked me senseless for six or so hours), but he'd also suggested I get a bottle of Quellada and douse myself in it before going to bed. Looking at the little scratch marks and sores around my groin and then listening to me describe how the problem seemed to date from when I'd moved rooms and started sleeping in a new bed, we both decided that the problem was probably bed bugs and that the sooner I did something about it, the sooner the problem would disappear. Simple. Logical.

Sydney's bugs were driving me crazy. Cockroaches were forever swarming all over my computer and my stereo. At first I thought I'd ignore them, mind over matter, but

I wasn't up to it and they soon had me screaming quietly. A week or so ago I'd gone out and bought a bottle of 'Kill 'Em Dead Number One' and bombed my room, but they were back again within a day. What on earth was a poor boy to do?

And I still hadn't bought the Quellada because I was bust (something you are well aware of by now), and my scratching was getting worse. When the welts had first appeared, dull purple bruises from where I'd been busy scratching, I'd had a moment's panic thinking of the calling card that is Karposi's sarcoma, AIDS ugliest harbinger, but remembered that I'd taken an AIDS test over a year ago, and that since that date I'd barely even looked at a poof, let alone had anything risky within reach of any of my orifices. No, this was fleas: it was plain, it was simple and it was horrible. Poverty has new tricks up its sleeves on a daily basis. Next dole payment I would treat myself to a bottle of Quellada and 'Kill 'Em Dead Number Two.' Oh, goody!

It was legitimately cold, even by the standards I'd learnt in Melbourne. I hurried my step as I made my way from the library to Simon's warehouse home. They were all there, Simon and Yvonne and Gary and Katie and their two cats, and Roseanne was on the box and Simon was serving out a simple but wholesome meal of rice and vegetables. It at least approximated heaven. But something was wrong. Simon didn't like that I was scratching cigarettes off everyone and wasn't interested in me loaning any magazines off him, and Seinfeld did little other than annoy all of us. And the sky had opened and the rain was bucketing down in the black outside. On Simon's floor I noticed a green and red umbrella, large and ornate.

"Oh, you found it," I said.

When I was in San Francisco in the winter of 1993, Clinton was being inaugurated and California was experiencing day upon day of massive rain. One night I got drunk and was picked up by a pimply Filipino boy who persuaded me to part with several of my scarce American dollars as we continued our drinking and cavorting, promising to pay me back in the morning. In one of our several taxi rides we had come across somebody's forgotten umbrella and taken it for our protection. In the morning he'd annoyed the hell out of me. For some reason I agreed with his mad scheme of renting a sports car and driving out to his mother's home across the Golden Gate bridge. He said that it would be his treat. When we were on the street, however, he suggested that we go direct to the car rental and that I should pay and that he would pay me back later in the day. I smelt a fish, a large one, and decided to get out from under his cloying hold immediately.

"No," I said, "we will go to a bank and you will draw some money and pay me back and we will leave it at that."

I thought he would cry. He was talking about me sponsoring his entry into Australia, for god's sake. It quickly became apparent that he had no money in no bank.

"Fine, my friend, but adios."

But he wouldn't go. He was crying on the street; he was pleading. When I threatened to punch him, someone attempted to intervene on his behalf.

"Fuck off," I muttered to his would-be protector.

"Same to you, buddy."

The situation was getting out of hand. The Filipino lad whimpered that he had nowhere to go, no money with which to get home to his mother's, his only safe haven in the entire USA. I escorted him to the train station and bought his ticket. He was still pleading with me, reminding me, entirely falsely, of the wonderful time we'd had together in the cot. I really did think I would have to punch him to wake him to the error of his sentiments.

Before parting, I had wrested the umbrella from his panicked grip.

"I'm keeping this. It'll be some compensation."

"I'll get wet," he whimpered.

"Fuck off," I grunted.

Last year, in Melbourne, I'd given that umbrella to Simon, some sort of token of appreciation for what he'd had to put up with when I was panicking and running around between Melbourne and Sydney and Perth. I'd asked him about it recently and he'd said that he couldn't find it. And now it was lying on the floor and Seinfeld had finished and it was raining outside and I could tell that Simon didn't much care for me this particular night.

"Can I have it?" I asked.

"You never should have given it to me, Owen", he said, "if you thought that one day you might want it back."

"Goodnight."

I left and made my way home, a bit cold, a bit wet. At midnight my dole would be credited to my bank account. That was still three hours away, but it was some consolation.

I crawled into bed and re-read old library books. At midnight I bounced up and walked around to two money machines, but both times the government's largesse had failed to materialise.

I went home and tried to sleep, but my life was troubling me, my bed uncomfortable and my fleas enjoying themselves merrily at my body's expense. At 2am I struggled up again and this time the money was there. I returned to my bed armed with soul food, coke and chocolate, but still sleep evaded me, finally coming at 4am.

Not for long, though.

At 5am I woke, in my mind the residue of a strange but friendly dream, forms and shapes coalescing into an attractive whole, apparently signifying a show that I was curating for the Museum of Contemporary Art at Circular Quay. It was an AIDS exhibition, a combination of pictures and texts.

I jumped out of bed smartly (something was meant to be done), and made my way down in the dark to Enmore's swimming pool, lapping and cavorting as the sun broke in the east and bathed the glassed enclosure of the pool in a soft pink light.

I was happy, deliriously so, and resolved to right whatever it was that could be righted in the course of a single day. I made my way down King St, pacing it impatiently as I waited for the shops to open. I bought a bottle of 'Kill 'Em Dead Number Two', cleaned my room, bombed it again, threw out all my old bedding, dressed myself in my plaid green suit, brown polo neck, brown suede shoes, green hat, bought myself new bedding from St Luke's op shop, packed the overdue library books in my black back pack and caught a train to Bondi Junction. I was alive and I was moving, the force with me. It was winter in Sydney and the sun was shining and the birds singing.

Everything went like a dream. The library had just the books I was after and Kelvin was home and willing to have me pay a call. Kelvin worked at the Museum of Contemporary Art. He was head attendant, not a position to be sneezed at. He was also a painter and my sometime friend.

In the course of a very pleasant conversation, Kelvin disclosed that the TV on which we were watching a Dave Graney music clip he'd found abandoned in the street. He offered me his old black and white telly. Only problem was that it only picked up the ABC. That was fine. We packed it in a box and I bade him farewell, catching a bus in to the Museum of Contemporary Art, armed with a pass supplied by Kelvin. I knew my friend Helena was on today and I wanted to see the exhibition of Czech art that was there.

I thought the bus driver was going to kill us. Wending its way through the curved streets of Paddington, the bus' wheels repeatedly mounted curbs and traffic islands. Added to which, the day had changed its course and decided to rain. Hell on eight wheels.

Helena was there, and she was fine, spirited company, moaning about life and her lack of stable love in her own inimitable way. Her troubles never failed to entertain and interest me. The Czech exhibition was deeply moving and I suggested to Helena that I might be interested in curating a show for the gallery, that I'd dreamed about such a thing. She seemed to think this a sensible idea (only she would) and she suggested I talk to her boss, Raymond, a man I'd noticed and respected and fantasised about (in decreasingly small measures), from a distance.

I told Helena that I was meeting Kelvin that night at Kinsela's and she agreed to come.

I took my TV and bag of library books and boarded the bus to Enmore. I'd intended to spend the afternoon occupied in editing my friend Bradford's autobiography, but was so delirious with joie de vivre and sleep deprivation that I decided I would be better occupied drinking and listening to records and toasting to my own glorious life. Three hours later I was pissed on two bottles of domestic lambrusco and dressing again for my night at Kinsela's. By the time I got there I was well and truly blind and have no idea what kind of fool I made of myself.

I woke the next morning at seven, still drunk, and cursing myself for yet again throwing away some of my hard-earned dole money on booze. When, oh, when would I learn? I had two hours to get myself across to Potts Point for my meeting with Bradford. I showered and dressed hastily, all in black, over the top of it a ludicrously bright sports jacket from Korea. Only last week, in the company of Helena, I'd stolen from the Bondi Junction Go-Lo store a $5 pair of sunglasses. I threw these over my belligerently red eyes and set off on a spirited fifteen kilometre walk, three times topping up my energy levels with coke and chocolate. My health could be damned: life was a never ending emergency.

I got there five minutes before Bradford. It was our most enjoyable breakfast meeting yet. Both of us were in rare happy form. I explained that I had no work with me because it was now pointless. I'd done as much editing as I would ever need to. The only thing for it now was to present it to him in disc form.

This would take money, money to have the hard copy scanned, money he would have to provide me with. He did so happily, slipping $250 into my eagerly proffered palm.

I set off for Central station. By the time I got there I was fagged. I slumped down on a seat waiting for my train to take me home to bed. This hangover would need curing. Dope would be nice, but coke and chicken and sleep would suffice. The new morn would see me right as rain.

Some hideous creature sat down next to me. He was thin, wasted, mid twenties, his feet in thongs, draped over his shoulders a pair of boots hanging by a shoe string. He asked me if I had any cigarette papers. I gave him the packet. In a strangely surreptitious move, he swiped two and returned them to me.

"I wanna roll a joint."

"Oh, yes."

We were being observed by a couple of old gents, pretty down and out themselves.

"Where you from?" he asked, as if I was an obvious tourist, an obvious rube. I get this question all the time, my voice a strange conflagration of American and English and Australian twangs.

"Sydney", I answered tentatively, deciding that after a year it was time I stopped saying Melbourne.

"See these boots?" he asked. "Bought them two weeks ago for $100 and now they're stained and the bastard who sold them to me won't take them back. Do you wanna have some of this joint I'm gonna roll?"

"I'd love to."

"Do you wanna buy some?"

"Maybe."

"Have you had any of this hash that's going around Sydney?"

"I haven't smoked any hash in Sydney."

It was true, plenty of head, but no hash.

"It's either Afghani or Lebanese. It's fantastic, mate. What's your name?"

He extended his hand. I took it warily. He shook it with enthusiasm.

"The name's Robin."

"Owen."

"So, wadda you say? Wanna buy some? I got $25 and $50 blocks."

"I might be interested in a $25 block. I'd have to see it."

"Sure, sure."

He got up and walked away. I didn't bother watching him. He returned quickly and sat down again. He now had a tattered copy of the Daily Telegraph in his hands.

"Have you read today's paper?" he asked.

"I've read the Sydney Morning Herald."

"I don't like doing this on a train station," Robin said.

"Well, that's where we are."

"Here, you gotta look at this," he said, shoving the paper at me, opened to the entertainment pages. Resting on it was a small plastic coin bag containing one decent sized block of hash.

"It's sticky like that, mate, because it's resinny. One blow and you'll go, mate, one blow and you'll go. It's usually $50, but for you I'll make it $40. Good stuff, mate, good stuff."

"Okay," I said, trawling $40 from out of my pants' pocket.

He pocketed the money while I pocketed the hash.

"Got a pen, mate."

"No."

"Maybe you'll want to buy some more, maybe your friends will want to buy some. I'll give you me number and you can call me. Got a pen?"

"No."

He looked around shiftily.

"Stay here. I'll go get one. Don't go anywhere."

He walked away. I didn't bother watching him. My train arrived and I got on and went home, completely zonked, but reassured by the recuperative force field I had secreted in my coat pocket. New money and new hash and good friends: what more could a poor boy need?

I got home and went to work, getting my room into some sort of order after I'd hidden everything the day before, bombing it. I was scheduled to photocopy my book later in the day. Then I was going to try and sell it. Life was sweet. I would have a joint and then I would get back on the train and go back in the exact same direction I'd just come home from.

I took the block of hash out of its bag. It felt funny. It was too pliable, soft and gooey. And then I smelt it. It was all wrong. It smelt like liquorice. I tried burning it, but nothing happened. And then I ate it. It was liquorice, forty dollar liquorice.

I laughed. Life was sweet and fate inexorable. I hope Robin enjoyed himself on Bradford's forty dollars.

That night I lay in bed completely exhausted, watching my new, free, black and white TV. ABC, of course. At 8.30 there was a science doco on fleas, on how wonderfully they have adapted to the human body, sourcing it every which they could. I simply couldn't watch.

WOMAN BORN OF MAN

Katherine Cummings

My ENDOCRINOLOGIST HAD prescribed a formidable regimen of hormones, both female and anti-male, to prepare my body for its future role and my emotions were reacting to these chemicals in a volatile and often unexpected and upsetting way. Tears were frequent and my emotions hit highs and lows foreign to my former even-tempered ways. Even in the few months between my first visit to Peter Haertsch and the date for my operation significant changes took place in my body, with my body fat redistributing itself under the coded persuasions of those mysterious drugs which made my waist reduce, my bust and hips enlarge, my body hair to vanish and my head hair to thicken. By the time 1989 started I was already physically more womanly than I had ever been and in January I left work for two weeks holiday to compose myself for the finale of my long march.

Katherine Cummings was born John Cummings in Aberdeen, Scotland in 1935, and grew up in the Gilbert Islands, New Zealand, Fiji, Scotland and Australia. She has travelled widely, studied and taken degrees in Sydney and Toronto, and lived and worked in the United States. Katherine is a reference librarian at Macquarie University Library and also writes regularly on a freelance basis.
The radio version of 'Katherine's Diary' was broadcast on Radio National for two years and was twice nominated for the Human Rights Radio Documentary Award.
Despite rumours to the contrary, Katherine has not worked as a lumberjack, sailed alone around Cape Horn or modelled for Oscar de la Renta. She has, however, worked as a payroll guard, sailed alone around Cremorne Point and modelled for Madame Lash.
'Woman Born of Man' is an extract from 'Katherine's Diary - The Story of a Transsexual.' First published William Heinemann, Australia, 1992; Mandarin, 1993.

I was constantly aware of the operation date creeping inexorably closer. Was I scared? You bet! Scared and excited and exhilarated and worried and apprehensive. Did I consider backing off, cancelling or postponing the date? Not for an instant.

When I returned to Sydney I had only a few days to fill before going to St David's for my operation. I contacted some friends who knew what I was doing, to give them final details. I left a letter of instruction for a friend in case I died on the operating table (you have to consider these things) and a letter for my family.

In my heart I knew that although I would appear much the same to the world when I emerged, this was the giant step into womankind, the one I could not retrace. The person I was about to become would no longer be the temporary, approximated daydream which had haunted me from earliest childhood but the concrete realisation of that dream, to be lived twenty-four hours a day, with the male memories and the male emotions and attitudes locked away as firmly as my female ones had been for fifty years and this would be the way of things as long as I both should live.

On February 5, 1989 I signed myself into St David's Private Hospital. I was received kindly by the hospital staff, who were used to transsexuals. One of the nursing staff confided that they usually saw one gender reassignment per week. This casts doubt on a 1988 estimate (Finlay and Walters) of four hundred post-operative transsexuals in Australia. Considering the number of hospitals carrying out these operations and the number of years they have been occurring, the figure is probably low by a factor of four or five...and this does not take into account those transsexuals who arrive in this country post-operative, nor those who go overseas to have their operations.

Signing oneself into a hospital has its own routines and St David's was no exception. I was weighed, measured, questioned and labelled.

The labelling was a wise precaution. I would not have wanted my operation given to someone else by mistake ... and he would probably have liked it even less. I was instructed in the geography and disciplines of St David's and treated with professional courtesy by the matron and sisters.

My room was small but light and comfortable and I spent the first night tranquilly.

Some months earlier I had been lunching at the Satasia after finding out my operation date and was euphoric with the knowledge that another major step forward was about to be taken. My lunch companion was congratulating me when Aleta asked why I seemed so happy. I told her and she said that she would have to remember the date and send flowers. I was pleased but thought it only a polite response, particularly as the date concerned was some months away and in a different calendar year. Yet on my second morning there was a beautiful arrangement of flowers in the room, sent by Aleta and Andrew, the first of many floral good wishes which soon threatened to give my bed the appearance of a catafalque. I have been amazingly lucky in my friends, who have demonstrated a warmth and compassion which have ameliorated many of the sad times.

I woke easily to the day when everything was to come together, or if you look at it from another point of view, everything was to come apart.

My surgeon and anaesthetist visited me and spoke words of friendship and encouragement. The day was warm and I dozed on and off between the visits from the kind, skilled people who were going to remake me the way I had always felt I should be.

I didn't enjoy the enema, although I could see the reason for it and I was calm, even before the sister came to pre-med me with an injection which made me even sleepier than before. Not for a moment did I feel any reluctance or doubt as I was trollied down to the nether regions of the hospital, dressed only in one of those comic gowns which opens down the back.

The operating theatre was as bright and sterile as I was, and the masked and gowned anaesthetist and surgeon and their assistants were my friends. One or two words from the surgeon and the anaesthetist put a needle into the back of my hand and said "See you when you wake up, Katherine." I started to drift off to sleep, then, equally slowly, felt my senses returning. Maybe the anaesthetic hadn't taken effect and I should say something quickly before they started to cut. Then I realised I was not in the theatre but in the recovery room and the surgeon leaning over me had pulled his mask down and was, therefore, not about to do anything surgical.

"I've done a good job, Katherine, you'll like it," he said and I am proud to say that from the depth of my anaesthetic fog I replied, "I've changed my mind. Put it all back."

Luckily we had met often enough for him to know my irresponsible and sometimes inappropriate sense of humour, so that he was able to respond with, "Too late, it's gone to the delicatessen."

Although I slept through all the most interesting bits of my operation, I needed details of the procedures for my radio series and my surgeon was kind enough to grant me an interview some weeks after I recovered. Peter Haertsch has developed highly advanced techniques and constantly seeks better methods. Some of his procedures follow the standard routines written up in most books on sex change but some, particularly the creation of the clitoris, appear to be in advance of work being done overseas.

Several kinds of surgeons carry out gender reassignments. Some are general surgeons, some gynaecologists and some plastic surgeons. Peter Haertsch is a plastic and reconstructive surgeon, which is appropriate since a lot of soft tissue reconstructive work is involved. The male-to-female operation is now possible as a single procedure although I have read recent accounts of operations taking up to seven hours.

The first stage requires the removal of the residual male organs, which have usually been reduced by a year or more of hormone therapy. As the male pelvis is not shaped for a vaginal cavity this must be created and having been made must be kept open, as there will always be a tendency for it to close up. Lifelong dilation is therefore necessary...but more of that problem anon.

After the penis has been removed the penile skin is retained as a lining for the new vagina for a number of reasons. Not only is the skin hairless and erogenous but when turned inside out it is an appropriate form for the vagina and can be packed with a dressing to create the new cavity. A small part of the glans is retained with its artery and nerves in order to create a clitoris.

If the penile skin is insufficient for the vagina then a split skin graft from the inner thigh may be required, as in the case of Renee Richards, of, 'Second Serve,' fame. Split skin, however, lacks the durability and sensitivity of penile skin. Some surgeons use scrotal skin, which has the drawback of being hairy, and some use a section of bowel as this retains the quality of constant moisture, which can be an advantage for lubrication but can also lead to problems of discomfort and odour.

The urethra must be repositioned so that urination can be comfortably carried out in a sitting position. When the necessary adjustments and reconstructions have been carried out the new vagina is filled with a packing dressing held in place by a suture across the buttocks. A catheter is inserted to drain the bladder and drains put in place on either side of the groin. In my own case the whole operation took just on two hours, which Peter Haertsch claims to be average.

And now to the matter of pain. There wasn't any. Discomfort, of course, what with drips and drains and catheters for the first few days but I don't recall taking any pain killers ... which is fairly remarkable if you compare my experience with those of other transsexuals.

Renee Richards writes of 'sharp, shooting pains of searing intensity...a tearing sensation...like someone was ripping at my organs with a pair of pliers' and Tula (Caroline Cossey) says 'It was if I was sitting on the edge of a cliff with my private parts hanging over and that a huge weight was attached to them, pulling them down'. April Ashley says 'I became aware of a most hideous pain...it was as if branding irons were being applied to the middle part of my body'. Neither Jan Morris nor

Christine Jorgensen refers to pain. I asked the surgeon whether I had been lucky or he had been particularly skilful but he modestly maintained that there is a wide spectrum of pain perception and one person's agony is another's annoyance. I should add, however, that I have visited several newly operated transsexuals since my own operation and one came and stayed with me during her convalescence and all seemed to suffer a lot more than I did. So pain must be a highly variable factor and I should not be so dismissive simply because I was fortunate.

One phenomenon I had not expected...a phantom penis. I had read of amputees who still feel their fingers or toes long after the surgical removal of the associated limbs but it had not occurred that this would apply to me. Sure enough, however, there was the unmistakable sensation of a ghostly appendage where my eyes and fingers assured me there was none. The feeling gradually diminished and virtually vanished by the end of the second day.

I spent the first days after the operation resting and being visited by friends bringing flowers, fruit and encouragement. On the third day Peter Haertsch came and removed the suture holding the packing in my vagina. (How new and wonderful it seemed to be thinking of 'my vagina'!). After the packing came out it was necessary for a new pack to be inserted, one which I could remove and insert as necessary. This caused the only serious discomfort of my convalescence. The pack was made from a condom stuffed with foam plastic and learning to insert it for myself was a necessary ordeal if I were to look after myself properly when I returned home.

The beastly thing wouldn't go in easily, partly because I didn't know my own new anatomy and partly because the foam would bunch up outside my vagina so that just when I thought it was in I would realise that ninety percent of it was still outside me. Even when I did manage to get it all inside the muscles strained to force it out again, lubricated as it had to be for insertion. This may all sound grotesque, or funny, depending on your point of view, but from my viewpoint it was frustrating, undignified, exhausting and very, very stressful. If I dozed off I almost invariably woke to find the pack had popped out and had to be painfully reinserted.

I tried everything I could think of to keep it in place. The One-Size-Fits-Nobody hospital pants were useless, stretch bandages failed and finally I resorted to wearing elasticised sports briefs at all times. Those concerned with administering the gender reassignment operation must give some thought to finding a satisfactory way of keeping the newly operated transsexual's vaginal cavity open without the constant strain of fighting a self-ejecting pack night and day.

I must, however, praise every other aspect of the program. On the third day the catheter and drains came out, the surgeon visited me again to check my recuperation and emphasise the need for twice-daily dilation of the vagina. I complained about the problem of the foam plastic packs and was assured that after I had been given a glass dilator matters would be much easier.

I was also guaranteed twelve months free aftercare. No matter what went wrong in the first twelve months I was to contact my surgeon and the problem would be remedied without charge. I asked if this meant twelve months or ten thousand lovers, whichever came first but he declined to commit himself.

Before leaving Haertsch said "I'm going to touch your clitoris, Katherine, to see if it is sensitive." As I clawed my way down from the ceiling I murmured "Thank you, doctor, yes, it does seem to be quite sensitive...". He gave me permission to check out of the hospital as soon as I felt well enough and left me to my thoughts.

And on the seventh day I went home, a new woman.

After my return from the hospital I was not in serious pain, although there was a good deal of swelling and bruising, so I spent most of my time lying down or standing for the first few days. I also spent a considerable time in hot salt-water baths and I think these greatly speeded my recovery.

The swelling receded and the bruising disappeared after two weeks. My visit to the surgeon for a checkup and removal of the internal sutures was no ordeal at all. Even driving a car no longer required a very soft cushion! Peter Haertsch examined his handiwork and pronounced himself satisfied, although there was a small web of skin he felt should be removed in a few weeks, just to perfect the job. He explained that if ever I wanted to have intercourse (which many surgeons recommend as a satisfactory way to keep the vagina dilated) then the follow-up surgery would be necessary. Although sex is not my mainspring and the thought of sex with men has never tempted me, I did want my new body to be perfect, so I agreed to the small additional operation and a date was set for a few weeks further on. I was then supplied with a set of three glass dilators in graduated sizes, looking like fat little test tubes. At last I was able to discard the hated stuffed condom packs.

The intervening weeks passed quickly. I returned to work the day after my checkup and life rapidly returned to its routines. My second trip to St David's would have been an anti-climax if I had not been made so welcome by the staff. One asked about my writing and others were interested to know how my new life was progressing. It was a bit like returning to boarding school after the Easter hols. ("I say, Angela, you are a brick!")

My second stay in hospital was much briefer than the first. I arrived on Monday morning, the operation was on Monday afternoon and I went home on Tuesday morning. A few friends asked me why I needed to go back so soon and I told them the second operation was so that I could have children. When they expressed astonishment or disbelief I would add "as long as they are male and over eighteen." But the fact is that my life is as celibate since my operation as it was immediately before. My transsexualism is and always was inside my head, not my loins. There is room for only one love in my life and she is lost to me.

Photo: Scott Wagon

Photo: Eros Candusso

THE BELTING PARAMETERS

David King

 H ERE I AM, STARING OUT OF THE
window, trying to write a story (but all too conscious that sentences are just lines of
signifiers against the dark semiotic web grounding them), when my eighteen-year-
old house border Brett slinks in. His expression combines sheepishness with something
that strikes me as odd – almost shifty. He clearly knows I found the joint under his
bed: but he is trying to tell me that I was meant to find it? Is he trying to add another
dimension to our rite?

Either way, my role is clear. I weigh down my sheets of paper with my copies of
'Dissemination and Justine'; then, collectedly, I stand, and go to the rack on which
hangs the belt. For a few moments, I contemplate it, and then I take it down, aware
of its large tarnished buckle and the cracks which testify to its frequent use. Then I
glance at Brett. He swallows; his Adam's apple goes up and down. He knows what
is going to happen next.

"Brett – you know why I'm doing this. I want you to lower your jeans and
underpants, and bend over the desk."

With an air of proud and defiant resignation, he does so. I pause, relishing his suspense;
then I double the belt over, take aim and there rear up before me The Belting Parameters:

---

*David King lives in Western Australia, where he is a part-time tutor at Murdoch University. He has a PhD in
philosophy. He lives with his lover of 12 years. He's been published in various literary magazines in Australia
and overseas. He enjoys the sauna aspect of the gay lifestyle.*
*"In 'The Belting Parameters' I wish to shock the reader commensurate with that experienced by the house border.
I'm using fiction to perform S&M on the reader."*

Duration

How long should a belting be? The ones administered to Brett's backside have varied in length from several seconds to several minutes, with a standard deviation of about ten seconds. Many times I've stood behind him, savouring the formerly intractable but now quivering adolescent male flesh as it recoils from the stinging blows, and wished I'd thought to buy a stop watch. But then, duration is only one of the Belting Parameters.

Intensity

At the shock of the first blow, the muscles in his backside contracted sharply, and he gasped. Now, a few seconds later, there is across both cheeks a rectangular red weal. It has long been my hypothesis that varying the intensity of the blows varies the rate of appearance of the weals, not their hue; and this blow confirms it, for it was very hard. "I don't ever want to find a joint under your bed again! I hope I'm making myself understood." The belt descends again, and the resulting rectangle links up with the first, making a capital 'V'. He shifts to one side; I imagine the foreskin is now rolling back from his hardening penis. It usually is at this stage.

Humour

That humour is not one of the Belting Parameters has been suggested to me by experience. Last week, for example, I'd decided to cane Brett instead of belt him. I'd toyed with the idea of saying "First the cane, and then the cock" (reaching in front of him to stroke his erect penis). I'd realised, however, that this sentence would have drained all potency from the cocktail of respect, fear, love, and sensuality we share. It would have been the same if I'd said "First the belt, and then the bolt." Humour razes the illusion of presence, and a cane gives even more of a sense of presence than does a belt. It's so much more painful - which is why I ration it.

Geometry

According to Christchurch Boys' High School, an ideal cane should be three feet long and half an inch wide. "The boys did not resent caning and preferred it to other punishments; they were actually proud of it." The prohibition of corporate punishment would surely result in the loss of a whole dimension from adult sexuality - unless, naturally, sexuality is genetic. But, in many respects, the issue is not dimensionality, but topology. Topologically, after all, a belt is deformable into a cane. Surely also significant is the fact that a stroke of a cane cuts *across* the backside while a cock goes *up it*, forming a pair of intersecting lines, or axes: an X of pleasure, or of erasure.

Frequency

"Step back, Brett." He does so, trying, as usual, to hide his erection behind one of the volumes on my desk. His face is red, and I can tell that at each smarting blow his eyes would have screwed up as he silently mouthed "Fuck" in pain. "How often do I have to keep doing this? Do you think I like thrashing you almost into unconsciousness, like some cheeky brat?" I pretend to lose my temper, and push him back over the desk. The belt makes a fleshy smacking sound as I reach with my other hand for the tube of KY.

Spacing

The interval between the blows is the time most to relish. It is the time to take in details, such as, around Brett's size 11 feet, the faded jeans and the cracked tan belt under whose bite, delivered with a cruel adolescent hand, I myself would give anything to bleed, if it were not for the fact that switching our roles would spoil them. It is a time when one can appreciate that a belting, like a story, never ends: when it seems to end it merely fades into another signifying practices. "I think you've learned your lesson, Brett." Silently, he nods, his eyes fighting back moisture. He carefully draws his jeans up over his hairy legs. At their apex, I tell myself, I have had my animal way, which is the way of all texts. I return to my desk, thinking now of the pleasure my projected story on beltings will bring: the shock it will deliver to my readers, and the humiliating mail that will, as a result, be delivered to me.

PERSONAL ADVERTISEMENTS

various queer authors

FITZROY NORTH 36YO, NON
SCENE, HONEST, INTELLIGENT,
CARING, SINCERE SMOKER. INTO
FILM, READING, MUSIC, FOOD,
TRAVEL ETC. SEEKS FRIENDLY,
GENUINE BEAR OR BEAR LOVER
(PASSIVE) FOR MUTUAL,
MONOGAMOUS, MARVELLOUS
MEETING OF MINDS AND FUR!
PHONE PLEASE. 440393☎

Editors Note: *Personal advertisments have an important place in queer culture. They document unique and diverse stories about seekers of lust, love and happiness. They also mirror the culture, health matters and other issues of our time.*

ingleburn/sydney 26yo, 5'7", blue eies, short brown hair, cute secretary. Seeking 26-35yo, tall, slim, attractive guy who is either a businessman, Fireman, Policeman, Army, Airforce or tradesman. 11414

BOXING Gdlooks & body slim 39. Seek fit non fat mates for going to boxing matches videos friendly horsing around with gear & leather gloves. Also into wrestling. ★711482 Reply 248104

CANBERRA Chubby guy 30s bald hairy body & uncut. Seek b'minded guy willing to come down for a hot time. Age open. Older guys welcome. ☎ if poss. Reply 248006

victoria Like to humiliate hustlers, street punks, macho types, through heavy S&M, B&D, W/S? Wish to contact other dominants with similar interests. Beer, smoke, overweight OK. Genuine only. 100143

inner west 36yo bi boy with gender identity problems, wishes to meet girl with, or interest in, gender identity problems. Purpose: Mutual enjoyment of so called problems. 901139

RECLAIM The night. Saw you at the Rally & then Exchange, you forgot your cigarettes, lets meet.

FEMININE 22yo dark eyes long dark hair & slim. Into live music books cafes magazines. Seek same for f'ship. Reply 248043

redfern Single white male, 22yo, stable, employed. Seeks similar, potential housemates (2), for move to house in Randwick/Coogee in February/March 1995. Jennifer Jason Leigh types need not apply. 13614

randwick If ABC and 2SER suits you fine, if a shy, quiet guy seems appealing, if notions of machismo bore you, if mid forties is not a liability, if love is something you're missing; soul mate? Momentous decision. 17015

GDLOOKING Guy 26. Into movies occasional scene dining out. Seek a gdlooking romantic with a savoir faire & finesse. Sensual love making. I need lots of affection. Any nationality. French a bonus. Reply 249078

bonnyrigg I'm a 21yo Chinese, tanned, solid and defined, 5'6", 58kg, loyal and romantic with wide interests. You should be medium to chubby or muscular to 40yo and non-Asian. I'm keen to be your friend, lover or a mate. Let's find out how far we could go. Contact me now! 13315

22YO Hdsome fit guy. Over my boyhood & couldnt care for meaningless encounters. Would like to build on thip. Wanting someone that feels the same. Age open. Reply 248021

ROMANTIC Submissive leatherboy. Seek younger dominant leatherboy. For long term pleasure day & night. Head to toe satisfaction. Tie me & try me. Any nationality. HIV+ OK. ALA ★694484 Reply 248058

SUBMISSIVE Need lover to take control. In return for complete loyalty. Your pleasure my aim in life. Tatts piercing amyl smoke leather BD SM restraints HIV+. All OK. ★727495 Reply 249107

I'M Looking for a dark hair/eyed goddess that wants the finer things in life that I'm willing to give. Passionate romantic 22yo dyke from West Sydney seeks the above. Reply 248065
INNER CITY Seek a together 40+ woman. Who enjoys the company of a sincere easy going intel woman with a variety of interests. Reply 248109

sydney Giving up? But you haven't met me yet! An articulate, fun loving, mid 20's Asian spunk, just waiting to meet you. Mr., I'm worth the effort. Dare & do soon! 13015

SYDNEY 6'4" fit hdsome intel masc passionate 36yo. Seek sim sincere intel attractive fit guy 25-38. Who happens to like men & dares to be real. Pics apprec'd. ★697497 Reply 249042

WHITE PERSIAN Male cat. Seeks new home. Me: Handsome, mature, good natured, desexed (sigh). You: Warm, caring. ☎ Gavin

sydney Hi sir. Cruising safe, sane, discreet sex? I guess it's time to meet me. I'm a spunky guy, seductive, naughty and keen to please. Out of town, mature gents, business or pleasure my speciality. Contact me anytime.

A TALE FROM THE BACKROOM

Nic Frankham

F OR SOMEONE NOT INTO EXERCISE, like me, cruising backrooms can be the most exhilarating circuit on offer. Many of my days are spent ascending black-lit stairs, anticipating thick afternoons that unbuckle, unzip and unfurl into a sweaty scene of cocks, tongues, nipples and lips. Usually, it takes a while before God happens along. But when the time comes, you'll know: when the body unwraps himself from the middle, jeans inch below the groin to display incredible thighs, his t-shirt climbs shyly beyond the camel trail to reveal taut, heaving chest.

Tentatively removing my shirt I get slipped a delicious tongue in my mouth, under my armpits, across the chest, into my navel and HA! I look down through the gloom to see a murky beauty going hell for leather, jawline momentarily ruined, serious eyeballs bulging up at me. I lean back against the sticky partition to avoid looking just as absurd. Bored, I swap roles for a tick. He starts spouting American crap. He's not American.

"Ooo yair, sock thaat cahk."

Great. I shut him up with a pash. But some 'str'acting' men don't know how to tongue with a sense of timeliness. Gag you, chew you, gag you. Still, the click of

---

This story was first published in the Sydney Star Observer newspaper as part of a series of stories submitted for 'Tales From the Backroom'. The AIDS Council of NSW solicits material from gay men as part of the 'Man on Man' project. The aim of the regular column is to encourage HIV debate on diverse sex experiences had in backrooms, saunas and beats. The hidden message: safe sex means such sexual pleasures can be had.

cognition, if and when it happens, is worth it. They are no longer obliged to pretend to know everything. Exploration begins, then it gets hot. Sometimes, however, anonymous sex can be anything but.

Like what do you do when a man comes into the cubicle – at your invitation – and instead of the initial routine described above he pushes you hard onto the porn monitor (so your nipples feel gaffered to the sticky 10" screen) with strong wrists and femur bones and forces his cock up your "I-have-to-be-relaxed" arse? Moreover, do you react when he starts dry-fucking you and all you can do, embarrassingly, is whisper "ow" and "stop" while he thrusts, pushes and manipulates your posture, rasps, gasps, pulls up his pants and does a flit before you can even croak "rape"?

Those and other questions struck me as I slunk from the sex shop onto the street, making my way towards the bus stop with my arse frighteningly sticky. I usually walked, no bounded, out onto the street with head high, ready to counter possible school friend interrogatives, as to my emergence from a filthy-dirty-sex-shop, with an even stare and a flat lie. Instead, I was used and defeated. I passed Videorama, recalling late-late movies, and considered douching with Coca-Cola.

What rape meant had become smeary. There was nowhere to clean myself because Oxford Street, it appeared, wasn't allowed to have public toilets. Rape was supposed to happen in a shopping centre car park, and be committed by gruff men with limps and balaclavas. I sported a hardon throughout – which is no mean feat in a stinking shipboard tardis with only celluloid femme tongue-play and a rapist for source material. I believed I must have somehow enjoyed it, without understanding the physiology involved.

Thus, with all the illicitness of a fuckbar, the episode was pushed to the backroom of my head. For a time. I never told anyone about it, and considered it an event of the past. Except when it came to HIV testing. It was probably that incident alone which scared me away from testing for three years. When I did go, it was the freakiest time in memory. But I survived the rape, the waiting time, and scored a negative test result. Next time anything like that happens, and believe me when I tell you it happens a lot - in backrooms, bedrooms, beaches, BBQ's – I'm gonna do everything I can to make sure it stops. Be alert, talk to your friends, figure out effective ways of negotiating sex safely, and how to get out of 'sticky' situations. Above all else: Screw etiquette.

CONJUGAL RIGHTS

Lance Price

T HEY WENT OUT INTO THE MISTED, densely humid night. On the ground, wet asphalt glittered; fast food cartons, beer cans, crushed cigarettes and soaked newspaper silted the gutter. The drizzle had lifted. Above them solitary stars were visible between dark banks of fast moving clouds.

Patrick said hesitantly, "I parked down here," as they turned into one of the series of streets converging at the back of StVincents Hospital. He glanced at Joshua anxiously. "You don't mind, do you? Coming back for a drink?"

Joshua smiled. "Of course not." He laid a comforting hand on Patrick's muscled shoulder, squeezing companionably. "Why should I mind?"

They'd met just one hour earlier, huddled in the smoke and noise of the Albury Hotel, crowded for a Wednesday night. An eternal hour, Joshua felt now, as he followed Patrick down the steep narrow street, in which his ardour dimmed perceptibly. It was always the same – the promise of a casual encounter less enticing in actuality than fantasy – a paradox he'd long wished would prevent him straying. But he had promised himself to Patrick for tonight; he would follow it through. Any familiar guilty thoughts of his partner he pushed away angrily. It was academic that

Lance Price was born in Newcastle, New South Wales, in 1968 and grew up in the Blue Mountains. He currently lives in Perth and has previously lived in Sydney's inner east and western suburbs. He is the Personnel Officer for the Faculties of Medicine and Science at the University of Western Australia.
'Conjugal Rights' is his first published work. He is currently completing a collection of short fiction.

between them each remain free to pursue contacts outside the main frame of their relationship, even if it was Joshua's fault Philip didn't know.

It was not that he didn't love Philip. No, he loved him deeply, so much so that as their fifth anniversary advanced inexorably toward them, Joshua couldn't envisage a life without him. There were innumerable sweet things about Philip which Joshua loved: the way each morning he'd fold Joshua into his arms, reluctant to separate so they could each face the day; his ribald, loud, emotive laughter; his inimitable sexual habits, the way he moaned and clutched Joshua when he was just about to come; his sense of the impermanence of things, so that if it all fell swiftly from them – the jobs, the car, the renovated apartment, the seventy two thousand dollar joint income, it wouldn't matter. Between them lay the core of something better – each other.

And neither had his desire cooled. Of course, as time had flung them further forward, there were dull weeks and months even, when between them physical affection was at best desultory. But an old match can still be struck; this Joshua knew. Something would happen – one would brush up against the other, lightly, accidentally, or Joshua would roll over in the middle of the night and wake to discover his body curled to conform to Philip's – and they found each other again. Just like the first time, wildly, with a little surprise. And Philip's laughter would burst from him loud and warm and endearing.

It was not dissatisfaction that drove Joshua to pursue the random encounter; he did not lack love; he wasn't lonely or sexually frustrated. His relationship with Philip seemed oddly complete, almost symbiotic, a strange confluence of wishes and dreams. Of course he knew there were some small faults – the largest his own continual acquiescence beneath the soft weight of Philip's stronger will. That same inability to assert himself that'd allowed them to proceed so far so smoothly. Not that Philip had ever overtly coerced him; it was the gentle touch of command in him before which Joshua submitted, quite willingly, a thin line of steel invisible to any outsider. And for years now their union had proceeded in the same structured manner. The very idea of change had become anathema.

He knew why he was driven to deceive Philip; he knew why he'd continue to deceive him, time and again. When they'd first met, Joshua had believed himself transformed by love. The old selfish habits, the addictive pursuits, the very things from which he'd begged for rescue – well, they too would be transformed by love into nobler, less intense, obsessive emotions. And so the long days and nights of their togetherness began, with Joshua hushed and expectant, awaiting the magic transformation. But his character didn't change; the conjugal life brought to him only another way of knowing the world. There was no one, great and all enduring love. There were many varied ways of loving; many means. He wanted them, too, as well as Philip. He wanted the hundred little momentary loves his previous assignations had brought him.

So, now a little shamefacedly, he stood beside a red Hyundai as Patrick unlocked the doors. He felt a wave of irrational nervousness. Patrick did not slide easily into the pattern of his previous contacts; too anxious, he thought, too panicked. He was tall, broad shouldered, bulky, casually but expensively dressed in jeans and a light rust coloured sweater. His face was arresting, bumpy, irregular, exuding strength and purpose. He'd have to be edging his mid-thirties, Joshua thought; Philip's age, possibly a year or two older. An odd thought struck him - he had until now avoided sex with men who reminded him of Philip, whether in age or quirky mannerism. The thirty odd men he'd been with these past five years had all been Philip's physical opposites. They'd had blond hair, red hair, blue eyes, green eyes; they were not tall, broad shouldered, particularly hairy or bent forward with that distinctive stoop of a scholar, like Philip.

Patrick had dark hair, dark eyes, like Philip. His voice was deep and resonant, recalling to Joshua the musical lilt of Philip's voice, rich currents of warmth. He was a stockbroker (thank God, Joshua thought - Philip taught primary school). He had an office and a secretary; he worked on Bridge street, down near the Quay. Each June he travelled to San Francisco to attend the annual Gay Freedom Day Parade. He had a dog, a terrier, called Lloyd. He'd grown up in Sydney's eastern suburbs; he'd attended Cranbrook. All this he told Joshua in the car, while they drove up past Edgecliff station and on into Woollahra, where Patrick owned a terrace. He kept glancing across at Joshua awkwardly in the darkened interior of the car. There was something so comfortably diffident about him, Joshua felt, the way he opened himself up for perusal. That same quality of vulnerability Joshua knew present in himself. Even the way he had hit on him had been slightly unusual, sliding up to him dexterously, inclining his head politely to ask, "Would you mind if I introduced myself?" Joshua had had to bite back the instinctive urge to say yes.

"Get off me, stupid mutt!" Patrick bawled at a ragged terrier who bounded up to them, quivering with excitement, when they entered the foyer of his house. Lloyd panted and barked alternately, while Patrick slid one hand up under the dog's collar, dragging him off. "Just a minute," he called shyly over his shoulder. "I'll put him outside." Various doors opened and closed, then Patrick appeared again, smiling apologetically. "Sorry about that," he said. He rubbed the palms of his hands together, agitated. "Would you like a drink?"

Joshua followed him into a large room opening off the hall. He peered around discreetly at what seemed to be antiques but could've possibly been fakes. Heavy red draperies shut out the glare trying to edge in from an outside streetlight. The wooden floors had been polished until they gleamed; an oriental rug wound with tufted colours lay centre of the room. Patrick stood by an oak paneled bar, fiddling with a pair of cut glass tumblers. Joshua sat down in an overstuffed armchair.

"Scotch? Brandy? Contreau?"

"Contreau sounds nice," Joshua said. He was watching Patrick's back, entranced by the way the muscles bunched in his neck each time he breathed. There was a certain unsettling energy about him, as if he were gathering strength before the effort to push himself forward. Gingerly, Patrick handed him the drink. They talked desultorily, sitting opposite each other on the overstuffed, uncomfortable armchairs. Patrick described his job; he spoke at length about interest rates, share options, the futures exchange. He chatted about his visits to the States, detailing the many leather bars he'd visited, the most amazing fist fucking he'd witnessed in a Castro bathhouse, the West Hollywood porn star he'd had sex with by default. He joked cruelly about the simpering antics of well known Oxford street queens. A low humming anxiety settled itself in Joshua, a warning he recognised instinctively. For such a shy and nervous man, he'd bet Patrick was a real bastard in bed. But he felt it already too late, too rude to attempt to leave. It would insult Patrick, possibly hurt him, and it would be a breach of sexual ethics.

Then Patrick asked heavily, "Would you like to take off your clothes?" An edge had crept into his voice, the soft supplicating tones, the politeness, gone.

"Here?" Joshua asked.

He nodded. "Right here. Please."

Joshua hesitated. Patrick had already begun jerking his thick dick with one hand, spreading spit on it with the other. He stared at Joshua intently, aggressively. There had commenced in Joshua a strange distancing sensation, as if he were edging outside himself, watching in disbelief. He stood up and began to disrobe. First his glasses, then his sensible shoes, the sensible white denim shirt Philip bought at David Jones in winter, his jeans and boxer shorts, his socks. The heavy gold Rolex. He stood before Patrick, naked, half erect.

"Jesus," Patrick muttered. "You're really beautiful."

This Joshua found difficult to believe. He knew himself: thin, angular, awkward, small. At twenty eight, he still sometimes felt like an adolescent, underdeveloped. The hairs on his legs might be dense and wiry, but on his arms and chest and stomach, they spread thin, pale, insignificant. No amount of sexual contact, nor one hundred pairs of hands, had brought to him an ease with his body; even with Philip there were still moments Joshua marvelled someone could crave him so much.

Patrick stood up; his expensive jeans slipped down around his expensive shoes. Joshua knelt down and began to suck him. Patrick talked dirty; he barked commands. Eat this. Suck that. Run your tongue along here. He grabbed Joshua's hair roughly and forced his dick deep into his mouth. Feeling it bobbing against the wall of his throat, Joshua gagged, choking, retreating. He did not want Patrick to come in his mouth. And he was a little surprised – and frightened – at how aggressive Patrick had become. He kept pulling his swollen dick from Joshua's mouth, slapping it against his face, urging, coaxing. His desire seemed an angry insistence which Joshua disliked.

And suddenly he felt his own sexual excitement dissipate, the swift contraction of an energy he'd always taken as a given right. Patrick continued unaware; a litany of smut poured from his mouth. But for Joshua there was a moment of fierce disgust, a savage awareness of kneeling naked on a polished wooden floor, his face sticky from his own saliva and the smell of Patrick's uncut dick, while this large frightening man hovered over him, grunting, groaning.

He pulled back and looked up tentatively. "Listen, Patrick. I can't do this."

Patrick looked momentarily confused. "What?"

"I told you," Joshua said, quickly putting on his shirt and nervously securing buttons. "I can't do this. It's not what I expected. I – "

Patrick hit him. He pulled back with a fully clenched fist and struck him again. The force of the second blow sent Joshua sprawling, back against the rosewood table on which their unfinished drinks lay waiting. A glass smashed; there was the hard repetitive tinkle of ice cubes striking the floor. A low ringing buzzed in his ears. He felt dizzy and unsteady and confused. Somehow he was on his hands and knees, half naked, trembling, patting the wooden floor in search of his glasses, certain that if he could only find them the room would stop its crazy tilting, he could grab his clothes and leave. Blood trickled from his nose. His lip had split; he coughed once and a spray of blood arched over the shiny wooden boards.

Patrick grabbed him. There was a brief frantic struggle, then Patrick had him pinned down over the arm of a red fabric covered sofa. He felt three fingers thrust roughly into his rectum, then part of a hand. He felt himself tear; pain ran like a knife up through him. Then Patrick was pushing into him, lubricated with a little spit and the leaking blood. He took hold of a fistful of Joshua's hair and lifted his head, stretching tight the muscles in his neck. He thrust hard, angrily, with a rush of intense excitement.

Through the fog of fear and pain and panic, Joshua heard the same curious words re-printing themselves in his mind. I am allowing this, he thought. This is me allowing this. He felt a sudden stab of longing for Philip, so intense he almost cried out. Then the pain took him up, higher, Patrick arching deep into Joshua's body, muttering through clenched teeth unintelligible words. He pulled back suddenly, barely inside Joshua when he came, and finally Joshua cried out in shock at the hot flood of semen filling him.

Patrick pulled out and stepped back. "Shit," he said, as if returning to himself. "Jesus Christ!" He seemed close to tears. "You bastard! You made me do that!" He dressed hurriedly, then turned away to the bar and began fixing a drink. "Get dressed," he snapped derisively.

Joshua eased off the sofa, picking his clothes from the floor. He was shaking so badly he could barely fasten the buttons on his jeans. He lifted three fingers to wipe his nose; they came away wet with blood. He felt faint and sat down abruptly, gasping in pain.

Patrick came hesitantly toward him holding a squat crystal tumbler in one hand, Joshua's gold rimmed glasses in the other. He looked frightened, dismayed, apologetic. His face twitched nervously; he trembled.

Joshua took his glasses and put them on. When Patrick held out the drink, he shoved his hand away angrily. "Go fuck yourself," he snarled.

Patrick quivered. "Christ," he said. "I'm really sorry, I mean it. I - I guess." He looked down at the brandy stain soaking into the oriental rug, his face suffused with shame. Then he murmured very softly, "Help me. Jesus, help me."

It was something in his voice to which Joshua responded, recognising in Patrick a symmetry with himself. Understanding gathered in him, a palpable weight. The future opened briefly, reflected in Patrick's dark eyes, his tense body coiled with frustration, loneliness and loss. He looked up and opened his arms wide in a posture of crucifixion or blessing. And Patrick, bewildered and frightened, came quickly to him.

★

Philip knew. He'd known for some time, he realised sourly, sitting in the darkened living room of their lower Macleay street flat, a knowing that had traced gently beneath the surface of their everyday life. It'd been apparent in Joshua's smallest acts: a new sexual trick offered with a laugh and innocent surprise; a note of guilt and entreaty in his voice when they lay close together, talking in the night; the odd moments when he'd caught Joshua watching him, as if trying to read some unspoken knowledge into the profile of his face. It all fanned out before him wide like a loaded deck of cards. Joshua had lied and schemed and tricked him. A slow burn had begun spreading in his chest, flamed by a little spurt of anger.

In part, Philip blamed himself. Over time, in his relationship with Joshua, things between them had settled into a pattern where Philip led and Joshua followed. Exactly how it had come about he'd never been entirely sure - Philip had not wanted to dominate or control him. When they'd first met, he had sensed in Joshua a wish to be taken in, a need to escape his bewilderment at what had come to him in the world. And because Philip loved him - he truly loved him, to a depth he'd never before realised himself capable of - he had complied. He'd coddled and cushioned him, wrapped him in warmth, in the same way Ruth as Joshua's mother had once tried to shield him, red robin with a broken wing.

But he'd learnt from Joshua, too. He was simply the most unashamedly affectionate, demonstrative man Philip had ever known. And a long silenced part of himself had opened to greet him, delighting in their tactile exchange. In Philip's youth, the endless cold years spent closeted in Sydney's west, he'd learnt to repress the need to display affection. He'd become stiff and reserved; many of his previous lovers had been similarly inhibited. But Joshua was different - the Polish-Jewish environment he'd grown up in had freed him from such restraint. He kissed Philip on the street, in the weekday morning crush at Town Hall station; he held his hand, oblivious to the stares of passers-bye, he caressed him; on nights when they sat quietly in front of the flickering television, Joshua often came to Philip unsolicited, laid his head in Philip's lap and murmured endearments. Tears would often well in Philip's eyes at such moments. He wasn't sure if he really deserved such unadulterated love.

He shifted in the armchair. He felt embalmed in the dark and silent flat, the ballooning emptiness punctured only by the slow persistent click of the gold French travelling clock. Distant, muffled sounds reached him from the street. It was nearly two am. They'd both have to rise early for work the next day. It was entirely out of character for Joshua to disrupt a weekday evening in this manner. Something had happened, Philip was sure. A guilty concern surged in him. If only he hadn't gone to visit his parents this evening - if only he'd told Joshua he'd be home early rather than late - if only he'd had the courage to confront him earlier. If, if, if! His mind churned ceaselessly. Why was this happening to them? He felt a burst of fury and indignation toward Joshua for threatening their conjugal togetherness with lies and deceit.

That Joshua had been unfaithful did not expressly preoccupy him. They'd never had a strictly monogamous relationship; he wasn't worried Joshua would leave him; he wasn't jealous. They did not purport to own each other in that strict heterosexual sense of the word. Philip himself had strayed on six or seven occasions over the past several years – an impromptu visit to a sauna on Oxford street, offers accepted without equivocation while away at teacher re-orientation programs, in Canberra, Wollongong, Brisbane. For Philip there existed a clear line of demarcation between love and sex; he did not award the momentary passion the same weighted meaning as Joshua. And each of his excursions he'd brought back to him, for perusal, acceptance. Joshua would laugh, kiss him, beg for details. In the retelling something sexual would often spark between them; they would make love with relief and familiar ease.

Joshua was more complex. Philip understood. He'd come away from childhood burdened with strict moralistic beliefs, a sense of duty to the complicated history that stretched back behind him, to Poland, the ghettos, the camps. He'd once been deeply ashamed of what he felt was an addiction to casual sex, to the thousand possibilities on offer nightly in bars and clubs, in saunas, back streets, beats, parks. Driven to pursue ceaselessly, he'd return haunted and shaken, wary as if all his murdered ancestors stood peering over his shoulder. In Philip, he stated repeatedly, he had found himself complete. All his needs and various demands were easily met and satisfied. That excess energy – a craving for sexual affection – had simply been subsumed into their union. Naively, Philip believed him. He had not thought to question or analyse. And as he sorted through the preceding years, he could recall only two occasions when Joshua had had sex with other men.

He was suddenly confused. What had changed between them? Maybe he had himself precipitated the sea change, unwittingly. He'd wrapped Joshua in a too idealistic love. And he'd narrowed the channel of communication as he marched forward to meet life, dragging Joshua by the hand.

He remembered a conversation he'd once had with Ruth. They were sitting in the small walled garden of her neat and modern townhouse. Joshua had gone inside to use the phone. She'd watched him depart, eyes narrowed with interest. And while a light breeze stirred the hot and humid air around them, she'd looked at Philip with compassion. "You'll never understand him," she'd said then, cryptically. "Believe me, I know."

Philip had felt irritation rise swiftly to anger. "What exactly do you mean?"

"He had a hundred different faces." She'd sighed and looked up cautiously into the darkened interior of the house. Heavy summer sunlight obscured one side of her face, as if she too had grown divided. "I've often thought I understood him, Philip, as a mother should a son. And each time I retreat with the same realisation. It's just another way – a different way – of knowing him that's begun."

★

They met in the newly renovated, hard redwood, cupboard lined kitchen. Philip, who had fallen asleep, was jolted awake at the sound of the front door opening. He sat bolt upright, tensed, hearing Joshua's shuffling footsteps on the new granite coloured linoleum, the clink of two glasses touching, the water tap running. A light came on; a chair scraped; keys clicked together with a light thud on the blond oak kitchen table. Philip waited. To assuage his stiffening pride, he wanted Joshua to come voluntarily to him, and explain. A humming electrical silence carried from the kitchen. And in Philip the voice of guilty concern rose: Go to him, fool! Ask him! He stood up uneasily and went out.

He leant against the kitchen door frame, about to ask coldly, "Where have you been?" Suddenly he stopped. Fright stabbed him hard once in the chest. "My God, what happened to you?" He went to him quickly, instinctively, cupping Joshua's chin gently in one hand, turning his face up slowly to catch the light.

"Jesus, are you okay?" Philip asked. "Are you badly hurt?"

Joshua shook his head. "I'm fine," he said. Dried blood coagulated in a flaky stain up under his nose. A bruise was swelling along his upper left lip, puffed and purple where the lip had split. His front teeth were speckled with tiny, rusty drops of blood. There were small patches of blood on his shirt, on his hands, spread thin across one cheek. Intermittently, his body shook, a strange irregular rhythm offset by his stiffly rigid demeanour.

With a squat sense of anguish, Philip knelt down and wrapped his arms around him. He pressed his lips to the fluttering pulse in his neck. And slowly he felt Joshua's body begin to relax, opening itself to him. His hand came up and insinuated itself in Philip's hair, pressing him close. He exhaled softly and then whispered dully, "Philip, I'm so sorry."

"Honey, what happened?" Philip prodded gently. "Tell me."

"I think I fucked up."

"Oh?" He tried to keep the surprise from his voice. "How?"

"I think I exposed myself to the virus."

Philip jerked back, astonished. "What? But -" Dismay transmuted itself to an acute fit of dizziness. Shock made his voice come out shaky and unsure. "What are you talking about? Christ, be specific!"

Joshua hesitated. When he'd been ascending in the elevator to their sixth floor apartment, he'd decided to tell Philip everything. The whole sordid exchange between himself and Patrick, and the other thirty odd libidinous expeditions he'd led these past few years. Upon these stark facts, their relationship might break. But there it was. Something had been irrevocably shunted from him during the scene at Patrick's house. He'd been raped and violently abused; he felt dirtied, devalued, used. But the shock of recognising himself in Patrick had changed for him all his preconceived ideas, especially those which concerned Philip. On the way home he'd kept visualising Philip's wide boned, handsome face, kept trying to recall the dry soft papery touch of his hands. If he could only reach him, he'd feel at once that instinctive relief; he'd see the wide safety net of their union spread beneath him. But the whole truth he'd have to tell him. He owed him that much, at least.

He began detailing the evening in a calm sure voice, clamping down irritably over his rising apprehension. He described Patrick, how they'd met at the Albury, how he'd willingly gone home with him to Woollahra, and what had followed. He watched Philip's face, ever the clear barometer of his emotional state, change from bewilderment to concern to angry disgust, then fury. He stood up and began pacing the confines of the kitchen, hands balled into clenched fists.

"I'm gonna kill that son of a bitch!" he burst out wildly. "Tell me where he lives!"

"Stop it, Philip. Sit down."

He turned to face Joshua. "Do you need to see a doctor?" At the answering disconsolate shake of his head, Philip said, "How do you know he has the virus?"

"I don't," Joshua replied.

"You didn't ask? This bastard beats you up, rapes you, comes in you without a condom, apologises, then drives you home – and you don't think to ask whether he's infected with HIV?"

"Like he's gonna tell me the truth? Sure, Philip," Joshua retorted hotly. "Just like he's gonna tell his secretary in the morning he raped a tax accountant from a big eight firm!"

Philip stormed back and forth. "Fuck! I knew something had happened to you! I knew it!" He walked up to Joshua and stood over him threateningly. "Why did you do this?"

Joshua looked up in amazement. "Do you think I asked him to rape me?"

"I didn't mean that." Philip sat down abruptly. "Why is this happening to us?" He reached over and took one of Joshua's hands in his. "I love you," he said simply. "What did I do that was so bad you couldn't tell me the truth before?"

He knew. Pain exploded in Joshua's chest. No! He couldn't know! But there it was written plainly on Philip's face: self doubt, anguish, rapidly swelling fear. His own apprehension dissipated in the wake of panic. How stupid he'd been! He felt rocked by the degree of his own self loathing and disgust. Really, he deserved everything, every approaching moment of pain that came to him from his actions. He was a twisted, incomprehensible fool, undermining the well of his own happiness, and Philip's. He looked at him in fear and confusion. "What do you want me to say?"

"Well," Philip said. "You could try explaining." He coughed once, nervously. "What did I do?"

"You did nothing."

He let go of Joshua's hand, ran his fingers in an irregular pattern once over the blond oak table. "I never cared about monogamy," he offered in a stiff, cautious voice.

"I know."

"It's not about where or how or who with."

He answered him evenly, "I know what you mean."

There was protracted, uncomfortable silence. At last Philip said, "Joshua, you'd better say something. Quickly."

"I – " He faltered. Then abruptly it all tumbled from him, a jumble of confused emotions and explanations. He made no attempt to instil order; he simply divulged everything. The many men he'd slept with; the elaborate subterfuges he'd entered into for concealment; his endless unsatisfied craving for sexual affection. The fact that he seemed unable to ever assert himself; he could never make a decision. He'd grown so accustomed to Philip's lead his own homing instinct had deserted him. And they'd grown so comfortable and settled together he'd often felt all the adaptability and versatility had disappeared. So he'd lied; he'd tricked Philip; he'd gone his own way without asking, and look, here is where it brought him.

"I didn't know what I was doing," he went on nervously, the better to cover his own dismay at Philip's wide eyes distress. "If I'd come to you in the beginning none of this would've happened – Philip, listen to me! – it was only coming home to you this evening that I realised the magnitude of my error. I did it. It's my fault. All of it. I didn't trust you enough. I didn't trust us! And why? Because you were the one in control – you always took the lead? But I so wanted you to do that, remember? I practically begged you, when we first met. And then I go and blame you! Jesus, I'm contrary! I wanted some crazy approximation of a bourgeois marriage and you gave it to me, you've gone on giving it, selflessly, without equivocating. And still it wasn't enough. I forced all sorts of changes in you. I forced you to become materialistic, to run after money and dumb objects and expensive clothes and cars and flats. You! Who never gave a shit about things! And what for? To satisfy my insatiable neediness? Philip, it's true to say that I've used you. Goddamnit, it's true. Don't look at me like that! I've used you to get all those things I knew I couldn't get by myself. I'm not strong like you. I've never been able to look after myself. And I've used our relationship, too. It made it easier than ever before to go out and fuck around. It didn't cost me any emotional energy. It was safe. I could just take take take and put nothing back. And you've often said so yourself, it's addictive. Maybe it's the element of surprise that sends me back, time and again. I really don't know. But it's still like a drug, the way a complete stranger can give himself in sex, entirely, a moment of abandon that's often so amazingly intimate. I want that. I've always wanted it – those little loves, and you too. And it may kill me to tell you, Philip, but it's the truth." He stopped, mouth open in astonishment, as if his own words were being replayed in his head.

He looked at Philip, confronted by what seemed an optical illusion. His face seemed to have narrowed, the wide heavy bones constricted. There was a light patina of sweat traced along both upper lips. Joshua swallowed. His face twitched anxiously. He said earnestly, "I always attempt to destroy all the good that comes to me. You know that. You've remarked on it before. It's like I'm some complicated piece of machinery that works fine up to a certain point, then swings wildly out of control. But I don't want that to happen this time, okay? I love you, very much. And I know you love me. There's more than enough between us to get past this, right?" To Philip's continuing silence, he added, "Jesus, Philip, say something, would you? What's with you? Why do you keep staring like that?"

And then he understood. Like a bolt of electricity it passed between them, that knowledge, that new adulterated way of knowing. Until now, Joshua thought with depressing clarity, it's really been easy. Until now he'd been protected by the idyllic naive love in which Philip had cushioned him. A holdover from the first blush of romance that had somehow lasted for five long years. Well, that romantic myth had been abruptly debunked. The gloss had gone. He'd risen to the thorny surface, into the poisonous air. He recalled a phrase in Polish his mother often used, which he translated swiftly into English. "Now the cobwebs are really gone," he said bitterly to Philip, "and the gas is on."

All the shimmering tension exited Philip's face, his lips twisting into an uncharacteristic grimace. Then he got up and went out of the room. Joshua heard him rummaging in the bathroom cabinet; the light in the main bedroom came on. He returned carrying the burgundy first aid box, and a couple of Di-gesic caps prescribed for his own painful lumbar scoliosis. He pulled one of the kitchen chairs closer to Joshua, and sat down. Their knees bumped together awkwardly.

"What are you doing?" Joshua asked, even though it was clearly apparent.

"I'm going to patch you up," Philip said. "And then we'll drive up to the police station in the Cross and file a report."

"What for?"

"Rape. Assault and battery. Whatever it is you want to tell them."

"There's nothing I want to tell them."

He opened the crinkled plastic covered box, extracting cotton balls and diluted disinfectant. Gently, he began swabbing the dried blood from Joshua's face, careful around the puffed and purple swelling on his split lip. Joshua flinched. Philip looked at him. His exhaustive explanations had left him unusually pale. But if he expected a quick revelatory transformation, none was evident. He still looked as he'd always looked, his fine boned, moderately tapered face so typical of East European Ashkenazim, as if his features had been lifted whole from an extant portrait in a photographic album of Vishniac's. Of course, the Diaspora and his lack of religious belief had expunged much of the homely warmth, an incorporeal quality Philip so admired in that old photography. But the lively intelligence was there, evidence of his silvery, razor sharp mind. The sad black eyes. And the stiff black hair he needed a wire brush to keep flat. Not even a hint of duplicity etched into his reserved, gentle features. And yet for a fleeting instant Philip felt a violent urge to crush that beautiful face between his fists. But he went on treating Joshua's lip. He bumped his nose accidentally, and a fine trickle of blood began to run again.

"Careful," Joshua warned.

"You can't sero-convert in one night," Philip said. He leant forward and surprised himself by kissing Joshua lightly on the lips. "Don't argue, please, let's go to the police."

"No." He could not explain it to Philip, what had occurred between himself and Patrick. It'd been like walking into an empty room and being confronted, suddenly, with a frightening future vision of himself. "I'm partially responsible for what happened," he said lamely.

"Why? Because you went home with him?" Philip looked angry and perplexed. "You sucked his dick? So what? How does that make you culpable?"

"It doesn't." All the warmth went out of his eyes. "But I don't wish to share it with the police." He met Philip's fierce gaze with determination. "And Philip, if we're going to go on together, you must stop subjecting me to your peculiarly gentle pressure. It's got to be different."

Philip smirked. "How could it be otherwise?"

"What does that mean?"

He felt a sudden, blinding fury, but suppressed the urge to strike him. "In one night you turn upside down everything we've had! You admit to using me. You've lied. And you've played on my love for you. How could anything be the same after that?"

"But I know you," Joshua said in a small voice. "And I know what you'll do."

"Well maybe you assume too much. Yes, you assume a great deal!" He stood up angrily and moved away. "How can I trust you? How will I ever know you? You're twenty different people, not one!"

"All that I told you, Philip, is not reducible to that."

"But it's not irreducible, either, is it?"

Joshua stood up. He started to walk out of the room, then abruptly turned and shouted in a hoarse voice. "What do you think it is we've been living here these past five years? Some fucking Cinderella fantasy? Some ideal little love affair that can only ever exist in the mind? Because if that's the case, Philip, you can go to hell. Now two people fit perfectly together. Real love is about challenge, and it's about commitment, and the other hundred smaller things that build together over years." He took a deep breath. "And don't you tell me this is all some sort of surprise. Fuck that! You knew what I was like the very first night we met! You've always known! I was vomiting up some old guy's come in a public toilet, and you came on to me! How many men would do that, huh? The truth, Philip, is not exactly salubrious, is it? It never is. So if you suddenly decide to only love one part of me - then - well - you can go fuck yourself, Philip, because - because, I don't want that kind of love." He went out trembling with anger, leaving Philip standing awkwardly in the centre of the room.

And he'd already undressed, showered, slid shaking into his pyjamas, and finished brushing his teeth before Philip came to him. He came stealthily, with unease, appearing behind Joshua in the bathroom mirror. Each studied the other's reflection briefly, then Joshua averted his gaze.

It was Philip who made the decisive move, who came forward purposefully over that last vestige of reserve existing between them. He stretched both arms out and wrapped them around Joshua, pulling his smaller body back to press gently against him. Through the thin walls of fabric Joshua felt Philip's heart beat, arrhythmically, it seemed. Surprising and unexpected tears welled in Philip's eyes. Joshua watched in warm astonishment. Philip rarely cried. He rarely offered up his vulnerability without hesitation. He never trembled like this, never held him with such urgency, as if willing, at last, to let go of the dreams, to let slide the wish it could be simpler, less changeable, less wrought with difficulty and uncertainty and fear.

"Is it what you want?" he asked him, very softly.

"Oh, yes." A shy smile. "I want you."

He felt simultaneously expansive relief and inestimable gratitude. The past seemed no longer an accidental construct of events through which he stumbled, but a continuum, a logical progression forward to this, to Philip, to a place where he belonged. With a sudden jolting clarity, he realised how inseparable they'd become. And before that knowledge, he felt a spreading sense of awe. He lifted one hand and caressed Philip's roughly bristled cheek, surprised by the hot stab of desire in his stomach. He said to him, his voice a little husky, "Really, Philip, you are the most beautiful man."

★

And, well, Philip didn't entirely agree. There was little beauty in what he'd done. There was symmetry, certainly; there was a willingness to commit. A surprisingly energetic willingness flowing in the wake of bitter disillusionment. There was also acquiescence before the inevitable. Joshua had slipped his familiar skin; the spectre of loss had invoked itself. And where it would take them, to what point they would grow, remained for him elusive and bewildering.

For Philip, the now existent threat of a HIV infection frightened him only insofar as it raised the possibility of suffering and loss. For too long it had been a subtext in both their lives to surprise him unduly. He had loved and buried nine friends and companions; Joshua himself was a committed Ankali volunteer. If it was to come personally to them, too, he could accept it as fate, he would attempt to learn from it as he'd seen so many other men do. Patrick might be unbalanced, from Joshua's account, and he had unforgivably assaulted him. But if, in that moment of regretted anger and loss of control, he had passed on a virus, well, Philip would not raise the finger of accusation. Patrick, no doubt already shaken and shamed, would punish himself far more severely and undeservedly.

In his stumbling, vulnerable way, Joshua had been right all along. No love could be perfect in the world. No honest love, anyway. And even the most awkward attempt - the briefest, the truncated, the dysfunctional - was equally real, equally valid and necessary. For what was love, really, except the very strangest alchemy of diffuse elements? Trust, friendship, compassion, passion; a yearning to communicate, a need to be touched. No matter if only momentary; no matter where or how or who with. Between himself and Joshua he felt a weighty accumulation of tiny strands that bound each to the other. And he understood, now, that was love.

Simply this: lying next to his sleeping friend in the last dark hour preceding dawn, watching him, listening to the soft sound of his breath escaping, thinking,

7 7

yes, I do love you, sweet man, perhaps more than you know. And maybe it took tonight, and all that it means for our future, to make me realise what it is about you I love the most. It's everything awkward, Josh, everything difficult and complex and frustrating. That's what makes you real for me; it makes you, you. And in the end, that's the only truth.

Eros Candusso

Eros Candusso

THE ABBA YEARS

Chris Wheat

1974
Waterloo

NORMAN HATED HIS NAME SO HE
changed it to Matt. He had toyed for a few weeks with Style, Moss and Bilbo but
the others were sceptical and finally the names were used only for Jenny's succession
of stray cats. So by the time he had turned twenty-two he had become Matt McKenzie
- which sounded cute and a bit machismo.

"Just as well your surname isn't Triculation," said Greg.

"Or Rimony," Jenny added.

"Or Finish," said Ray.

Those sort of jokes made him feel inferior. His friends were all at uni, and were
quick and funny. He could usually beat them at card games but not at repartee.
There were four of them: Jenny and Greg, who slept in the same bed but maintained
they weren't a couple; Ray, who slept alone and usually until eleven; and Gail who
slept with a lot of people. Matt hadn't yet slept with anyone, because he didn't
count masturbation with a middle-aged man in a toilet block at South Melbourne
beach as having serious, in-love, sex.

Chris Wheat is from Melbourne and has been writing gay short fiction for four years. He has had stories published in 'Brother Sister' and the 'OutRage Anthology.'
The ABBA Years draws on a number of coming-out experiences in his life but is largely a work of fiction. It is as much about being young and in turmoil in the seventies as it is about coming out gay.
Chris Wheat is a teacher in Melbourne's western suburbs. He has travelled in China, Europe and the US. He lives happily with his partner of twenty years in a pet-free suburban house.

The invitation to move into the house came from Greg. They had grown up together in Bulleen and had attended the same secondary school. In mid-November, just after the others had finished their end-of-year exams, Matt arrived with six cardboard boxes of belongings and his old bed. The house was a decrepit Hawthorn mansion with rats in the walls, two mould-ridden bathrooms, a mulberry tree under which Sir Robert Menzies was reputed to have proposed to Dame Pattie, beautifully etched and coloured glass around the front door, and each of the bedrooms had a different carpet pattern – all with the same musty smell. A deep veranda ran around three sides of the house. The garden was large, overgrown and romantic. It seemed perfect to Matt, who had lived all his life in his parents' ordinary weatherboard.

On the first day they abandoned unpacking and went nude sunbathing in the back yard. Matt had never shown his naked body like this. He had been brought up strict Church of Christ and every school rebellion and sexual fantasy was accompanied by a load of guilt. But the nude sunbathing turned out to be quite a discrete activity. The grass was so long they were able to make little nests in it and crouch behind the stalks laughing and shy. They passed joints over the grass walls and talked until tea time about the fun they were going to have.

Matt (nee Norman) decided to make his announcement that very night.

"Could we have all the lights off and the record player turned down?" he said. "I want to speak to you about something really important. Just the candle. I don't want to look at your faces." True confessions were an important aspect of participatory democracy.

"I'm gay."

"I knew at school," said Greg. "Doesn't worry me man." He and Jenny were sprawled on the couch, their bare legs entwined.

"I knew already too," said Gail. "Feminine intuition." Gail had been to Nimbin and danced naked in front of thousands, according to Greg.

"What you do in the privacy of your own bedroom is strictly your own business," said Ray. Ray was stoned most nights.

"Let's celebrate you being gay," said Jenny. "Greg, get the Green Ginger Wine."

For half an hour he was special. They didn't chuck him out, as he feared they might. They were sympathetic. He told them he was going to tell his parents soon. No one at the post office knew: he was a bit worried about losing a job he'd only just taken up. Gail wanted to know what gay people did. Matt wasn't a hundred percent sure himself. Greg confessed that he'd once had a dream that Mick Jagger had tried to get into his bed with a standard lamp. Jenny said she had a friend who was converting to lesbianism as a protest. Gail said Matt belonged to an oppressed minority. And Ray said he couldn't really imagine having it off with a bloke, but free expression was everyone's right. They went to bed at three, after listening to Nina Simone and sharing two joints.

Matt settled in to this communal house quite easily. Although the others were students they included him in everything and seemed proud that they were living with a worker. When he came home in the evening in his purple suit and shiny platforms they asked him about his day. He was a sort of mascot - but sometimes he heard them refer to the public as cretins and crypto-fascists. On New Year's Eve Matt woke to hear the sounds of someone singing Waterloo in the shower and from the radio a summary of the year's most significant events - Cyclone Tracy, Nixon's resignation, Billy Sneddon's defeat. He felt wonderful. He knew the next year would be his year of love and liberation.

1975
S.O.S.

So Matt decided he had to have real sex. Apparently the Dover was the place to go. He had no one to go with and felt nervous but he was determined. He climbed the stairs of the pub with shaking legs and entered a blaring, whooping world of animated faces and smiling eyes. He stood paralysed near the door until a middle-aged man, calling him 'honey', took him by the arm and manoeuvred him into the crush. He found himself at the centre of a group of playful men in their thirties and forties and received romantic proposals from all of them. Toward midnight he plucked up his courage and went home with a handsome, swarthy man called Joel who was wearing a green kaftan.

"I'm rather big," Joel murmured as his kaftan dropped to the carpet. And indeed he was. Matt didn't know whether it would fit. In Joel's large bedroom, Matt took off all his clothes too and stood shivering, covering his genitals, while Joel put the Carpenters on and got out some amyl nitrate.

"Don't shiver," Joel said gently. "Just relax." But it didn't fit at all. Joel kept spitting on it for lubrication. It was like trying to shove a salami down a worm hole. Matt bit the pillow and squeezed tears from his eyes while Karen Carpenter warbled: "We've only just begun, white lace and promises ..." Afterwards, in the Volkswagen on the way home, his sphincter burned and ached for hours and he wondered if he would ever make a true homo.

Every Saturday night after that he went to the Dover and tried to find someone. He found several older men but although they were considerate and generous, real love didn't rattle the pots and pans until Greg's birthday barbecue in March.

Gabriel was a friend of a friend of Jenny's. He had dark eyes, olive skin, long black hair and he wore a white shirt with ruffles, undone to the waist, and green velvet pants. His chest was glowing pink as it caught the light of the setting sun. They were all outside in the backyard getting boozed. Through the speakers, which had been turned around to face through the open back windows, Stevie Wonder crooned 'You Are The Sunshine Of My Life.' Matt stared. Gabriel was laughing. Gabriel was an archangel. In Matt's eyes the party contracted quickly and soon there was only Gabriel floating among anonymous faces in a shimmering sea of laughter.

Matt began drinking straight whisky. "This is desire. I'm going out of my mind; I think I'm going to be sick," he whimpered to Gail. "He's sure to be straight. Please speak to him." Gail soon had his attention and Matt swooned at the way Gabriel smiled and seemed so intensely interested in whatever she was saying.

Then someone put on 'Time Warp' and there was a stampede inside. Gabriel threw off his shirt and became a power drunk transvestite - so did Matt. Gabriel had a lovely body and very slim hips. Matt danced like a maniac. "Just a jump to the left!" they all screamed, their arms flailing. "Just a jump to the right!" Finally he positioned himself in front of Gabriel. They held each other's eyes and competed with one another in outlandish gestures. This was love, pure and simple.

In Matt's virginal bed Gabriel confessed that he hadn't decided whether he really wanted to be gay or not but he was interested in trying it out. He had a girlfriend but they were having a break from one another. And he was a worker too, a draftsman, so Matt didn't feel he had to compete. Gabriel didn't want to do anything, so like a puppy chewing its master's hand, Matt gently chewed Gabriel all over. He was proud he was so naturally erotic - he even chewed Gabriel's eyebrows. Gabriel lay passive, moaning occasionally.

Pretty soon Gabriel had decided he was going to be gay and he and Matt were seeing one another every day and Gabriel was sleeping in Matt's single bed every night. Matt had to put extra money in the kitty for him, but he loved the mutual rush to get ready in the morning and the way they kissed good-bye. He had a wonderful feeling of elation in the train coming home. It was like a little marriage. They even shared undies.

Then came November the eleventh. Gabriel didn't care who won the election but Matt was infected with the outrage of the house and went on rallies after work and stayed up late worrying about a military coup. Gabriel was invited to an election eve party. Matt had voted for Gough but Gabriel wouldn't say who he had voted for. Matt went along to the party. It turned out to be a gathering of gay Liberal supporters and Matt felt furious. When Whitlam came on to concede defeat Gabriel lifted Matt up and he hung above the revellers feeling stupid and unable to cheer. He grew more and more angry when Gabriel wouldn't put him down.

"Gabriel, it's all over. I can't have a relationship with a Liberal supporter," he said quietly as they drove home. Gabriel was cold. He said he was going back to his girlfriend anyway.

"I gave up love for Gough," he said miserably to Jenny. He thought he was going to cry.

She put her arms around him: "You're one of the few who is really maintaining his rage," she said consolingly.

1976
Fernando, Mama Mia, Dancing Queen

He now realised that Gabriel and he had never quite been in love. There had been a sort of happiness in each other's company but there had been little sharing in the sex and Matt realised now that it was over he was relieved. So after Christmas he started hunting again. One night in late January at Society Five he saw a new boy talking to a drag queen – a huge outrageous Maori who was showing him her left breast. This boy had an animated cheeky face, a strong lean body, and confidence. Matt spied on him for much of the night and finally went up to him and asked for a dance. The boy grinned, nodded and as they danced they sang to *Fernando*.

"I'm sunburnt," Matt said self-consciously after the song finished. They had all been at Half Moon Bay for the day.

"It's a glowing tan," said the boy and they exchanged names and danced again. Darryl invited Matt back to his flat. He was a part-time art student at the RMIT, funny and forthright.

"You know what attracted me to you?" said Matt coyly as Darryl rinsed two mugs. "It was when you looked at that drag queen's breast."

Darryl laughed. "What was so impressive about that? She shows them to anyone," said Darryl. "The things I like best about you are your curly hair and your almost all-over tan." He kissed Matt's navel and Matt was in love again.

One Saturday afternoon there was going to be a full eclipse of the sun in Melbourne, so despite the anxiety about looking at the phenomenon while tripping, they all decided to take LSD. One hour into the trip Matt found himself feeling strong sexual desires for Style, one of Jenny's cats. He stalked the creature through the house on his hands and knees and eventually cornered him in Ray's darkroom. He fondled the cat affectionately and tried to restrain his desire to take her to his bed. Gail appeared in the door and immediately metamorphosed into a giant S.

"Jenny and Greg are on the front lawn trying to swim," she said. "We have to rescue them. There's a rip. What are you doing to Style?"

"I love him."

"I think he's straight." she said. "Take him down to the sea with us."

"You're a giant S," he said picking up Style.

When Darryl arrived he found them all scattered across the lawn. Greg and Jenny were lying on their backs panting, Gail was doing backstroke and singing *Love Will Keep Us Together* and Matt was giving artificial respiration to the cat.

Matt looked up. "Darryl, I think I'm freaking."

"No you're not," Darryl answered. "Be still and watch this, then we'll have sex. Is there any acid left?"

Darryl took some too and they sat on the lawn and waited for the street lights to come on. Jenny and Greg hid behind a geranium bush. Ray and Gail sat cross-legged and chanted the Om. Darryl cuddled Matt and Matt cuddled Style.

"This is really weird. Listen, the birds have all stopped singing," Darryl said. And they sat still and Matt felt terrified but safer in Darryl's arms.

"I'm having this total bummer," he whimpered. "I don't like eclipses." He snuggled closer into Darryl's arms and felt as if he were a baby monkey.

When the sun came back out Darryl watched while they all did a dance of welcome around the house, then he grabbed Matt's hand and they went off to bed. In the bedroom Style squirmed free of Matt's grip and bounded out the window. It was peculiar sex. At one stage as they lay side by side, their erect penises, which appeared to Matt to have little animated faces like gnomes, had a dialogue about hydrofoils. As he came down from the LSD later on that evening, Matt sighed. He nuzzled Darryl who was sprawled beside him chanting repetitively, "Mama Mia, here I go again, my, my, how can I resist ya?" because he felt sure there was a cryptic message encoded in the lyrics. Matt felt a peace and joy which could have only come from finally being in a steady, sane, relationship.

1977
The Name of the Game

To celebrate the Queen's Silver Jubilee Ray suggested they have a bed-in. They chose Jenny and Greg's bed. Gail brought in an extra, a friend called Kevin, whom

Matt found very handsome. Darryl was away on the day of the bed-in.

They all filed nervously into the darkened bedroom and climbed in. Matt ended up on the edge. Pressed coyly against one another in the dark the others made small talk about university politics. He could hear hands moving and limbs sliding over one another . There was a gentle rustling and giggling. No one discussed what they were doing. For the first time Matt felt a woman's breast. It was Gail's. He was sharing it with another hand. Someone groaned and everyone tittered. He got an erection thinking about Gail's new boy Kevin whose leg may or may not have been rubbing his. A hand came down and touched his penis then drifted away. Finally someone got out, then another, then another. There was an etiquette for this demure orgy. Afterwards everyone was particularly sweet and Gail bought them all Choc Wedges.

Two days later there was a crabs outbreak. They all blamed Gail's friend Kevin. Darryl caught them too. "How could you give me fucking crabs!" he yelled. "Who else have you been sleeping with?"

"I didn't do anything." Matt reeled back surprised. "We don't have to have World War Three over a couple of crabs," he complained.

"Get me a Marlboro. I have to think through our relationship," Darryl ordered.

1978
Take a Chance On Me

"Can I borrow that wig of yours?" he asked Gail. "I'm going in the Miss Society Five Contest."

It was really cross-dressing - protesting against stereotypes. A male in a frock but still a male. He decided on a long pink negligee, carpet slippers onto which he sewed plastic pink roses, a crocheted shawl which he found in an opportunity shop and Gail's blonde Sixties wig. He shaved his legs but didn't wear false boobs.

Matt walked around in circles with the other contestants to the soundtrack of *Saturday Night Fever*. But he didn't place. The winner, a boy with a broken front tooth, burst into tears as he received the gold cardboard crown. Darryl loved him dressed up and was all over him most of the night. Matt felt he needed to do it occasionally to add spice to the marriage. They were a couple in the household and accepted. Matt was happy.

But the seasons turn. After Jenny turned vegetarian the house disintegrated.

"It was a mongrel of a meal," said Greg one night after Jenny had cooked red kidney bean casserole and beetroot in batter: an entirely maroon meal.

There was silence around the table. It was against the house's unwritten code to be so blatantly aggressive. Jenny and Greg were having big hassles. "Oh, typical male response!" she screamed.

"I'm going out!" Greg muttered.

"Another male cop out!" she called to him, her voice breaking. "You're supposed to do dessert tonight! Pig!" And she threw the rest of the casserole at the wall.

Matt sat and watched the beans streak slowly down the wallpaper. He waited for the door to slam and then said: "I thought it was quite nice Jenny."

"Thanks Matt. Gay guys are so much more sensitive and understanding," said Jenny and burst into tears as she fled the room.

Soon after that Ray said he couldn't cope with the bad vibes any more and left for Queensland to get his head together. Finally Greg and Jenny split up. The house had to fold. They all went their own ways, promising to keep in touch. Matt moved in with Darryl. Bikies took over the lease.

1980
The Winner Takes It All

One Saturday afternoon they were driving past the old house. It was being pulled down.

"I loved that place," said Matt. "There go some of my best memories – gone with the wind. Like ABBA!"

"It was squalid," said Darryl.

"Well, there were more important things than cleaning."

"I meant emotionally squalid," Darryl responded.

"It sure was," he answered with a smile. "Thank God!"

ALL THE WAY OUT

Melinda Waters

E VERYONE ASKS "WHEN DID YOU KNOW you were - you know - GAY?" Fourteen is when I started consciously denying to myself that I was a lesbian. In fact until recently I couldn't even say the 'L' word out loud. It conjured up images of rough women with bad tattoos in leather jackets riding on Harleys. No offence intended, I was naive. I have since met some warm, caring individuals who fit that image.

At fourteen I met 'Vicki'. Words fail me, but we've all been there. The person who makes you involuntarily inhale to maximum lung capacity, makes your pupils fully dilate in bright sunlight, stops time and space and turns you numb to all outside proceedings. Well, that one to me was Vicki. I was fourteen and she was twenty- one. Sounds like a 'bent' school girl crush, doesn't it? I had friends my own age but I didn't seem to quite fit in. I wanted to ride motorbikes with my brother and his friends, not read Dolly magazines and practice applying make-up. My hair was too short to French braid and I didn't transform into a giggling fit when a member of the opposite sex walked past. In hindsight it is all very obvious.

Melinda Waters was born in a large Queensland town with a small town mentality. She lives with her partner, two dogs, a cat and a bird on a small acreage block, 45 minutes from Brisbane.
Melinda (Lou) has not been published before.
"To begin with no one calls me Melinda. For as long as I can remember everyone who knows me has called me Lou. I'm unsure of the exact origin of 'Lou'. I'm commonly described as 'practical' to a fault. This is inherited from my mother. I would like to think I also inherited her real strength and sense of humour which I didn't know about until I left home."

All my heroes were heroines.

Vicki had a sister my age who was best friends with my twin sister. That's how Vicki and I met. Vicki's sister invited my sister to their farm for a weekend and the invitation was extended to me. Most people believe it proper etiquette to invite both twins. I enjoy the outdoors and since my grandmother sold her farm, I hadn't enjoyed the rural atmosphere for which I held fond memories. While our sisters did girlie stuff in the house all weekend, Vicki and I did farm stuff outside.

Vicki had a friend Shiree, who worked on the farm and lived there as well. (No romantic attachment though). Shiree was an 'I don't care what others think' kind of person. That's a brave attitude to have and I liked her for that. I couldn't explain it at the time but I was a little jealous of Shiree.

I'd never had a 'best friend' at school, but in a matter of a few months Vicki became my closest friend. I saw her only at softball fixtures and practice twice a week, and occasionally she'd give my sister and I a ride home from school if she was in town. She had looks, confidence and a metallic green sports car. I was impressed.

One day Vicki confided in me that she was gay. I tried to appear unphased and replied, "That's OK, but I may look at you a little differently tomorrow." Like she was going to grow horns over night. She understood my lack of tact and I grew up enough to position that piece of data away from the forefront of my mind. Her sexuality wasn't frightening. If she hadn't told me she was gay I could have convinced myself any weird things I was thinking or feeling were a sick game our bodies play on us at puberty.

Vicki began to creep into my daydreams and for the first time, the role I played in those dreams was ME. Not the world's greatest athlete, rock star or actress. I was thrilled to be me because that was who Vicki wanted to know. I'd spent my life trying to gain recognition on a solo basis instead of being a half of a set of twins. I didn't fully understand what was going on but I didn't want it to end

I don't know all the details, I doubt I ever will, but one night Vicki's mother and sister arrived at my place with an agenda. Mud slinging and accusations hit the fan and in the end I was told I was to have nothing to do with Vicki or Shiree - period. I thought it best to burn my diary. It wasn't incriminating but I feared that someone else may decipher my confused thoughts and realise what I was denying to myself - I really felt something for Vicki. Now I couldn't see her, my devastation brought an end to my confusion and I weakened. What confidence I'd gained in myself through Vicki's attention and caring faded and I ached for her. If I saw her my heart would leap to my throat in anticipation and then, with the realisation she was out of reach, crash back down from where it came.

Some months later Vicki's sister arrived at school and announced she was going to be a bridesmaid - Vicki's bridesmaid. Twist the knife in my heart another half circle. Vicki was marrying the farmer next door - the father of the baby she was carrying.

I was shocked, even more shocked than 'I'm gay' shocked. I knew in my heart it wasn't what she wanted, but at fifteen I was helpless. I wished I could grow up overnight, and steal her away and protect her. I wanted her to confirm the feeling in my heart. I was a little scared my perception of the events of the preceding months wasn't right. At fifteen you don't understand outside pressure and influence and I didn't understand why she was doing this. It just wasn't her.

Time passed and I tried to force my memories to the back of my mind, but often Vicki would be in my thoughts, especially when I heard Shiree had been killed in a car accident. I knew Vicki would be hurting and again I wished I could steal Vicki away and console her.

At eighteen I ran into Vicki again. The four years since I'd spoken to her were four seconds and we were completely at ease in each others company. She'd borne a son, divorced her husband and was living alone in my home town. I'd finished school, moved to the big smoke, done a year at college and dropped out. I was unemployed, not exactly a good catch, but at least my bra size had improved from 10A.

We talked for hours and she gave me her address. Six months later I visited her. Six months is a long time to leave it but I realised that life as I knew it would never be the same afterward. I wanted to be totally independent, not the restricted fourteen year old of before. So, at nineteen, I went to visit her. She had company so I didn't stay long. Her company didn't pose a threat, but again I was a little jealous. I had no claim on this woman but I was jealous all the same.

My second visit, two weeks later, was a baptism by fire - yes, we slept together. I'm far from a 'fast' woman, it's just that I knew this woman. Some of my knowledge came from years before and some was just there, its origin unknown to me. My previous sexual experience had arisen from mere curiosity and was limited to a couple of brief and less than memorable tumbles with the opposite sex.

Although Vicki and I saw each other only on weekends (due to distance) our relationship grew quickly. Sunday's parting such sweet sorrow until Friday came around again. We had a very secret romance. 'Coming Out' to our families was not a step to take lightly. How many mothers have aspirations that their children will grow up to be gay?

I have often wondered what it would be like to have full family support. What it would be like to have them share in your excitement in falling head over heels, poured tea in the sugar bowl, in love. What it would be like to have them show pride in your decision to buy land and build a house. To greet both you and your partner with sincere warmth on visits. To feel fully at ease in each other presence. Frankly, I'd really like to know just how close we can sit on the lounge without being considered degenerates.

Vicki's mother even went as far as removing all photographs of Vicki from the picture wall and family albums. My mother isn't quite so cruel, however she has but two photographs of me taken in the time I've been with Vicki and no it doesn't include Vicki. I don't receive a birthday card from Vicki's family, nor she from mine. They were unsettled by our relationship and took refuge in their own ignorance. We consoled ourselves with the thought we didn't require their approval. We had friends (straight), Vicki's son and most reassuringly each other. This was a false sense of security, another danger was looming.

Ever heard of the seven year itch? We got it at seven years, give or take a week. We got it bad. We separated and I went to a friend's place for a couple of weeks. (Tip - don't go to a re-born Christian's house when you have relationship problems if you're gay). Vicki went to a couple of counselling sessions. The counsellor saw the problem right away - we'd lost our identities. This is not an uncommon occurrence in same sex relationships but we had no idea as we didn't know anyone else in a same sex relationship.

We were as one literally - went everywhere together, wore each others clothes, checked with one another on every little decision and generally lost ourselves in compromise and concession. Vicki was no longer the woman I fell in love with and I was no longer the one she'd fallen for. The old Vicki and Lou were trapped within this one being who agreed with herself on everything.

It has taken a great deal of self discipline to regain our identities. We are each close to our former selves now and our relationship has strengthened from this, as it has from many adversities. We are closer and it really shows. Rebuilding our relationship required a certain amount of selfishness. Stopping yourself from continually seeding a compromise is difficult but we've made it. If I particularly want Kentucky Fried and she particularly wants Maccas we just go to two drive throughs. It's not that we don't compromise anymore, we're just not extremists with it nowadays. Circumstances have even forced us to work different hours and it's kind of like the old days of weekend romance. Besides, it gives me time to play my old Nolans tapes.

I refuse to ever walk on eggshells, skate on thin ice or pretend in any way any more. It makes no difference if you wear the most demure dresses or a leather jacket, drive a five door hatch or ride a Hagley. If you are gay you're gay. Unacceptance doesn't come in varying degrees. It doesn't matter if you try to appear acceptable (straight) or go to extremes to promote what you are. If people don't accept you for who and what you are, changing your appearance and modifying your behaviour won't alter their inability to get past that one unsurmountable barrier - YOU'RE GAY.

This has been tough lesson to learn and has taken longer than it really should have. You can't isolate yourself from the rest of the world or live two separate lives, one being honest to yourself and the one lived purely to suit others. You must accept what you are, yourself, and then you won't feel a need for approval from others. This search for approval nearly cost us our relationship. Besides, being a lesbian has its advantages. No awkwardness at that crucial moment when birth control is usually addressed. No one to leave the toilet seat up. And there is always someone to understand and accommodate your PMT.

Photo: Eros Candusso

BRIDE OF PRIDE

Pamela May

I T WAS A FRIDAY EVENING IN EARLY March. The air was hot and heavy. Fiona McGrath (ex-Bainbridge) was driving from her home in northern New South Wales to Sydney. The air-conditioning in the Commodore had been broken since 1986. Fiona was feeling tense. Her two children were telling jokes and quarrelling in the back of the car.

"Shut up!" said Fiona. "How can I concentrate on driving with you two yelling like that?"

"We're not yelling," protested her daughter Amber. "We're cybermice. They squeak a lot."

"Cybermice are hungry. Can we stop at McDonald's soon?" asked Sam.

"No." said Fiona. "You've been eating junk food for the last hour solid."

"When are we going to get to Sydney?" Sam whined.

"Soon. Haven't you got anything to read? What about playing I Spy?"

"Can we have the radio on?" said Amber.

Fiona switched it on. Music crackled out as she twiddled the dials looking for a local frequency band. A Madonna retrospective was in progress on the FM station of the town which flowed past the windows of the car.

Pamela May lives in Newcastle with her two children. She has published several short stories and a lesbian novel, 'Easy Come, Easy Go' (Womens Redress Press, Sydney, 1990). She is currently working on a feminist sci-fi thriller. Under another name she has another life as a tertiary academic.

She believes strongly in the diversity of queer culture, and continues to exist on the cutting edge of the domestic and the dangerous, which she regards as a spiritual path.

"Turn it up!" shouted Amber.

"Where's the party?" wailed Madonna. "I want to free my soul. Where's the party? I want to lose control."

Fiona's stomach gave a lurch, half excitement and half fear. Her palms were sweaty on the steering wheel. She silently asked herself yet again why she had allowed herself to be persuaded to go to Mardi Gras this year with her young friends from the Health Centre collective. It was not just a matter of going down and looking on, either. She had agreed to make up the numbers in the parade contingent when one of the original volunteers had fallen sick. This meant dancing about in front of thousands of people wearing precious little but a tutu. And it did not end there. She had paid quite a lot of money to attend the all night dance party at the showgrounds too. Fiona shuddered. She really didn't know why she had said yes in the first place. Perhaps because it was something just so completely different from the rest of her life. When Greta had asked her she had agreed at once, as if it was somehow fated. She had been excited by the thought. She had imagined things. Now however, driving towards the seething metropolis of Sydney, she was having severe doubts. She told herself she was too old and too straight for this kind of thing.

"Madness, madness, madness," she muttered to herself as she drove on in the gathering dusk. And Madonna went on wailing.

At about three o'clock the next day Fiona kissed her two children goodbye and gave their grandmother last minute instructions on baths, sleeping and medication. She bundled her Mardi Gras costume out of the house in a green garbage bag and stowed it in the boot. She got into the car wearing her customary Indian-print hippy dress and massage sandals. She drove away through the quiet suburbs where northshore conservatives were mowing their lawns. Driving over the Bridge into Sydney she believed, for a moment, that she was on the brink of a great adventure, but then she took the wrong lane for the western suburbs, and fell back into believing it was all totally stupid.

Fiona finally found her way to Glebe and parked the Commodore with some difficulty between a Harley Davidson and a Farrago. She checked the address and went along the street to number nine. Charles, a middle-aged gay friend she had known since art school days, had recently sold his townhouse in Strathfield and moved in with his new lover, a twenty-five year old accountant. They had bought the house in Glebe together and were furiously renovating, or so Charles had said on the phone. It didn't look like it though. The one storey terrace was immaculately painted and pristine. Perhaps they had done it all in the last three weeks. Charles opened the door when Fiona knocked. He was wearing an Akubra as usual, to hide his balding crown. "Me and Molly Meldrum," he always said, "We're men who know the real value of a hat."

Fiona and Charles sat in the tiny courtyard garden at the back of the house. The traffic roared in the streets beyond the French-washed walls. Charles brought out smoked salmon foccacia and Dom Perignon in tall glasses.

"To you Fiona," he said, toasting her health. "Your first Mardi Gras."

Fiona looked down at her hands. They were lined and the veins stood out. Thank goodness she no longer wore her wedding ring. "I feel like an imposter," she said quietly.

"Why?" asked Charles, knocking back the champagne. "Just because you were married for fifteen years? Look, I know you've been completely celibate since you left Doug. You've told me often enough. But before you married Doug you went out with girls. I remember that butch one with the dark hair who was studying to be a lawyer. What was her name?"

"Kay. But that was almost twenty years ago Charles. The whole scene is different now. I don't know what to do ... And anyway I'm past all that. Going to the Mardi Gras Dance Party is silly. I'll stand out like an old tourist in a lion park."

Fiona drank her champagne in small, nervous gulps. The gay couple next door, both psychiatric nurses, were having a pre-Mardi Gras late brunch in their courtyard. Noises of talking, drinking and laughing drifted over into Charles' garden. A bunch of pink and mauve balloons rose up beyond the dividing courtyard wall then were pulled back down again to delighted shrieks. "We could go over and join them I suppose," said Charles. "I was invited. But they're really friends of Shane's."

"Where is Shane?" asked Fiona. "He is coming to the party with us isn't he?"

Charles pulled a petulant face. "No." he said. "He went to Wagga Wagga for a family wedding! He couldn't make up his mind, then at the last minute he went. It's hard to credit that he'd deliberately miss Mardi Gras, but there you are. He comes from one of those awful close families. I'm sure that evil niece of his chose this date with the sole purpose of luring dear misguided Uncle Shane away from big bad Mardi Gras. In any case, maybe it will be a good thing after all. This will be my first solo Mardi Gras in six years. I went with Shane last year and Hassan for the five years before that. " He toasted himself.

"Do you still see Hassan?"

"No. I just heard that he's scored a transfer to Canberra so with any luck ..." Without finishing his sentence, Charles began to eat a foccacia.

"The problem is, Charles," said Fiona. "I'm really too old for this kind of thing."

"What kind of thing?"

"Prancing about in a tutu in front of thousands of people! Going to an all-night dance party! I usually watch television on Saturday nights."

"Hey!" said Charles. "No-one is too old for Mardi Gras. You're just nervous. You'll be fine when you get there and set eyes on all those gorgeous young dykes."

"That's not why I'm going! I don't want to meet anyone. I like being single. Anyway, I'm sure you worry about your age."

"No I don't."

Fiona shrugged. She didn't believe Charles. "Maybe it's different for men," she said sarcastically. When Charles did not rise to this, she asked, "Do you promise to stay with me all night? Till morning?"

"Yes. But I told you. We can't meet until one o'clock. I won't be there until then. I'm going to the Midnight Shift with my boss."

Fiona fretted with a finger at the edge of a foccacia. "You see, these women I'm going with ... I don't know Greta and Tash and Aveline all that well. We just work together."

"You'll be alright with them until one o'clock. They won't have left by that time. No-one will go home until after Kylie's big number at two. Eat your lunch." Fiona had not touched the food. She was feeling too nervous.

"What are you intending to do with this? You can't leave it like it is." Charles remarked, picking up a dangling lock of hair from Fiona's shoulder.

"I don't know. I haven't thought about it. What do you suggest?"

"A beehive. Come inside and I'll do it."

For someone who had not much hair Charles knew a great deal about hairdressing. He piled Fiona's hair up into a tall cone, lacquered it heavily and clipped a fringe to fall on her forehead. "There," he said, taking the teasing comb out of his mouth. "Just like Priscilla Presley on her wedding day. You will be a lovely Bride of Pride."

Charles dropped Fiona off in Broadway at about five o'clock. He took the Commodore away to park it in Surry Hills near the showgrounds. The stairs of the seedy hotel in Broadway smelt of stale beer and 1950s aftershave. The door upstairs was open. Greta and Tash had rented a room shaped like a half moon on the first floor. They were anxiously peering out of the window at the sky, wondering whether it would rain before evening. Fiona threw her garbage bag down on the floor.

"Well I'm here," she said.

Greta and Tash were clad only in their underwear. It was very hot in the hotel room. Not saying much they offered Fiona some Japanese take-away and beer. Perhaps they were wondering why they had invited a middle-aged mother of two to march with them at all. They did not comment on her hairdo. Fiona picked at the sushi rolls. She was still too nervous to eat but she was determined to keep calm. After all, it was very kind of Greta to have invited her. She hoped she would not prove an embarrassment.

The three other parade volunteers arrived carrying a six-pack of Tooheys. Aveline patted Fiona's beehive approvingly. The other two did not comment. They seemed to have been arguing about something before they arrived. Fiona sat on the lumpy double bed listening and watching as Greta, Tash and Aveline talked, showered, applied make-up and cantered about in their underwear. It was too hot to put costumes on yet. Outside in the city the heat of the day was pulling gradually away from the hard surfaces of roads and buildings. The traffic, if anything, was getting heavier. Finally Greta announced it was time to get dressed. Fiona pulled her tropical blue tutu out of the bag and got into it, standing cautiously behind the bed so that none of the younger women could see the stretch marks on her stomach. She went into the bathroom to put on the sequined bra top, but returned to arrange her veil and train in front of the mirror with the others. When they were finished they stood in a group to admire themselves. Fiona stood at the back.

"We are beautiful brides," Greta announced. "Beautiful Brides of Pride. Bum bags on? Check! Tickets? Check!" With one, sweeping, glorious movement, the Pride Brides sashayed down the seedy stairs and out to where the traffic was roaring up Broadway. Horns honked and fellow travellers en route to Mardi Gras waved encouragement. The Pride Brides posed for a passing photo, then dashed across Broadway between cars. Fiona admitted to herself she was feeling excited.

"How are we going to get there?" asked Tash as they stood on the footpath opposite the hotel.

No-one had thought of this. A taxi? They waited for a couple of minutes, but there were no empty cabs. It was nearing the time for parade participants to marshal up near Whitlam Square. Most of the taxis that went by were filled with revellers and enormous frocks. Just as the spirits of the Brides of Pride were starting to waver and sink, a bus came along. Fiona seized the moment. After all she was a mother. "Come on," she said, "We'll all catch the bus. Lift up your skirts."

Fiona shepherded her fellow brides onto the bus and sorted out fares. People on the bus stared. Some smiled and made comments. Others continued to look out of the window. Fiona found herself grinning. It was actually quite thrilling to stand up between two seats of billowing tutus, swaying from side to side, making eye contact with people who smiled back in degrees of appreciation. Fiona discovered in that moment that Mardi Gras was not just a matter of dressing up and shocking people. It was really a celebration of the deliberately and outrageously queer. A glorious yet eminently unnatural festivity which touched the edge of the extraordinary. Yet it included more than it offended. Her spine tingled. Her bum twitched. She felt contingently dangerous. She sensed great danger of losing or gaining something momentous. It was scary and wonderful. She thought of Madonna and hummed to herself, "Where's the party? I want to free my soul."

However, the euphoria did not last. Fiona's mood plummeted again when she and the other Brides arrived and found their places in the parade assembly area with the rest of the local contingent. The sea of staring faces beyond the barricade made her feel exposed and silly. She sat on the ground with the others and watched the police keep a group of homophobic protesters at bay. It was embarrassing. There were television cameras. Fiona hid her face, worried that her children might see her on the news. Or worse, her ex-husband. Greta and Tash began a stupid argument about money. Fiona slipped away from the prying cameras and walked around among the floats. As she was passing an enormous silver snake with fifty or so human legs she was startled by a shout. "Fee! Fee!"

She peered under the silver carapace. It was breathlessly hot inside the snake. Two old friends from her pre-marital days, a lesbian couple called Gig and Paddy, were strapped in and smiling sweatily. Fiona had not seen them for many years. They were astounded and delighted to see her. She chatted with them for a while, then a parade marshal came along and informed everyone that the snake would not be leaving for some time, so they might as well unstrap. Fiona went with her two friends to a nearby hotel to buy mineral water. While they were there, Paddy tipped her a wink. "Are you feeling a bit tense Fee? About being here for Mardi Gras I mean?"

"Oh yes. This isn't really me you know. I've been a stay-at-home country girl for too long. Right now I don't really want to be here. But I don't want to let my hometown girls down you see. Otherwise I'd probably just pick the kids up and go home."

"Don't do that." Paddy turned to Gig and they had a whispered conversation. "Would you like a little something to make you feel better?"

"Yes. OK. A little something like what?" Fiona followed Gig and Paddy around the back of the hotel. They huddled conspiratorially in the alleyway.

"Here." Paddy gave Fiona a tightly compacted piece of tissue paper. She turned it over in her hand as her friends popped similar things into their mouths. "There's a line of speed in there," Gig explained. "And some crushed up ecstasy. Just eat it up Fee. It's a present." Fiona hesitated. "Well if you don't want it," Paddy began.

"I do. I do." Fiona crammed the chalky tissue paper into her mouth and coughed dreadfully as it caught in her throat. Gig and Paddy looked at one another and laughed. Gig went to fetch a drink while Paddy thumped Fiona heartily between the shoulder blades. "Get yourself together Fee!" she ordered between thumps. "Just go with the energy. You are whoever you think you are, you know."

"Well who am I then?" gasped Fiona. "And what am I? That's what I'd like to know. I haven't known the answer to that question for years." Gig brought back a can of beer and Fiona sipped cautiously between diminishing coughs. They sat down on the greasy cobblestones together until Fiona had fully recovered. "I have to get back," said Fiona. "The parade must be leaving soon. Will I see you at the party later?"

"Look for us in the Dyke Bar. Take care."

There were many peculiar visions on the way back to Greta and Tash. A giant hairy man in a crinoline offered Fiona a joint. His accomplice, a bearded woman in a dinner suit, complimented her on her freestanding beehive. She told Fiona it was far better than a semi-detached beehive. Fiona did not get the joke, but moments later her beehive was flattened by inches when she fell over a gigantic rat, which was being hoisted up as the figurehead of a float entitled SEWER. A nun of indeterminate gender picked her up, set her on her feet, and sprinkled her with holy water. Taking a wrong turn between the lines of floats, she found herself looking at a completely authentic flying saucer. It was a case of rub your eyes and look again. A second glance only confirmed Fiona's first impression. She went slowly up and touched the smooth silver surface. She could see no wheels underneath the ship, yet the saucer did not appear to be touching the ground. She was just bending over to look more closely at the means of propulsion when the saucer began to hum, a panel opened in the side and some green and yellow aliens pranced out. Fiona never found out whether she was witnessing the first public landing of alien life forms on earth or whether it was just a particularly well constructed float. Suddenly music blared from all sides and the first floats and marchers moved out into Oxford Street. Fiona ran up the street, searching frantically for her fellow Brides.

"We thought you'd chickened out!" Tash and Greta hugged her. The rest of the local contingent arranged themselves behind the Brides and a banner bearing the name of their town.

"Hey," called one dour woman with a familiar army backpack. "What are you doing here Fiona?" She glared at Fiona with angry eyes. "She's not a real dyke!" she yelled, pointing Fiona out for the benefit of everyone within earshot.

"How would you know? Anyway what's a real dyke?" scoffed Fiona, angry.

"She's a Bride," said Greta, rushing between them. "A Pride Bride. A Bride of Pride. She came with the rest of us Brides. We're a Pride of Brides." Greta held out her arms. Fiona and the other Brides rushed in. They all hugged together. The dour woman and her friends went to stand further back in the parade.

"Stuff her," said Greta. "What a harpie. Come on Brides. Let's get our trains arranged."

Fiona stood still as Tash arranged her rainbow train. Now it was almost dark the air crackled with multiple sound tracks. The crowd behind the barricades let out a roar like a space shuttle climbing into the stratosphere and the whirr of chopper blades overhead mixed with the strains of 'Go West'. The vast Egyptian float moved ponderously out, preceded by a hundred garish slaves. When their turn came the Brides took hands and raced up into Oxford Street. Fiona was amazed to find crowds behind the barricades cheering and waving at their small group of rural marchers. The mechanised floats were so much more spectacular, but then perhaps people walking along at road level were easier to relate to. Or maybe the people behind the barricades were amused and interested to see queer people from a country town. Afterwards Fiona could never really remember much about the actual march. It was certainly a marvellous feeling to dance and walk for miles between vast walls of cheering people, but it went by so very quickly. What seemed to be merely seconds after the Brides had left the assembly point they arrived at the dis-assembly point near the showgrounds. Fiona was speeding. She lay down on the ground for a minute then rushed over to have a photo taken with the Absolutely Fabulous Patsy look-alikes. After all, it was her favourite show. When she got back Greta looked her up and down curiously.

"You're in a good mood Fiona."

"Too right!" Fiona lay down again on the car-park tarmac. Greta sat down beside her. "A friend gave me some speed," Fiona whispered. Greta smiled knowingly. The sky was clear. The stars were bright. The music of Mardi Gras wafted over them both. People were bidding each other farewell. "Merry Mardi Gras and a Happy New Year," said someone nearby. Fiona wondered whether the population at large knew that the institution of Christmas had taken a dive.

After a few happy snaps of the local contingent (Fiona took care not to stand near the dour woman who thought she shouldn't be there), Greta, Tash, Aveline and Fiona walked down the road towards the Party. The other two Brides had gone off to Oxford Street. "Wasn't it wonderful?" sighed Fiona. "Just wonderful?"

"Yes." said Greta. "You did well Fiona, for a ring-in."

"It's too early to go to the party," Tash complained, "nothing will be happening at eleven o'clock." Nevertheless they went in because there was nothing else to do. Tash was right. There were not many people about yet. The Brides wandered around playing tourist. Fiona had her glasses with her, but she had not put them on once since arriving at the hotel in Broadway. She thought they made her look old and besides, she actually preferred things in the distance to possess the rare fuzziness of an Impressionist painting.

For this reason, she could not at first make sense of a vast mound of heaving green which was edging its way along a footpath making feeble cries for help. Tash was laughing and pointing. The Brides began to run towards it. Fiona followed, screwing up her eyes to focus. It turned out to be a grounded mermaid. A man's head, made-up and bewigged, stuck out of a huge padded costume which ended in a thick and stumpy fishtail. "I was on a float," he gasped. "They sewed me in."

"How did you get here?" asked Greta.

"They carried me here. And now the bastards have gone off and left me." He gasped again. Under the foundation his face was red and flushed. "I can't move, and I can hardly breathe!" His arms were free and looked quite strong. Fiona could not understand why he couldn't tear himself out of the costume by ripping the stitches apart. "I haven't got anything on underneath my costume," he explained coyly.

Greta took a dim view of this excuse. "Do you want the Brides to help you or not?" she asked.

"Well yes," said the mermaid. "I don't know when those bastards will be back. They went in there." He pointed into the pulsating hive of the Hordern.

"Right," said Tash. "Let's do it then."

Ignoring the mermaid's protests, the Brides began tearing at his costume.

"You see," said Fiona kindly, "We can't leave you like this. You can't move and you can hardly breathe and you're too hot."

"But I can't walk around with nothing on!" the man yelled. "Get off you bitches."

"Ssssh," said Fiona. She put a finger up and touched her mouth, "Zip up lips."

After one final effort of pulling and shredding, the man emerged pale and naked from his green satin prison. "There," said Aveline. "You're fixed. Now come on Brides, I need a scotch."

"Wait," said Tash. She tore a length of satin off the costume and handed it to the man who was using his hands to shield his genitals from public view. "Wrap this round you like a loincloth and go to the Drag Bar. You'll be right. Someone will buy you a drink if you keep your wig on." The man clutched the fabric around his hips and sprinted off in the direction of the Drag Bar, leaving his costume in a sparkling heap on the footpath.

"Come on," said Greta, kicking at the dismembered tail. "Someone will take this away tomorrow." The four Brides went into the Hall of Industries and ordered champagnes all round. Aveline also got herself a straight scotch.

"Should we go somewhere else?" Fiona enquired, as they stood at the bar drinking. Both Tash and Greta were looking sombre and anti-climactic. They shook their heads. Fiona felt her own mood plummet again. The parade had been terrific and the mermaid was funny but she shouldn't have come on to the party. She thought she would just stay until she met up with Charles at one o'clock. In the meantime she wondered what the Brides could do to amuse themselves. Tash suggested they dance. In a desultory fashion the four of them went out onto the dance floor and bumped around. Fiona was embarrassed. She couldn't dance like the other three. Her style of dancing belonged in the discos of 1974. She tried to move her arms and legs as little as possible. After about thirty minutes of this, Aveline cursed. "I gotta get up and outta this mood!" she cried. "Wait over there by the wall. It's time I did some shopping." She came back in about ten minutes time smiling. "Come on girls," she said patting her bumbag. "Guess what I've got?"

Fiona presumed this was a rhetorical question. "Where are we going?" she asked Tash in a whisper as they left the Hall of Industries.

"Dyke Bar toilets," Tash told her. "There's too many people around now to have it anywhere else." It was true. Since midnight, the crowd had been growing. People surged in all directions between the various dance halls. The Brides tried to stay together, but Aveline and Tash got separated. Greta and Fiona made it to the Dyke Bar together.

"Oh no," said Fiona, "We've lost them." They stood on the steps and gazed out over the crowd. Fiona shivered. It would be horrible to be lost in this place. She wondered if there was a lost persons stall at the Mardi Gras Party like there was for children at the Royal Easter Show.

"No we haven't lost them," said Greta. "They know where we're going. They'll be along directly. Let's wait inside." Fiona's jaw dropped when she went in. A lot of women were dressed in black leather. They sported boots and underwear and lipstick and shaved heads. "Check them out!" said Greta. "You never see anything like this up home."

"No. Never." Fiona had to agree. She had never seen women like this in her life. When she was in her late teens and hanging out with a gay crowd in the 1960s, there had been butch lesbians and femme ones. She had never had any trouble distinguishing one from the other, particularly since she had played femme to Kay's dark and handsome butch. In this crowd, however, there was no telling what was going on. She shook her head. She could not read the codes. Girls in leather were wearing lipstick. Girls in tight satin dresses had muscles and Doc Martin boots. Not many women were dancing, but a great many were either playing pool or looking on. There were bikie types at the bar and girls with chains and boots and G-strings and tattoos sitting at tables. Two leather clad girls dancing were linked together by a silver chain which ran between their nipple rings. Another woman appeared to have something long and pink swinging down between her legs. Fiona could feel herself blushing.

"There are some tough girls here," said Greta. "Don't let them see you staring!" Fiona tried not to but found she couldn't help it. Eventually her eyes caught Aveline and Tash on the other side of the dance floor. She and Greta went over to them.

"Sorry," panted Tash. "There was a kind of traffic jam outside. Some guy freaked out. He was thrashing around. The medics had to hold the crowd back so they could grab hold of him and hog-tie him to get him out. OD I reckon. Too many drugs. That's the problem with these dance parties in Sydney."

"Let's go up to the toilets now," Aveline suggested. All the cubicles were occupied. The Brides milled around outside, waiting. Fiona stared at the plastic bags which were taped all around the mirror and above the basins.

"Don't stare," Greta warned her. Then she explained in a whisper, "They're lesbian safe sex kits."

Fiona was astonished. "Lesbians? Safe sex?" she whispered in horror.

"Well there's a risk of HIV infection when lesbians have sex," said Greta.

Fiona considered this for a minute or two. "So do you and Tash use those things in the bags to have sex every time?" she asked.

Greta and Tash exchanged glances. "Well no," said Tash. "But if I started a relationship with someone else I would for sure. Especially," she added, "if it was a woman from Sydney."

Greta left her place in the queue and took one of the kits off the wall. She threw it to Fiona. "There you go," she said, "just in case you get lucky."

Fiona was mortified. She thrust the mysterious package into her bumbag. She did not look back at the women in the queue behind her, but she was sure she heard them snickering. When a cubicle became free the four Brides packed themselves into it and closed the door. There was a different species of plastic package on the cistern. Fiona had no trouble identifying these as needle kits. "Oh good," said Aveline, "how thoughtful." She took up a package and slid out a syringe and spoon.

"Don't!" said Tash, "at least not while I'm in here. People giving themselves needles makes me want to spew."

"Oh," said Aveline, "all right then. I'll wait till you guys have snorted yours and then I'll have a hit." She took out a tiny plastic pouch containing white powder. This made Fiona very nervous. She was too shy to ask what it was. She told herself that it must be speed. Surely Greta and Tash would not take a really dangerous drug like heroin. She would just have to trust her own judgement of character. Aveline cut the white powder into four neat lines on two credit cards with her pocket knife. Greta rolled a new fifty dollar note into a thin tube and closed off one nostril with her thumb while she inhaled the line up through the tube into her other nostril. Fiona was embarrassed because she didn't know how to do this. She watched Tash and Greta closely. Aveline noticed her agitation and helped Fiona when it came to her turn.

"Thanks Aveline."

"No problem. Now will you all piss off so I can use this needle without Miss Sensitive there emptying the contents of her stomach?" Fiona was not sorry to leave the cubicle. For one thing it was frightfully crowded and smelly. For another she was horrified by the idea of Aveline poking a needle into herself. Worst of all, two women in the next cubicle were making the most dreadful squelching noises, and groaning. She looked at her watch with relief as the three of them headed down the stairs which lead from the toilets to the dance floor. "What shall we do now?" she asked, swallowing a number of times. Her mouth was dry and there was a strong medicinal taste at the back of her throat. Greta and Tash did not answer. They rushed out of the Dyke Bar and into the sparkling night. The crowd had swollen massively. Fiona followed her friends into the throng like a body-surfer.

The three of them came up for air outside the Dag Bar. "This is where we belong in a way!" shouted Tash. "We're daggy dykes from the country!" They ran in and joined the crowd of enthusiastic dags jumping up and down to *Puff the Magic Dragon*. Fiona felt completely at home in this place. She often danced to songs like this in the lounge room with her children. A long while later she needed to go to the toilet. They were clean and there was only a small queue, so it was quite a pleasant experience. However, when she came back, Greta and Tash were nowhere to be found. Fiona searched the Dag Bar and food stalls opposite, but to no avail. "Oh dear," said Fiona to herself. "Now I am lost." She walked slowly up towards the Dyke Bar, feeling lonely and a little desperate. Fortunately she glimpsed a familiar face through a ragged gap in the surging crowd. It was Aveline. She was standing on the steps of the Drag Bar apparently waiting for someone. Fiona went over rather hesitantly.

"Have you seen Tash and Greta?" she asked. At close quarters Aveline's face looked definitely peculiar. She slowly swivelled her head to stare at Fiona with huge luminous eyes.

"No." she said finally. "Have you lost them?"

"Yes."

Silence. Fiona wondered if she ought to slip away, but Aveline caught her wrist and spoke in a husky, slow voice. "How are you feeling in your heart? You look sad. Your eyes are low."

"Well," said Fiona uneasily. "I am feeling a little down 'cos I've lost Greta and Tash but it's not that bad."

"Come with me," said Aveline solemnly. She led Fiona by the hand to a relatively secluded corner near the medical centre. She pressed a small white tablet into Fiona's hand. "Take this."

Fiona had to laugh. "I feel like Alice in Wonderland," she said. "Will this one make me grow bigger or smaller?"

Aveline took the question seriously. "It will make you aware," she said, "You will see things as they really are. Take it."

Fiona pretended to swallow the pill but pocketed it instead. As they walked back into the main thoroughfare Aveline melted away so quickly she didn't see her go. One minute she was there, the next she was not. Her place had been taken by a hybrid robot pixie covered in metal spikes. "Damn!" Fiona said to herself. Now she had lost Aveline as well. She should not have looked away for even a second. She was all alone again now and there was no lost persons tent, of that she was sure. The best she could do was to search for someone, anyone, by walking around from bar to bar.

What happened then was quite a long period of wandering around by herself, which she did not like at all. There probably were other people walking around on their own but it was hard to tell. Every other person by themselves looked purposeful. She felt as if she was the only one wandering haphazardly. During this time she waited in a long queue for mineral water and a hot dog, and found herself nearly in tears. She was insatiably thirsty and she had eaten almost nothing since breakfast. The other people in the line seemed to know each other and she was the only one not talking to someone. She felt old, haggard and well past her allotted 'use-by' date. Her beehive was starting to disintegrate and she did not have a comb. There were still forty-five minutes to go before she was due to meet Charles. She fingered the tablet in her pocket which Aveline had given her. Seriously, in her present condition she did not know how she was going to make it through the night until Kylie's big number, with or without Charles. With a gesture of finality she threw back the tablet. She had no idea what it was, but she supposed it might help. Just at that moment a rumour flew down the queue that the stall was closing up for lack of food and drink to sell. Fiona gave up. She headed into the Hordern and bought a double scotch and soda. Because she was thirsty she threw it down quickly, then bought a beer so she could dance and drink to pass the time. Dancing by herself was an unusual experience. She had thought that people might stare at her, but they did not. After a while she noticed that quite a lot of people were dancing alone, and moving around, not staying in one place. They seemed lost in the music and the movement, almost unaware of those around them. This suited Fiona. She became one of the nomads of the dance floor, bopping about with a beer in one hand, closing her eyes at times to blot out the laser lights that left after-images on her retina.

At last it was time to meet Charles. She headed off in the direction of the front gate. As she walked, thousands more people flowed in through the gates towards her. "Phew it's getting crowded," she muttered. "At least I'll be with Charles soon." She stood near the cloakroom and watched the party-goers pour in, the gorgeous, the deliberately ugly, the dressed-up and the dressed-down. Most were young, but some were not. "Good!" Fiona said to herself whenever she saw a particularly wrinkled oldster. Charles came sauntering along just after one o'clock. Fiona was very glad to see him. He was feeling fabulous, he said, and thoroughly intending to enjoy his Mardi Gras solo. They went together to the Dome to dance. Fiona was happy. She was with someone at last. Even if it was only Charles.

After about twenty minutes on the dance floor Charles excused himself and went to the toilet. Fiona waited, dancing by herself again. Fifteen minutes went by, but Charles did not come back. Suspecting he might have met someone in the toilets she went over and waited patiently outside the door. Men came and went. The door swung to and fro. Finally, in desperation Fiona stuck her head in the door after a man came out. To her surprise, all the cubicles were empty. Charles was not there. "Oh no!" she groaned, "I've lost him." Or rather, she hastily corrected herself, he had lost her. Perhaps deliberately. This created a serious problem. Charles had not told her where he had parked her car. When he had dropped her off on Broadway in the afternoon, she had given him her wallet, credit cards and driver's licence to mind. He had not given these back and she had not remembered to ask him for them. She had no money left in her bumbag except a five dollar note and some coins. Obviously she had to find him before she could leave the party, but perhaps this might be easiest when the crowds thinned out towards morning. Surely Charles would not actually leave the showgrounds without finding her again. She decided strategically to make her way back to the Dyke Bar. After all, she might find

Gig and Paddy, there, if not Greta and Tash. She wondered, briefly, what had become of Aveline.

Fiona was halfway up the main thoroughfare on her way to the Dyke Bar when she realised she had made a colossal misjudgement about Aveline's little white tablet. The world went crazy. She was hallucinating wildly, all alone, in a crowd of tens of thousands of people. Her footsteps slowed until she was standing still. The huge noise from the two pavilions shrank away to mere titters on the horizon. The sea of bodies around her was not exactly hostile, but there was no getting away from the fact that she was surrounded by alien life forms. It felt like the entire dance party had left earth and was hurtling through space. The stars came down at her like stilettoes. She was in a new and completely frightening dimension. A tiny part of her wondered how she was ever going to get out of it again.

She slowly turned round and round, changing her mind every second about which way to go. Lots of people banged into her and hurt her legs and flailing arms. She took a few slow steps, then stopped. This was not the way to the Dyke Bar. There were buildings around her which might have been familiar, but she could not recognise any of them. In fact, she could not see them clearly at all. The crowd was pressing down on her from every side. No-one had a human face. She fumbled for her glasses and put them on in the hope of glimpsing the real world again but they only made things worse. Alien faces stood out in even sharper focus. She took her glasses off with a groan and fought rising panic. A strange woman in the crowd passed by and said something to her, but Fiona could not understand the words. The woman had the face of a monster. She took Fiona's arm and tried to pull her through the crowd and between two buildings where there were fewer people, but Fiona twisted away from her. She ran a few steps and then stopped again. Fortunately the crowd closed in and she lost sight of her assailant, who might only have been trying to help her. Something warm ran down Fiona's face and tasted salty in her mouth. Tears. She had to find somewhere to sit down.

Slowly, like someone treading in seaweed, she made her way through to the edge of the roadway and sat down on the kerb. She pulled her tutu down over her knees and rested her chin on her hands. She ignored the occasional kick. She did not flinch when someone fell over her and completely destroyed what was left of her beehive hairdo. Bravely, she forced herself to observe the alien tumult of stomachs, knees, kilts and boots that surged back and forth. It was scary but it was certainly better than shutting her eyes and watching the rings of Saturn swirl in limitless space. As she watched, she caught a flash of apricot orange and tangerine tulle. Greta and Tash walked by in the dead centre of the surging tide of partygoers. To

Fiona, their fluffy skirts were the loveliest things in the world. She bullied her way through the tumult of people and hobbled up to them, shouting in a feeble voice. "Excuse me, I'm not having a good time."

"Aren't you?" said Greta amiably, "then come and dance. Where have you been?"

"No. No. You don't understand!" Fiona waved her hands at the crowd around them. "Aliens. Aveline! She gave me something." She took Tash's hand and sank her face into Greta's shoulder.

Over her head, Greta and Tash exchanged meaningful glances. "What did she give you?" said Greta. "Ecstasy? Acid?"

"Don't know."

"There's no way of telling what she's had," said Tash to Greta. "Fiona doesn't know. How could she? She's probably never had anything like it in her life before."

"I'm not having a good time!" Fiona wailed like a child. "I can't hear properly and I can't see very well and everything looks completely bizarre."

"Well stay with us," said Greta reassuringly. "Don't go off by yourself again." Fiona felt vaguely that this was not the way things had happened, but she could not find the words. "We're going back to the Dyke Bar." Greta went on. "You'll like being there Fee. Soon you'll feel much better."

The trip back to the Dyke Bar was a slow march. Now that she was in the comforting presence of her friends, Fiona began to take pleasure in the weird things she was seeing. This meant she stopped every second or so and said "Look at that!". Greta and Tash lost patience with this. They put a hand each under her armpits and pulled her along. As they drew closer to the Dyke Bar, it became apparent that something was going on inside. Women were pouring in through the doors. Fiona could hear sounds properly again. The smooth, mellifluous tones of k.d. lang's song *Constant Craving* poured out from the dance floor. Fiona gasped. It was not a recording. This was live.

"It's her!" Fiona turned a shining face on Greta and Tash as she pulled away from them and began to run. "It's k.d. herself. She must be a mystery act. Quick! Come on or we'll miss her."

Dimly, she heard Greta and Tash calling out behind her, but Fiona took no notice. She ran into the Dyke Bar and up to a low stage on one side. There, in the flesh, was k.d. lang. Fiona sank to her knees in front of the stage. "k.d." she moaned. Tash and Greta came up quickly. Tash took hold of Fiona's arm and tried to pull her up. "Get up!" she hissed. "It's not k.d. lang. Take a good look at her Fiona."

Fiona ignored this. Her eyes were fixed on the singer and she was humming along. Greta laughed and laughed. She took Tash to one side. "She's hallucinating Tash," she whispered. "Let her think it's k.d. if she likes."

Just at that moment the song finished. Fiona could see right away that the singer was not her idol. She stood up. "You're not k.d. lang," she said to the woman who was about to start another song. "I thought you were."

"Thanks."

"Fortunately she took it as a compliment," said Greta, as they walked over to the bar.

"I feel sick," said Fiona all of a sudden.

Her friends sat her down and looked at her carefully. "You won't be sick if you just stay here and avoid getting excited about anything," said Greta. "Tash and I will get you an orange juice and something sweet to eat. They don't sell orange juice or food in here so we'll have to go outside. You'll be alright here until we get back. Just don't move and don't stare at anyone!"

Fiona propped her elbows on the bar. The singer had gone and dance music was pumping out again. Someone sat down next to her. Someone said, "Hello Mrs Bainbridge."

Fiona spun her head around in shock. Who could possibly know her by that name here? The multiple worlds of her life reeled and spun in her mind. She tried to focus on the face that was smiling at her. She was fairly certain the face was young and pretty. Blinking her eyes Fiona established that the woman had cropped hair and was wearing a denim shirt. At least she was not in leather. That would have been too much altogether. It was strange that although the young woman had addressed her by one of her names, Fiona did not recognise the face at all. "Don't you remember me?" the young woman asked in a very friendly way

"No," said Fiona slowly. Then she whispered, "You'll have to excuse me, I'm not feeling very good."

"Like many other dykes around here," the woman laughed, "Talking is the best thing you know. It'll talk your mind off your head."

Fiona thought about this. "O.K." she said slowly. "That sounds reasonable. Well, who are you, anyway? Where do you know me from?"

"My mother did one of your cake-decorating classes, about ten years ago. I used to come with her sometimes. I would have been about twelve. You used to let me have a go at the cakes sometimes."

It was a long time since Fiona had taught cake-decorating. She shuddered to think of those days. This was embarrassing. "See if I can remember your mother.

What was her name?" she asked, trying to concentrate through the waves of hallucination.

"Pauline. And my name's Tegan." Fiona had no memory of either name. Her face remained blank. Tegan laughed. "It doesn't matter. Can I buy you a drink?"

"Um no. I mean yes, I suppose so. I um ... I'm waiting for my friends to come back, you see."

"Are you with someone?"

"No. I mean yes. I'm with two friends." Tegan ordered the drinks. Fiona's brain suddenly gave sharp turn. She put her head into her hands and groaned.

"How are you doing? Too much of a good thing eh?" asked Tegan.

"Well," said Fiona, "It's not my fault. I made a mistake a few hours ago. A friend gave me something and now I'm hallucinating. I think it might have been L.S.D. or something like that."

"You're certainly not the cake-decorator I once knew," giggled Tegan. "I bet you don't even go to church any more." Their drinks came and they sipped on them. Tegan took Fiona's hand and squeezed it with a smile. Fiona was silent. What was going to happen now? Was this what Greta had meant about getting lucky? What were Tegan's intentions towards her? She touched the safe sex kit in her bumbag with horror. "Do you want to dance?" Tegan asked after a while.

"Um, yes." Fiona was so pre-occupied with worrying about what you were meant to do with the different parts of the safe sex kit that she forgot her promise to Greta and Tash. She and Tegan got up from their stools. Tegan was still holding her hand.

"Not here." said Tegan. "Let's go to the Drag Bar. It's not so crowded." Once inside the Drag Bar however, they did not dance. Tegan lead Fiona to a dark corner and started kissing her. Once Fiona got over the initial shock she thought this was wonderful. It was a very long time since she had kissed another woman and Tegan's lips were soft and full. She wanted to go on kissing her all night. She liked it even better when Tegan put her hands on the bare skin of her stomach and nibbled at the top edge of her bra top. Fiona put her hand between Tegan's legs. She had not given a single thought to the safe sex kit since Tegan's lips had touched hers. Suddenly, just as she and Tegan were becoming passionate and involved, a drag queen resplendent in red lamé came over with an angry looking lesbian in tow.

"There they are!" he/she shouted. "I told you Madge. I've told you and told you that that girl is nothing but trouble."

Tegan sprang away from Fiona. "I have to go," she said. "Sorry Mrs Bainbridge.

It's been nice." Tegan's girlfriend grabbed her forcibly by the arm. As they walked away Fiona could hear Tegan saying, "But she used to teach me cake-decorating ..."

Feeling extremely flat, Fiona went back to the Dyke Bar and waited. Half an hour went by. Fiona spent the time thinking about Tegan. Greta and Tash did not come. She began to think that they had been and gone while she was in the Drag Bar. Finally she decided to find orange juice and sweets for herself. She spent her five dollar note on these refreshments and consumed them at a table by herself. As the effects of the drug diminished she began to see her situation more clearly. She had lost everyone and even missed Kylie's big number in the Hordern. Charles still had her wallet and all her identification. The location of the Commodore was still unknown. So, as she had no intention of arriving in Mardi Gras costume at her ex-mother-in-law's place in the wee hours of the morning and demanding the taxi fare be paid, she was effectively trapped until dawn broke. She was sure that she would find Charles then. However, right now she was lonely. She could always return to her earlier role as a nomad of the dance floors, but this did not appeal. She decided she would make a grand attempt to find a friend by touring all the smaller bars. But she had no luck. Was it possible she just kept missing people by minutes? Finally in the Dome toilets she glimpsed a familiar face. Believing her bad luck had broken she rushed over. "Oh, I'm so glad I've found you!" she cried, hugging furiously. She was pushed away.

"Now listen," said the woman she had hugged. "I've never seen you before in my life." Fiona looked at her, blinking furiously. The face was that of a complete stranger.

"You're right," she said, backing away in embarrassment. "I'm sorry." The other women in the toilet queue laughed behind their hands. Fiona fled. She went into Hall of Industries where laser lights were flashing hypnotically and sat watching them for a long time. Eventually she thought she might as well dance to pass the time and headed for the Dag Bar where her style of movement might be appreciated. Just outside however, by sheer chance someone called her name. Gig and Paddy were walking by.

"Oh, I'm so glad I've found you." Fiona hugged and was hugged in return. She cried a little too.

"What's the matter Fee, have you lost everyone?"

"Yes. A friend gave me a tablet and I took it without knowing what it was. I've been off my face. I lost Tash and Greta. Then I lost Charles. Then I lost Greta and Tash again. I met a nice girl called Tegan but her girlfriend took her away ..."

"Poor Fee! You'd better come along with us," Gig said. "We've volunteered for a little job. You can help. It will give you something to do." Paddy had a friend who was organising the distribution of safe sex and needle kits in the women's toilets all over the showground. Gig and Paddy were helping her. Paddy came over to Fiona and dumped a large cardboard box in her arms. "These are for the Dyke Bar toilets. Off you go. There's sticky tape in the box. Give them out to anyone who asks."

"Do I have to go by myself?" asked Fiona. She dreaded losing Gig and Paddy.

"You'll be alright Fee," laughed Paddy. "Meet us back in the Dag Bar when you've finished. O.K.?"

"Where in the Dag Bar?"

"On the far side of the dance floor. I promise we'll wait." Fiona set off on her assigned task. She had to admit it gave her a sense of purpose which had been sadly lacking while she was wandering about on her own. Nevertheless it had a down side. The toilet floors were covered in used needles and spoons. She crunched about on them, cursing, hoping no needle would rebound up and jab her in the ankle. She had just finished the toilets designated LADIES and was moving over to the toilets labelled GENTS when she saw Tegan's girlfriend Madge coming towards her. "Hey, you!" she called.

Fiona turned to run, prepared to throw down the box of remaining kits if necessary. "Wait on," yelled Madge, "I'm not gonna punch you."

She came over and looked into the box. "Oh great," she said. "I need a new fit. They're all used up in there." She took out a needle kit. "Who are you anyway, the bloody needle fairy?"

"Yes." said Fiona. It was not an accusation she could easily deny.

"Well I like you for that," said Madge, weaving slightly as she spoke. "Hey you know that Tegan," she went on, "Well you can fuckin' have her if you like. Me an' her are finished. She is nothin' but a slut."

Fiona smiled nervously. "I have to finish this job," she said and pushed past. Madge accompanied her into the GENTS. While Fiona was distributing kits, she went into a cubicle and locked the door.

"When I come out of here," she yelled. "How's about you and me have a dance, eh?"

"I'm busy," said Fiona.

"Now you just wait for me at the bottom of the stairs," Madge continued as if she hadn't heard, "An' I'll be down in a minute." Her speech had become slurred. She drawled the last few words.

"Bye for now," called Fiona and fled. She threw the empty box into some rubbish in an alleyway and sprinted for the Dag Bar. On the way there, however, she saw Greta and Tash waiting in a line to buy a coffee.

"There you are!" said Greta. "Jesus I got sick of carting that bloody hotdog around."

"Have you still got it?" asked Fiona, suddenly hungry.

"No." said Tash. "Greta ate it after an hour or so." They made a place for Fiona in the queue. In the furore of telling Greta and Tash about Tegan, Fiona momentarily forgot about Gig and Paddy. She forgot them even more completely when she suddenly glimpsed another familiar face in the distance. Greta was just saying how impressed she was that Fiona had had a brief romantic encounter at her very first Mardi Gras, when Fiona gave small cry of horror.

"Hide me!" she cried.

"Who from?" asked Tash, peering in the direction Fiona had indicated. "Who do you mean? That woman over there with the grey hair?"

"Yes," whispered Fiona. "It's Kay. An old girlfriend of mine. From way back before I was married. I can't believe she's here. She's a famous legal eagle these days. Very respectable. QC I think. I can't see who she's with. Can you?"

"Yes," said Greta, standing on tiptoes and craning her neck. "Hey I recognise that woman's face! Who is it Tash?"

Fiona gasped as Tash named an equally well-known newspaper editor. "Hey they're coming this way." Tash said in some excitement. "Don't you want to talk to her Fee?"

"No. What could I say after all these years? After all, I dumped her for the man who became my husband. A chapter of my life I'd rather forget." From behind a set of stairs the three of them covertly watched the two women stroll by. They were necking and smooching as they walked.

"I could make a fortune in blackmail if I had my camera," sighed Tash.

"Which is why they try to stop people bringing cameras in," said Greta harshly. "I'm against that kind of thing." Tash took issue with Greta's tone of voice. She said she had only been joking. An argument began. Fiona backed away as Greta and Tash became more and more angry with each other. She had listened to enough of their quarrels at work to know this one could last a while. She suddenly remembered Gig and Paddy. What had happened to the time? Leaving her friends to argue she slipped off the Dyke Bar. It was almost dawn. The Dag Bar was practically empty and Gig and Paddy were not among the few remaining dancers. Fiona tapped her feet for a while to the hits of the sixties and seventies, among fewer and fewer people, but in the end it was too depressing. When she went outside the sky was quite light and the air was cold. She shivered in the pinkish glow of early day. When she got to the Dyke Bar it was just closing up. Tegan was standing by herself on the steps. You could tell from her face that she had been crying. Fiona watched her for a while then went up hesitantly.

"Hello."

"Hello Mrs ..."

"Please don't. My name's Fiona."

"Really? I had a horse by that name once." Tegan laughed and her face looked better. "Are you going home right now? Do you have a car? Can you give me a lift?"

"Well, no. I'm sorry," said Fiona. "I haven't lived in Sydney for years and I'm afraid I don't know where my car is right now. I have to find my friend Charles who parked it yesterday afternoon. And I haven't seen him since just after one o'clock this morning."

"I see." Tegan fumbled in the pocket of her jacket. "Do you have a pen and a piece of paper?" Fiona provided her with these. "I'll write down my phone number and address. Call me next time you're in Sydney. We could go out for a drink."

Fiona took the piece of paper and looked at it. "Don't you live with Madge?"

"No way," said Tegan. "Anyway we're finished. Unfortunately though I have to get a lift home with her on the motorbike. All my other friends have gone home and I've spent all my money," she glanced furtively around. "Quick Fiona. Give me a kiss goodbye before she comes out." Fiona obliged, thinking how nice it would be to see Tegan again. She thought she might drive down to Sydney next weekend. Then Tegan pushed her away. Fiona concealed herself behind a group of women just in time to see Madge stride angrily out of the Dyke Bar and grab Tegan by the shoulder. They went off into Sunday morning, sullen and silent.

Fiona went and sat down beside the main thoroughfare with a discount coffee. She yawned. She told herself that if she just sat here long enough, someone she knew would come by. Not long after, Aveline struggled past. Her eyes were puckered and red. She was not walking properly, and she had lost her tutu. Her pink underpants were drooping. Fiona called out but Aveline did not seem to hear her. Fiona was glad to see that a tall girl in full leathers was helping her friend along. She let them go by without calling out again. There would always be time to ask Aveline what had happened when they were back at work on Monday. Finally, as the morning wore on, along came Charles, hobbling, the morning sun shining on his bald pate.

He had lost his hat and he seemed to have something wrong with his left leg. Fiona hugged him and he winced. "What's wrong with your leg Charles?"

"What happened to your beehive Fiona? Your hair has gone into dreadlocks." Fiona shrugged. She had given up worrying about her hair some hours ago. Charles propped himself up beside Fiona and massaged his patella. "I think it's called housemaid's knee," he said. "I spent too long kneeling on the concrete floor down there." He pointed to the men's toilets below-ground which were set up for sex.

"Well, did you meet anyone nice down there?"

"I didn't ask. Anyway, my heart is true to Shane. Now why did you go off like that when we were dancing? I could hardly go looking for you in the Dyke Bar." Fiona rolled her eyes. She was about to protest her innocence, but then decided not to. After all, who was to say who had really lost who? "Now what about you?" Charles went on. "Did you have a good time after all? Did you meet anyone nice?"

Fiona gave a small, secret smile. "Yes."

Charles patted her hand. "Tell me about it later when I'm not in pain. Let's go fetch the mighty Commodore and go home for breakfast. I'll get the nurses next door to bandage up my knee before I go on to the recovery party."

One of the pretty boys in the cloakroom tent had put on his pyjamas. He yawned mightily as he handed over Charles' coat. "See you next year," said Charles.

"Yeah." The cloakboy blew them a kiss. "Same time, same place on this crazy planet."

"Planet?" Fiona repeated, suddenly remembering the flying saucer in the parade. "What planet are you talking about?"

"Planet Mardi Gras," the boy said. He flashed them an atrocious wink. "Touch down safely!"

COMEBACK

Graeme Aitken

AS SOON AS I NOTICED HARRY standing there, back from the bar, leaning against the wall, I turned away. I hoped he hadn't seen me. Ordinarily, I would've walked straight out of the bar. Even being in the same room as him was enough to provoke a flurry of heated emotions in me. Fury. Jealousy. Hurt. Had I not just paid a ridiculous price for a gin and tonic, I would've left.

I rarely buy spirits. In fact, I seldom drink. I hadn't bought a drink in a bar for years, which is why I was surprised by the price. I'd had to dig in my wallet for a larger note. My change was delivered to me on a saucer, which I considered an insult, given what I'd already been charged. I snatched it up and stared defiantly at the barman. He returned my gaze with grand indifference. It was then that I noticed Harry, over the barman's sculptured shoulder.

I couldn't believe it. Harry. I took a swig of my drink to calm myself. Actually, I could believe it. Harry had a knack for ruining my plans. For it was one of those rare nights when I felt that a drink, in such a bar, where the chance of intimacy or at least some company lurked, was what I needed more than anything else. I had been at a funeral that morning, a funeral that had been profoundly depressing. I sipped my drink and felt the sting of the liquor flush through me. I resolved to stay.

Graeme Aitken was born and educated in New Zealand. He has lived in Sydney for the past seven years and works in the book trade. His short stories have been published in several local anthologies and magazines. His first novel will be published by Random House in July 1995.

I would finish my drink. I would not let Harry ruin my evening, the way he'd ruined years of my life. I didn't even care if he saw me. I would finish my drink and then perhaps go to a different bar, and order another.

But I couldn't help worrying what Harry would think seeing me in such a place. He knew I wasn't a drinker. Not like him. Harry had always been an absolute lush. He'd presume I was there trying to pick someone up. Such an assumption was almost enough to make me walk out of the bar there and then.

"Hey," a voice behind me said loudly.

I ignored it. There was only one person it could be. I went to take another sip of my drink but discovered I had drained the glass. "Hey there," said the voice, louder, more insistent.

Slowly, I turned round. To my surprise, Harry was still standing where he had been before. The only person nearby was the barman. He was flicking shots of liqueurs into a blender, but his eyes were fixed on me. When he put the bottles down, he beckoned me closer. I looked around. Surely, he must be looking at someone behind me. But there was no one there. The barman's expression had become more impatient. "Me?" I mouthed silently.

The barman nodded. I was thunderstruck. I couldn't believe he wanted to talk to me. It was inconceivable. He was at least ten years younger than me. Blond, ruddy, muscles prominent through his teeshirt. He was the type who generally regarded me with utter disinterest or even outright disdain. I couldn't believe my luck. Now I felt pleased that Harry was in the bar, a witness to my success. I glanced quickly across the room, and sure enough Harry's eyes were trained upon me.

I walked over to the barman and he handed me a drink. Another gin and tonic. I was so surprised. Why had he given me a second drink? Was it happy hour? Two drinks for one. It couldn't be. It was far too late in the evening for that. The barman must have bought it for me. There was no other possible explanation.

"For me?" I asked coyly.

The barman nodded, preoccupied. He was still busy with the blender. I was all aglow. I had never had a drink bought for me by a stranger and to have one bought for me by this youth, the focus of the entire bar, filled me with a fierce sense of pride. It was something I thought was confined to happening in the movies.

I was still so surprised by his gesture, I didn't know quite what to do. I sank down onto one of the bar stools and raised my glass to him. As I sipped at the drink, I tried to think of some suitable conversation, something original and interesting. Then, I remembered. I hadn't thanked him. I couldn't believe that I had completely forgotten my manners. "Thank you. Thank you for the drink," I blurted out loudly.

The bartender turned and stared at me. He'd been laughing with a man in a business suit who I noticed had just laid a five dollar bill in his saucer. He turned towards me. The good humour drained out of his face, as his gaze rested upon me. "Don't thank me, mate. Thank the gent over against the wall. He paid for it."

Oh the shame, the shame. Harry had bought it. Of course he had bought it, hoping he could atone for the gross betrayals of the past by buying me a drink. I would've refused it if I'd known. But it was too late now. I'd already taken a sip. I glanced at the glass and was shocked to see that I'd downed about half of it in the elation of the moment. It was too late to send it back. I glanced across at Harry. Of course, he was still watching me. I felt like throwing what remained in the glass across the bar at him but instead I put the glass back down on the bar and turned my back. I would never make such a public display. As it was, I had already made a complete fool of myself. I picked up my umbrella and bag and was about to walk out, when suddenly, there he was, standing at my elbow. Harry. "Hi ya, Sunshine," he chirped.

That name took me back. I hadn't heard it in years. Of course I hadn't. It had been Harry's name for me. I'd forgotten that. It astonished me how good it felt to hear it again. It was rather like the feel of that double gin slipping down my throat. Warming, soothing, slightly bitter.

I didn't want Harry to think hearing that name had affected me. "I'm surprised you've got the nerve to even talk to me," I said tersely, without turning to face him. "Let alone call me ridiculous old nicknames."

"Sorry. Still think of you as Sunshine. It just seemed natural. Sorry."

He didn't sound sorry. He sounded his usual confident self. I was sure he'd used that name deliberately to try and stir up some sense of nostalgia in me. I was determined he was not going to succeed. I was surprised at his gall. He hadn't dared approach me in years. I supposed he was drunk. Once Harry being drunk had been fun, but I gathered from what people insisted on telling me, that these days going drinking with Harry was grim. His moods were unpredictable. Increasingly, the booze brought something vicious and insulting out in him. He lashed out at people. Or so Nina told me. Sometimes I wondered if our estrangement had driven Harry to drink. I rather hoped it had.

"I was just about to leave," I said.

"You haven't finished your drink," said Harry.

"No," I said coldly, finally turning towards him, though even then, not looking him in the eye.

In the past Harry had never failed to overwhelm me. I'd been hopelessly attracted to him for several years when we were both in our mid-twenties. Once, just looking into Harry's eyes was enough to make me lose all sense of purpose. I'd agree to anything he said without really listening. His eyes had always been eloquent. They seemed to say a thousand things, everything I longed to hear but never actually did.

Yet I'd always known my feelings were destined to go unrequited. In the ranks of beauty, Harry was a colonel while I could only dream of one day being an officer. I never allowed myself to declare the anguished state of my heart. Even when we'd come to this very bar all those years ago and Harry had grown more tender and affectionate with every schooner, his arms creeping round me, his beery breath whispering in my ear, "I love being here with you, Sunshine." By that stage, I'd be drinking mineral water and though I'd allow myself to wallow in his arms, I knew it was wrong. That it was doing me no good. Merely stoking the passion I'd been struggling to stamp out.

Meeting Harry again, after all those years, was like a breath of wind on the embers of that passion. It might blow those embers away, scattering them irretrievably or somehow manage to cajole a last glowing cinder back into flame. Had those years of utter estrangement finally cured me of my infatuation?

I raised my eyes to meet his. They were as blue as ever. I noticed the lines beneath them that hadn't been there before. I saw the bleariness of several drinks there too. We were the same age. Thirty five. I had hoped to see more signs of damage in his face. I'd imagined him going to seed, but I was disappointed. Like most queens, Harry was committed to the cause of self-preservation. Despite the rumours of his binges and excesses, there was no real evidence of them in his face.

I stared at Harry and waited for that familiar ache of longing to stir in me. His gaze wasn't as steady as it once had been. It wavered and I felt a small sense of triumph. Perhaps Harry had some sense of shame after all. He began to talk, his usual nonsense, discomforted by the directness of my gaze. I hushed him. Touched my fingers to his lips and he stopped mid-sentence. He was so surprised. I let my fingers linger there a moment, convinced that touching him would surely awaken something. I had longed to touch him so many times, yet never had the courage to do so.

I let my fingers fall away. *Nothing.* Looking at Harry. Touching Harry. I felt nothing. I was surprised. I'd never held any faith in the belief that time heals every wound but it seemed to be true after all. I felt no desire, but no anger either. Finally coming face to face and speaking with Harry had been an anti-climax. That anxiety when I first noticed him across the bar had completely seeped away. I only felt indifference.

I smiled, pleased to have achieved that state. It was a victory over my own emotions. Harry grinned back. "I'll get us another round," he said.

The smile died on my face. I might have been indifferent, but I wasn't forgiving. I had no intention of allowing Harry to get me drunk, stage some sort of soppy reconciliation and insist on picking up the pieces of our friendship. I picked up my bag instead. "I don't think so."

"Sorry to hear about your Mum."

I turned on him. Furious. "How'd you know about that?"

He stood there, shrugging, fumbling for an answer.

"Friends keep me informed," he finally muttered.

I knew who that was. I resolved never to breathe another word to her.

"Of course, if you stopped screening your telephone calls and spoke to me when I rang, Nina wouldn't need to tell me what's happening with you."

"You never called. There were never any messages from you ..."

"I didn't ring to speak to your machine. I rang to speak to you."

"Well you'd have better luck getting my answering machine to accept your apology than you would getting me to."

At that point Harry did something extremely unexpected. He laughed. When he should have been striving to find the rejoinder to cap mine, instead, he began to laugh. I stared at him in surprise, and then increasingly with disgust as his laughter became louder. He was drunk. He had to be drunk to behave so senselessly.

"Can you believe this?" he grinned. "The two of us. The grand feud. Years of silence. Sniping at one another behind each other's backs. How did we ever get to be such drama queens?"

Harry seized my hand and turned those eyes of his upon me. "Perhaps it was inevitable we'd end up like this, considering where we met?"

"I shudder to remember," I said coldly.

But Harry was grinning at me and then he started to hum a tune. Softly. So only I could hear. That song took me back. I couldn't stop myself from smiling too. Harry had always been so impossible to resist. We'd known each other since we were ten years old. We were child stars, or at least our mothers thought we were and their friends insisted we were too. Child stars of the local musical society shows. We started out at age ten as part of the brood of the King's children in 'The King and I'. The next year, we were the von Trapp brothers in 'The Sound of Music'. I was Kurt. Harry was Friedrich. Then at twelve, they made us rivals. The musical society decided to do 'Oliver'. But which of us would be the lead?

After our auditions, we were sent to the empty dressing room while the committee made their decision. While we waited, Harry showed me the hairs that were growing round his cock, then insisted that I show him what I had. "Nothing. I've got nothing to show," I protested. But Harry pulled down my pants anyway. He studied my genitals, then grasped my cock and his own in either hand and watched them swell. "I've got hairs. And my cock's bigger," he finally announced with satisfaction. I stuffed mine away in my pants while Harry began to count his hairs. He was only halfway through and had already counted twenty two when Mrs Lister called us back.

I knew the part would be Harry's. As we walked out to the stage, I acknowledged his merits. As well as his superiority below the waist, he was also blonder, better looking and more confident. I was faster at memorising my lines and I could reach high C whereas Harry couldn't come near, but somehow I knew that wasn't going to be enough. Mrs Lister took me aside before she made the announcement and asked me to understudy the role. My mother appeared at my side. "We'll think about it," she snapped, sweeping me out the door, so we wouldn't have to witness the triumph of Harry and his mother.

I cried into the collar of my mother's fur coat all the way home on the train. I felt so inferior. Harry had everything. The lead role and superior looks and physique. I re-read the book my mother had given me that told me all the things that were *supposed* to be happening to me. But reading that book made me recognise an opportunity. It was possible, it was just possible, that Harry's advanced physical developments might also spell his doom. Oliver was a soprano. Yet it was far from certain that Harry would remain one for much longer. I had my mother ring Mrs Lister the next day and inform her I would understudy the part.

In my bedroom I practised black magic, trying to accelerate the growth of Harry's Adam's apple by chanting the witche's speech from 'Macbeth' over the script of 'Oliver' and one of Harry's pubic hairs, a symbol of his bodily transformations. That hair had taken some procuring. I'd tried to persuade Harry that if he shaved them all off they'd grow back faster and longer. But Harry wouldn't hear of it. He was proud of them just as they were. Finally, he conceded to pluck out one as an experiment. While he was distracted, moaning about his loss and the pain it had involved, I was secreting the hair between the pages of my copy of the script.

I said my spell faithfully every night for a week. At rehearsals, I studied Harry's throat, longing to witness the cartilage swelling within it. I was so jealous I not only wanted it to grow, I didn't want it to stop until it had choked him to death. But all I noticed from scrutinising Harry's throat were several long dangling hairs a little further up. Harry was going to need to shave soon. Everything the book said would happen was starting to. Except his voice. It continued to soar, pure and sweet, even looming close on occasion to that high C.

Then on the day of the first dress rehearsal, Harry croaked in the middle of 'Food Glorious Food'. Mrs Lister rushed onto the stage and swept him into the wings. When they tried the song again, some minutes later, Harry was pale and unsmiling. He croaked again only a few words into the song. That night, Mrs Lister rang to say that Harry was unable to perform and that I had to be Oliver and save the show. My mother was thrilled and instantly accepted on my behalf. "Just a moment," I said. "There's still a problem."

My mother stared at me in surprise. I could hear Mrs Lister's voice gulping on the other end of the line. "What? What? What he's saying?" I had given this scenario a lot of thought. I had played this possibility over and over in my mind hundreds of times. "If I am going to be Oliver, then it has to be my name on the poster and on the front of the programme." My mother relayed this information to Mrs Lister nodding her approval to me. "But they've already been printed," Mrs Lister wailed. "They've been put up all over town." "Well, they'll have to be reprinted and put up all over again, won't they?" said my mother.

After a long silence, Mrs Lister finally conceded that perhaps they would have to be.

I still have that poster. When everything blew up with Harry, I rummaged round in all the boxes under my old bed at my mother's house, until I found it. I had it framed and hung it in my bedroom. It might have seemed an immodest thing to do but it made me feel better. After what had happened, I knew there'd be no one sharing my bed for quite some time. No one to remark on the poster and make me feel ridiculous. Seeing that framed poster, made me smile a little on those nights when I climbed into that bed, the bed I bought with Tim.

We were at that stage of buying furniture together. It was a futon bed, with a queen size mattress. Too large for one person. I should have got rid of it as soon as he left. Except it was brand new. That was what I told myself. It was too new to throw away. The truth was I didn't get rid of it because I kept on hoping, hoping for far too long, that Tim would come back and clamber in beneath the sheets on his side of that bed.

Now the mattress has a distinct slump in the middle. From the weight of me over the years. I've tried my best to get rid of that slump. I've rolled the futon up regularly in every possible different way. I've shaken it out as best as I could by myself. Once I even tried to beat it back into shape with my old tennis racquet. It was useless. The slump remained. Whenever I changed the sheets I noticed it and invariably felt depressed. For it seemed the only way the mattress could ever be righted was if I had someone to share the bed. Someone to sleep on the other side of the slump so that eventually the mattress might get flattened out.

"Have another drink," Harry was saying in my ear, reaching for his wallet.

It was this bar where we met again, twelve, thirteen years after 'Oliver'. Our mothers' friendship didn't survive that show. Harry and I went to different high schools. His parents separated. Harry and his mother moved away to a swanky, waterside apartment. Our paths never crossed. Until that night, when he'd come up to me in this bar, and said hello. I wasn't able to respond. I was so in awe of how good-looking Harry had become, and flattered that he'd even remembered me and bothered to talk to me. Then I noticed the boy. Standing just behind Harry, his fingers caught through the belt loops of Harry's jeans, petulantly tugging at him.

I quickly learnt that there was always a boy hanging off Harry. I'd been jealous of them at first, but after a while, after seeing so many of them come and go so fast, some of them genuinely heartbroken, I began to lecture Harry on being fickle. It wasn't only for his benefit but also for my peace of mind. When Harry was single, I couldn't help hoping that *this time*, finally, he'd recognise my worth and pick me.

It was agony, every time he failed to. Eventually I realised that I had to save myself. I had to find my own lover and get over Harry that way. Harry was buying me another drink. He placed his wallet on the bar and flipped it open. There was a photograph beneath the plastic sleeve, opposite the change purse. Was it Tim in Harry's wallet? *Harry's* wallet. He hadn't noticed me looking. Harry was waving a twenty dollar note at the barman. I strained to see. I had photographs of Tim, but none of the two of us together. There had never been anyone else to take photographs of the two of us. We'd spent our days alone together. Just the two of us. I avoided Harry's invitations for as long as I possibly could. I didn't want to watch him and Tim together and inevitably begin to compare them. When they did finally meet, I watched Tim swoon as Harry's eyes frankly assessed him.

I could hardly blame Tim for falling for him. I was guilty of the same desires. I blamed Harry. The photograph in the wallet wasn't Tim. It wasn't any of Harry's many lovers. Harry carried round a photograph of himself at twenty one. I turned away and walked out of the bar. I should have known it was impossible. He was as vain and heartless as ever. He would betray me again without a thought if the opportunity ever arose. But I would never give him that opportunity. I turned down the side street in case he should follow me. He would look for me on Oxford St, if he bothered to look for me at all. When he noticed I was gone, probably all he'd do was shrug and throw back my drink as well as his own.

The side street led in the opposite direction to my apartment. To avoid the possibility of running into Harry meant I would have to walk right round the block.

It was dark and drizzly. The rain on my face reminded me that I'd left my umbrella in the bar. My new umbrella. My expensive new umbrella from David Jones. I stopped. Should I go back for it? I turned, but still I hesitated, unable to decide. I looked back up the street towards the bar on the corner and there it was, bobbing towards me. My umbrella, opened out, with Harry beneath it. He pulled me under my own umbrella, his arm cradling me against him. "Sunshine, you worried me. Don't do that. Disappear on me like that."

I couldn't believe he'd found me. I kept my face down, not wanting to betray my pleasure that he had. I mumbled some excuse.

"Is it your mother?" Harry asked, all concerned.

It was easiest just to nod.

"Where are you going?" he asked gently. "It's too wet to be wandering round."

I had to say something. "I'm going to Mum's. I've got things to do there."

"Now?"

I nodded. "Well, you can't walk to Wahroonga. We'll get a taxi."

Harry waved down the next taxi and ushered me into it. "You can't be by yourself tonight, Sunshine. You just can't. I'll help you do what you have to do." I tried to protest but Harry wouldn't let me say a word. I had been about to point out that a taxi to Wahroonga would be a terrible price. But Harry paid. He insisted on paying when we got there and I didn't argue. Once we'd got in the door, Harry turned to me. "Now what is it you wanted to do?" he asked.

I didn't know.

"Do you have to go through her things?"

I nodded dumbly.

"Well, if we're going to do that, we're going to need a drink. Where's the liquor cabinet?"

I pointed to it and Harry strode over, flipped it open and began to exclaim over its contents. I drifted past him, down the hall, to my mother's bedroom. It had been weeks since she had slept in her own bed and now she never would again. I had made the bed up myself with fresh linen before I drove her to the hospice, knowing it would prove to be a waste of time, but determined to do it nevertheless. My mother had sat at her dressing table, watching me in the mirror, her expression betraying nothing.

I sank down onto her bed and buried my face in the pillows. I was relieved then that I had changed the linen. All I could smell was the fragrance of the laundry detergent. The scent of my mother and her suffering had been erased. I heard the clink of glasses behind me and rolled over. Harry stood in the doorway, the brandy bottle in one hand, two glasses in the other. "You just lie there and tell me what you want done," he said.

He placed the bottle and glasses on the mantelpiece and waited for his orders. When they failed to come, he marched over to the wardrobe and flung the doors open. He half fell in amongst the rack of frocks and coats, embracing them. "Your mother always was a smart dresser," said Harry.

He righted himself and stared into the wardrobe. "Ah," he exclaimed, pulling out a black and purple ankle length evening dress. "I remember this dress somehow."

Harry's brow creased trying to recall why.

I could've told him if I'd felt able to trust myself to speak. My mother had worn that dress to the opening night of 'Oliver'. She had bought it especially, along with new shoes and gloves. Topped the outfit off with her fur coat.

The fur. What was I to do with the fur? I couldn't give it away to charity. It was worth thousands. But there was no friend I could give it to. Who would accept it? I couldn't keep it myself. A dead animal's skin that had belonged to a woman now dead. I shuddered. It was too macabre. I began to regret that I hadn't thought to bury her in it.

But then Harry discovered the fur, pulled it out of the wardrobe and began to put it on. "I can't resist," he gushed.

He was very drunk.

He had one arm in, when suddenly he stopped, turning to me, his face knotted in concern. "I'm sorry. I'm being silly. Do you mind?"

I shrugged. "Put it on. Have it if you like. I don't know what to do with it."

"Have it?" Harry was indignant. "Sunshine, you can't go giving this away. You've got to keep it. This is the sort of thing that gets handed down in families."

"Amongst the women," I pointed out.

"Honey, in this case, you'll do just as well." Harry held the coat open for me. "Go on. Slip it on."

I stared into its grey silk lining. "I can't."

Harry stared at me. Hands on his hips. "Because she's dead? Sunshine, haven't we both been through enough deaths now to have given up on all those niceties. All the bullshit. Why not try a few things on as we go through her wardrobe? Have ourselves some fun."

Harry poured himself a drink and one for me. He passed me the glass and then clinked his against mine. "After all, it's not the first time we've done it. Dressed up in your mother's clothes. Only this time, we don't have to worry about her coming in and catching us."

I laughed but even to my ears it ended up sounding more like a moan. Harry swept to my side, brandishing the coat. "Darlin', don't carry on so. Here snuggle up in this. You're shivering."

He spread the coat over me as if it were the tartan rug my mother had kept pulled up to her chin as she sat in her chair by the window at the hospice.

"You just lie there and leave everything to me."

It was simplest to demur and do as I was told. There was something comforting about that coat. So many times in my childhood I had snuggled up to my mother and felt the sensation of the fur against my face. Years ago. In more innocent times. When wearing a fur was the height of glamour and not a crime.

It was true we had dressed up in my mother's clothes before. Back then, neither of us had dared to put on the fur. We'd been in awe of it. We were almost scared to stroke it. I had chosen one of my mother's nighties to wear. Harry, who always had to be the best, put on her Sunday church dress and the hat she'd had specially made to match. We stood there in front of the wardrobe mirror, Harry wobbling in her shoes, me in her fluffy slippers. "You have to take your underwear off," Harry said. "Women never wear their underwear under a nightie. We have to be authentic."

Harry said this last sentence in the British accent he was so good at imitating, the accent he had used in the 'Oliver' audition. "What if someone comes," I protested.

"Then we'll be caught looking authentic," said Harry coolly.

He began to rummage through the make-up my mother kept on her dressing table. He selected a lipstick, breathed into the mirror with a sigh and traced the brilliant red over his own thin lips. Then he picked up my mother's powder puff and dusted his face. He stood back to admire the effect, his startling new mouth smiling with satisfaction. Then he glanced at me. My fingers were on the elastic of my jockeys. Harry gave an exasperated sigh, a perfect imitation of my mother. Then he pursed his lips exactly as she did when she was impatient. Reluctantly, I peeled my underwear down. My penis stuck out comically through the flimsy material. "You've got a stiffy," Harry observed.

"No, I haven't," I said, refusing to look down.

Harry wobbled over to me in his shoes. He grasped it through the fabric of the nightdress. "Yes, you have," he whispered.

He fondled it, until it was too late to tell him to stop. I had my first orgasm all over my mother's nightdress. All I could do was cry. Harry took charge. He mopped it all up with the nightdress and then buried the incriminating garment at the very bottom of his schoolbag, promising he'd destroy it. When my mother returned, he looked at her with an expression of such wide eyed innocence, that even I was struck by his performance. He deserved the part of Oliver after all. Even if he couldn't hit high C.

Harry was rummaging through my mother's wardrobe for the second time in his life. "Sunshine, none of this is going to some dreary second hand shop," he said firmly. "It's too gorgeous for that. We'll have a stall at Paddington markets. A drag stall. We'll sell it all off and donate the money to the hospice. Isn't that a super idea? Wouldn't your mother like to know that her frocks were passed on into good hands? Honey, no one would appreciate these frocks more than queens and that's the undeniable truth."

I was sure my mother would be horrified by the idea. But it had always been impossible to stop Harry once he'd started. So I said nothing. I let him run on, though I knew the next day I would throw it all into some suitcases and take it to St Vinnies. Including the coat.

"And you and I'll man the stall, dressed in the finest items. Oh, won't it be fun. Aren't you glad I came to help? Now, what will I wear?"

Harry started pulling out frocks. "I don't know if I'm going to be able to get into these. Well, maybe, with a few adjustments."

Then his hands seized upon a stiff floral dress. He turned to me in triumph, holding it up high, his eyes shining. "What does this remind you of? Remember Sunshine?"

Harry started to sing. It took me a moment to place it. Something from 'The Sound of Music'.

"Remember? Don't you remember? It's the curtains dress. The play clothes for the children that Maria made out of the curtains. Your mother already had a dress made out of the exact fabric that the costume woman found. You pointed it out to her. `Mummy, you've got a dress just like the curtains' and your mother looked like she wanted to throttle you."

I smiled at the memory. "She never wore it again. I thought she'd thrown it out."

Harry began to fling off his clothes. His shoes. His jeans. His jacket. His teeshirt. For a moment, he stood there in his underwear. When he bent his head forward to slip the dress on, I saw the regrowth in his hair. Harry kept the blond in his hair with chemicals. But even more amazing were the hairs all over his chest. He who had always insisted that he *had* to be smooth chested, no longer bothered to shave them off. It had been years since I'd seen Harry half naked. He wasn't as slim or as tanned as he once had been. But it was winter after all and he was thirty five years old.

Before our estrangement, we'd still been clinging to our youth, trying to be boys. Dressing young. Acting young. Lying about our age and dancing till dawn to prove we still could. Now it was completely undeniable. We had grown into men.

It was only a glimpse of him before he plunged into that dress but still it stirred something in me. Desire? Affection? I couldn't tell. The emotion vanished so quickly. Perhaps it was merely nostalgia, something I'd denied myself feeling for years. I'd clenched Harry's betrayal so fiercely inside myself, poisoning the memory of 'the good old days.'

Harry shook himself into the dress. "Do me up. Do me up," he commanded, playing with the fabric, smoothing it out over himself.

I shivered as I slipped out from beneath the coat. My fingers were trembling as I reached for the zipper. I placed a hand on Harry's back to steady myself and he jumped, startled. "Your hands are so cold," he moaned.

I mumbled an apology and bowed my eyes. The dress gaped open. I could see the white of his underwear. The curve of his buttocks. I jerked my gaze away and pulled the zipper up. Harry began to hum the overture to 'The Sound of Music'. The zipper was stiff after years of never being touched, and there was more of Harry than there should have been. I could only get it halfway up.

Harry didn't care. His hands rose in the air. Arms spread wide. He began to twirl round and round and began to sing. Harry could still sing. After his voice broke, it mellowed into a baritone. Mine faltered and was lost. Forever.

My audition for the high school choir was devastating. The music teacher only allowed me to sing a few bars before telling me, "No." I stood there staring at him, disbelieving. He had to shoo me out of the room. I was bereft. Such a grievous loss. I no longer had anything that made me special. My gift had been snatched away and I was just another plain, skinny kid, indistinguishable from so many of the others.

When the nurse told me about my mother, I felt the same hysterical denial welling up in me, that exact same emotion as all those years ago when the music teacher guided me out the door, his hand gripping my neck.

I never tried to sing in public again. Not even 'Happy Birthday' round a cake. I'd whisper the lyrics. I couldn't bear the sound of my own voice. It grated too much. What it had become. The irony was I still had the desire to sing. That failed to wither away and vanish with my voice. It lingered, reminding me of the destiny I'd always imagined for myself and that everyone - my mother, her friends, my audiences - had assured me would be mine.

Only when I was alone at home would I sing. I'd play my favourite records, show tunes, at top volume so the true vocals drowned out my own efforts. Or I mimed. In front of the mirror. All the emotion. Without a sound. But there in my mother's bedroom, Harry silently cajoled me. His hands stretched out to me, urging me to join in, his eyes wide and encouraging, his head nodding. Tentatively, I began to hum along. Harry pranced about the room. "I always wanted to be Maria," he confided in between verses. When he finished the song, Harry burst into a wild applause. Whooping and cheering. "It's our comeback doll. After all these years. Our comeback." Comeback. Come back.

The words I whispered down the phone to Tim. That was all I managed to say before I began to cry and couldn't stop. I cried into the phone until I realised that he was no longer there. He had hung up or perhaps Harry had hung up for him. That is what I believed. Tim wouldn't have done that. Hung up on my tears. But Harry would've. He liked to take charge. He would've broken the connection.

Why had Harry stolen him? He wasn't Harry's type. He wasn't bold and glossy like Harry's other boys. He was ordinary. Impressionable. Very young. Almost ten years younger than me, and Harry. I had been his first lover. Had Harry taken him merely to prove to me that he could? As if I hadn't always known that.

I didn't know how long they lasted together. I'd refused to let anyone mention Harry to me and though friends were always disobeying, they never actually told me what I longed to know but was too proud to ask. I wanted to be told that it hadn't lasted. That Tim - ordinary, suburban Tim - had been the one who *finally* hurt Harry.

Memories were heaving through me like orgasms. I was giddy. My limbs twitching. I could feel the tears swelling in my eyes. Finally. Tears. They had refused to flow when the news of my mother's death was broken. Seeing the body hadn't provoked them either. Even at the grave side, when the coffin was lowered deep down into the earth, I remained dry eyed. But my tears were poised. I knew it. Over the previous three days I had felt them. The weight of them. Clogging up my head. Making it ache. I hadn't cried since that day on the telephone speaking to Tim.

I threw myself onto the bed and sobbed into the fur collar of the coat, just as I had all those years ago after the audition for 'Oliver'. Suddenly, there she was. My mother. Beside me. Bending over me in her favourite floral frock. Stroking my hair, soothing me, telling me to let it all go and that everything was going to be alright. Wrapped in her fur, her voice softly whispering in my ear, I could almost believe her the way I always had when I was a child.

But of course, it wasn't her. That dress. The emotion of the moment. The tears in my eyes... it was so easy to make the mistake. It was Harry. I knew it was Harry when he picked me up off the bed and enfolded me in his arms, crooning the song in my ear like a lullaby. I rested my head on his chest and he clasped it there, his fingers running through my hair. He began to sing a different song. I knew it well. Knew the different parts. It was a duet. Harry's heartbeat was all the accompaniment I needed.

UP IN SALVADOR

James McQueen

I TAKE SOME PAINS TO BE BACK AT THE hotel each day by mid-afternoon. By then the small pool is in shadow and it is pleasant to sit by the water and drink a beer or a coffee and do nothing else at all. I am often alone, because it is the hottest time of the year, and there are few guests at the Villa Romana. Of these, not many will stay more than a day or two; except for me, Paul and the French girl. Her name is Marianne and at the moment she is lying supine by the edge of the pool. She wears a swimsuit which is much too brief for her solid body. She has been motionless for fifteen minutes or so, except for her hands, which move languidly, stroking the tops of her breasts above the halter of the bathing suit. Apart from the waitress, a very black girl in long blue skirt, white blouse and red headscarf, who comes regularly out onto the terrace to replenish my

James McQueen was born in Tasmania and worked at a number of jobs - factory hand, window dresser, ship's cook, weather observer, fruit picker, truck driver, accountant - before he began writing full time in 1977.
He has had thirteen books published including 'A Just Equonox' (novel, Macmillian, 1980), 'Hook's Mountain' (novel, Macmillan, 1982; reissued by Penguin, 1989; published by Viking, USA, 1990), 'The Franklin : Not Just A River' (non-fiction, Penguin, 1983), 'White Light' (novel, Penguin, 1990; Book I, Clocks of Death trilogy), 'The Heavy Knife' (novel, Heinemann, 1991; Book II, Clocks of Death trilogy), Travels With Michael & Me' (short stories, Random House, 1992). In preparation are: 'The River King' (short stories), 'Island People' (short stories), 'Acts of Mercy' (novel).
He has won a number of national and international short story awards and has received several; fellowships from the Literature Board of the Australia Council.
He lives in rural northeastern Tasmania. His hobbies are golf, fishing and silence.

glass or merely to inspect us, apart from her, we are alone, Marianne and I. We do not acknowledge each other's presence, but we are both very much aware of each other, all the same. Paul is absent, and we are very much aware of that, too. And I am not dissatisfied.

Salvador de Bahia sits on the horn of land opposite the curve of the African slave coast, and the blacks have been here for a very long time. Dark skin is common on this littoral, and negroid features, and a certain vital earthiness in the music. This morning, by the Lacerda elevator, I saw a man in bathing trunks dancing up the street, a pineapple in one hand, a blaring transistor in the other. And a boy, very negroid, with protuberant nipples, like a woman's. This is not uncommon here; perhaps there is something in the diet, some unsuspected abundance of oestrogen, as in kangaroo apples.

Beyond the stone parapet of the terrace, somewhere down in the shadowed alleys, a trumpeter has begun to practice riffs. I have heard him before. Soon a trombone will join in, and they will play idly, easily, for perhaps half an hour as the day dies. I will eat alone this evening. Perhaps I will go down in the hot night to the Avenida Oceanica and drink a beer and watch the crowds. Perhaps not. Perhaps I will go to bed early instead, read for a while, think about what is happening to Paul.

Marianne is still stroking herself.

Paul loves the beach, and spends as much time there as he can. My skin is too fair to bear the sun for long, and anyway, there is too much of a meat-market about Brazilian beaches, and a kind of mindless sunstruck sensuality that is dangerous. So while Paul is swimming or lying on the sand among the brown bodies, I sit in the shade of the old Portuguese lighthouse on the knoll that stands at the southern end of the Barra beach. Sometimes I eat an Argentinian apple, crisp and cool, a small taste of more temperate climes. Sometimes I take a taxi, go to the big square by the Lacerda elevator, lean against the stone balustrade, watching the pimps and illegal currency dealers harrying the tourists. They don't bother me anymore, they know me now. Sometimes I take the elevator down to the lower town, go into the Mercado Modelo, climb past the stalls and shops, go out onto the balcony and drink a cold beer. There is a sea breeze, usually, a poet or two selling their clumsily printed booklets. Sometimes a flautist comes by, plays for ten minutes for the price of a drink.

It was by the Lacerda elevator that I first met Pedro when he approached me, waiting to buy travellers' cheques. I shoo-ed him away, but not before he tried to interest me in girls, boys, emeralds, cocaine, Candonble, Capoeira.

It was a week before I thought of him again, after Marianne had begun to insinuate herself into Paul's company.

She is staying here for three months - so she says - to improve her Portuguese. In return for teaching French to the children of the landlord, she has free meals and lodgings at the Villa Romana. But it is the slack season, the hot season, and I think she is bored.

We had not intended to stay for more than a few days in Salvador, Paul and I; but there is something about the city that has kept us here far longer than we expected. An atmosphere, an ambience ... the calm sea, the long hot days, the slow pace ... the old town, mouldering under its stained tiles, the music - everywhere the music ... the smell of dende oil, the bare dark bodies, the frenetic nights.

And something else. The city has a certain sinister quality ... things are different here, slightly skewed, seem always on the edge of something secret, something a little depraved and vicious.

Like Pedro.

I eat alone in the large dim dining room. The wooden floor is highly polished and the room is filled with dark heavy furniture, with black beams overhead. The shutters are open to admit the slight breeze. Both the waitresses wear the traditional local dress, with bright headscarves. One of them smiles at me, the other, the prettier of the two, is sullen, and will never look at me directly.

After dinner I walk up the narrow stairs, along the bare polished corridor, past the wooden chests and African masks to our room. It is very large, sparsely furnished with the same dark furniture. There are two beds, a great wardrobe, a dresser, a dressing table. A door leads to the bathroom. The single window faces north, looking out over the terrace and the pool. It is very quiet.

I read for a time, lying on my bed, and fall asleep over the book. It is midnight before I wake, undress, crawl into bed. Another day, perhaps two.

In the morning, when I wake, the room is already flooded with light. I look out the window, down at the pool. Marianne is already there, in her bathing suit, with the landlord's children. There is a boy about six, and a girl perhaps two years older. Marianne is in the pool with them, playing and splashing. Watching her, I have the curious feeling that she knows I am at the window, although she has not raised her head. There is a slightly artificial air to her movements, a forced quality, as if she is playing to some unseen audience.

She began the process of attaching herself to Paul a few days after our arrival. I am not unaware that Paul sometimes finds girls attractive, enjoys their company. After all, he is only twenty. And usually it does not worry me. But Marianne is different. There is a certain arrogance to her, and an intrusive slyness. Suddenly, on about the third day, she began to haunt us. Everywhere we went - to the park, to a restaurant, to the cafes on the beach – she was sure to be there, smiling, a little way off. And at the Villa Romana, of course, in the dining room, in the pool, on the terrace. And Paul began to notice, began to feel flattered, began even to encourage her.

She began to accompany him to the beach. She knew I could not, would not, go with them. And there was about her a kind of knowing scorn, as if she had put me in my place. I watched them through the binoculars from my place by the lighthouse. On their second trip to the beach she wore a tanga, the string bikini that all the local girls wear. But she is plumper, heavier than them and the tanga simply made her look ridiculous, heavy and bovine, among the slim dark girls of Salvador. I think she realised this, because she wore it no more, even by the pool.

By then I was growing a little nervous, and more than a little irritated. We could have moved onto another city, of course, but in the long run that would have solved nothing. So when, on the fifth evening, I saw her kiss Paul hungrily by the pool, I knew that I would have to do something. And remembered Pedro. Of course, I didn't know his name then. But I remembered his face, and his list of pleasures.

I wait by the Lacerda elevator, leaning on the stone wall in the bright sunlight. Out beyond the naval base the breakwater curves gently, enclosing the yacht anchorage. The water is shallow, pale green, dotted with an array of small boats. It is no more than half an hour before Pedro appears, strolling across the wide square. He is tall, taller than I am, and slim and sinewy, despite his age – which must be sixty at least. His skin is very brown, his hair silvery-grey, a mat of crinkled curls cut close to his narrow skull. Today he wears white slacks and a pale green shirt, open halfway to his waist. He sees me watching him, nods, approaches.

Standing before me he smiles widely, showing three gold teeth.

"Changed your mind perhaps?" he says.

"Perhaps," I say.

I tell him what I want, and he laughs briefly, sharply, a sardonic and unsurprised bark. I think that nothing would surprise Pedro. We agree on a price, half down, half later. It is a great deal of money, but well worth the cost, I think.

"Where?" I ask.

He gives me the name of a cafe on the Avenida Presidente Vargas, by the beach, and a time. Ten that evening.

Then he is gone, crossing the road, disappearing beyond the big pink building that houses the tourist agency. He is like Salvador itself, in some ways; knowing, amused, a little dangerous.

The cafe faces the beach, and tables extend out from the open front onto the footpath. At ten o'clock it is crowded, noisy. Everyone seems to be drinking beer, sweating, shouting. The music is loud, insistent, and the evening is just beginning.

Paul and I sit alone at a table near the edge of the crowd. Paul is reluctant, a little surly. He wanted to see a Candonble ceremony, and I have had difficulty in persuading him to abandon his plans. It has also taken some ingenuity to shake off Marianne.

It is twenty minutes after the hour before Pedro appears with the girl, approaches our table. I introduce Pedro to Paul, Pedro introduces the girl. Clara is her name. I look at her with some interest. Her physical type is not uncommon in Rio, but rarer up here in Salvador. Her skin is olive, her hair honey-blonde, her brows dark, her eyes brown. Her teeth are perfect, and very white.

Pedro and I make small talk. We are old acquaintances, for this evening at least, engaged in a theatre of the absurd, inventing mutual friends, recalling past meetings, laughing at private jokes which do not exist. And while I talk I watch Paul, who is very silent, watching Clara.

She is worth watching, of course. Her face is almost beautiful, her body splendid, not yet overblown. She is perhaps twenty five. And there is about her an almost tangible aura of sex. Her smallest movement - lighting a cigarette, touching her hair, sipping her drink - is endowed with an incredible sensuality. Even I am not completely immune to its message. And Paul, of course, is enthralled. I nod to Pedro, congratulation on his selection.

After our second drink I rise to visit the toilet. In a minute or two Pedro follows me, leaving the other two alone, a tiny intent island in the hot crowded cafe.

We are alone in the small smelly toilet, Pedro and I. He raises his eyebrows at me, smiling. I nod.

"Where will she take him?" I ask.

"To her place," he says. "A house in Terreiro de Jesus."

That is a part of the city, I know, that is full of brothels.

I hand Pedro a wad of cruzeiros. He counts the notes quickly, slips them into his pocket.

"Three days," he says. "Maybe four. OK?"

"OK," I say. "Tudo bem."

"I come to the Villa Romana," he says. "In three, four days. You pay me, he comes back, OK?"

"OK."

He lights a cigarette.

"Better we wait a few minutes, give Clara a chance."

When we emerge finally from the toilet, Paul and Clara are no longer in sight. The table is empty.

"You're sure she knows what I want?"

"Sure, sure," he says.

"I want him disgusted, totally disgusted."

Pedro laughs, loudly and with great amusement.

"Don't worry," he says. "Clara will do things to him that would disgust even the devil."

He pats my arm and walks off, pushing his way through the crowd, disappearing into the darkness.

Marianne passes me on the stairs the next evening.

"Paul, où est-il?" she says.

It is the first time she has ever spoken to me directly.

"Il est parti pour quelques jours," I say.

"Où est-il allé?"

"Séjourner chez dez amis."

"Quand sers-t-il de retour?" she asks.

I shrug, continue my way down the stairs. The pool and the terrace are completely shadowed now, and beyond the stone wall the afternoon light is flat and brassy. The black girl comes out, fills my coffee cup again. Down in the shadows the trumpeter has begun his gentle riffs. Soon the trombone will join in, and a tune will slowly take shape.

One more day. I will be very gentle with him when he returns, very gentle and understanding. I suspect that he will not want to be touched, not for a time, anyway. Marianne is still lying by the pool. As I watch, her hands move again, her fingertips caressing the upper slopes of her breasts.

We will move on soon, I think, perhaps to Recife or Fortaleza. But not for a day or two. I must have a little time, after all, to enjoy Marianne's discomfiture.

THE BUOYANCY OF A GEMSTONE HEART

A G DeVan

ONE MORE UNWELCOME LETTER, this time delivered by hand. Condensed venom. It dares me to open it, but I'm not about to. I've had enough, baby. I surrender. Your emotional inanition has worn me down. Every lover is a warrior, and Cupid has his camps. Ovid said that, and he never even met you.

I had another a dream about you last night, but I knew it wasn't really you. The sweet imposter made the telltale mistake of giving love and passion equal to mine.

I didn't think you could do anything more to shock or hurt me. I thought I had managed to grow a kind of shell around my heart, an immunity to you. Safely indifferent. The sight of the familiar scrawl on the envelope mocks that notion, telling me I was mistaken. Fooling myself. Nothing new there.

They say nobody can cause another person to feel a particular way, at least not without consent. I disagree. From the day I met you, you began putting me through all the primary human emotions, and most of the subtle shades in between. Looking back, I realise I spent the greater part of that time at the end of the continuum where misery and its company are kept. I don't remember ever giving you permission to do that.

A.G. De Van, originally from Montgomery, Alabama, has lived quite happily in rural Queensland for a number of years. So happily, in fact, that living anywhere else is all but unimaginable.
Taking time out only to earn a living, writing has been the sole (pre-) occupation of A.G. Devan since childhood. Inclusion in 'Divertika' marks this writer's public debut.

I'm writing this to you, but I wouldn't send it even if I had your address. I'm doing it because there are too many things I should have said but didn't. Couldn't. A burden of personal business unconcluded, a tangle of hurt feelings left unspoken because you would forbid me with a sharpened glance. A wordless threat of love withheld. I feared that look in your eyes; it could cut laser-straight through me, and out the other side. Burn marks on the wall. I'd feel offensive, diminished, invisible. Such was your power, and didn't you know it!

Given the chance, I wonder if I'd be able to speak my mind now. Even when you still lived here, I usually had to make do without you. My thoughts and fantasies of you coalesced into a kind of ghost, a comely hologram, sometimes at my command, sometimes not. It was easily conjured from an image of you always just behind my eyes, superimposed on everything, part of every single day. It's not as bad as it sounds: that ghost has always been easier to get along with than you ever really were.

Long after you left, the ghost stayed on. Even after I gathered up and burned all the tangible reminders of you; every photo, every note or letter, some clothing you'd forgotten. Like some primitive ritual, a personal auto da fe, I was hoping it would rid me of you: out of my heart, my head, my life.

I felt a wicked, if temporary, satisfaction when the pieces of your mean-spirited farewell note hit the flames, the one I found in your otherwise empty room. I never did read it - I only scanned over enough of the preamble, and a few lines of the subsequent ten or so tightly packed pages, to get the drift of it. As if your words might burn me, I didn't want to look too closely. I remembered several instances when a person had fallen from your favour. You'd state that as far as you were concerned, that person was dead, not to be spoken of ever again. And you meant it. I never knew of one single reprieve. I was certain those words were in there somewhere, a malignant curse. I couldn't risk it, vaguely afraid that if you pronounced me dead, it might somehow be true. I ripped it up right then, lest I be tempted to inflict it on myself in an unguarded moment. So, however long it took you to write all that invective and recrimination, it was time wasted, unless it made you feel better. Did you honestly think I'd read on as you catalogued my faults and failings? I'm sure you did. But I know my faults, and I'm aware they are abundant. At least it could be said, in my defence, that I don't stride through life recklessly hurting people, using them up and tossing them aside. And I'm never disrespectful of love.

Once I was in such awe of you that I couldn't see the extent to which you hated yourself. You were adept at concealing your insecurities, a paragon of confidence. I wished I could be like you, be you. It must have been lonely in there. You never let anyone get close enough to see behind your perfectly painted mask.

Instead, you'd encourage me to reveal myself to you. What a listener you were! It gave the sensation of great intimacy. Only much later would I realise that you knew everything there was to know about me, but I knew almost nothing about you. A dangerous imbalance; I had handed you all the ammunition you'd ever need.

The fire was gratifying while it lasted but as I said, it didn't work. The ghost was still there. Not that I didn't keep trying to get it to leave, or at least fade. To my distress, I found that if I forcibly banished thoughts of you from my conscious mind, you would then invade my dreams. That was much worse, because I could touch your skin, and smell your hair, and, and .... wake up alone feeling a heartache so intense that it hurt to breathe.

That just wouldn't do. The only sensible action was to compromise. Learn to live with it, negotiate terms of a truce. The ghost would stay, inhabiting some roomy spot to the back of my head, forgotten, but not really. I would think about you at least once a day, and by this the ghost was appeased. At least most of the time. As with live embers, there is always the danger of flare-up, especially at the unexpected mention of your name. Fully blazing now, in fact, and impervious to tears.

I always fight to hold the tears back. Best not to let them get started, but sometimes they break loose despite me. Grief knocks me to the floor, and I find myself at the mercy of my emotions, trying to catch my breath between waves of convulsive crying. The sound of a vestigial soul that never learned to protect itself. Impossible to contain or console; it just has to wear itself out, and me along with it.

I have re-run the whole story in my mind many times, wondering if there wasn't something I could have done differently, looking for a reason why things went wrong. Whatever it was, it didn't happen that first brilliant day.

You danced into my life on a crisp autumn afternoon. I worked as a cook in an infamous grease trap of a restaurant. I carried out my duties over a fiercely hot grill situated in full view of the clientele. They were uniformly nondescript; cheerless, and unencumbered by taste, completely unable to discern good food from bad. That revelation came one day when the mince had turned. The boss, who'd never throw anything away, showed me how to rub white pepper into the meat to kill the odour. I was certain at least a few hamburgers would be rejected, but not one was. After that, I absolved myself of the ethical dilemma of serving spoiled food to the unsuspecting. It happened too often, and I needed the job. The exception was that I warned my friends never to order before discreetly asking for my recommendation.

Customers sat at a long counter that curved right around me and the burger forge. Alternatively, they could sit in one of a half dozen booths with cracked vinyl upholstery the colour of dried mustard. The place was fifty years old and had not been renovated, or even cleaned with any serious intent in all those years. It was an unapologetic dive, the diner from hell.

I was drawn from the back room, where I washed the dishes, by the sound of your voice. It was incredible, the aural equivalent of velvet stroked down the nape of the neck. I looked to see the source of such a voice, and there you were. My heart stopped. It was thirty minutes to closing time, and there was no one else there but the head cook. She was your Aunt, the person you had come to see.

Your Aunt used to really give me a hard time. Hostile in temperament, and twice my size, she refused to even pretend to get along with me. She'd try to pick fights, growing even more aggravated when I declined to take the bait. She belied the tenet that it takes a quorum of at least two to argue. She'd carry on perfectly well all by herself, call and response. She'd refer to 'my little world', as apart from her own. She meant "You don't understand real life." She resented me, aware I was only passing through. One day I would be finished paying my way through university, by means of that hard, dirty work, and I'd go on, presumably to better things. She was right, of course.

"All you white people are in the same boat!" was a favourite pronouncement of hers, uttered in way that sounded like the preliminary to a vigorous spit. I didn't think that was fair, as her sweeping statement set me afloat with all kinds of objectionable types, from vile neo-racists, to comparatively benign wastes of air: indolent wastrels personally known to me, partying their way through expensive schools. Yet dispute was futile. In a way, she was right about that, too. I was locked into the Protestant work ethic, believing in it, without realising that it does tend to work best for Caucasians. If I had a future, race was undoubtedly a factor. She was over forty, barely literate, at the summit of her earning potential, and she knew it. Reason enough for being permanently indignant.

Yet if I irritated her, you drove her straight up the wall. She couldn't make sense of you, least of all your exuberantly eclectic thrift shop wardrobe, an improbable blend of textures and bright colours. You never wore anything the same way twice: you were a brand new work of art each day. That afternoon you were incandescent, shimmering in contrast with the lacklustre surroundings. You wore a floaty yellow confection of a ball gown cut indecently short; pink heels, canary tights, a navy boy's school blazer, and a fuchsia scarf long enough to have strangled Isadora Duncan. Prism shards collided off the smudged stainless steel.

I had to get near you. I'm normally quite shy, but that was abandoned along with any common sense I may have had. You had the loveliest shade of skin I'd ever seen: a warm, glowing colour, hard to describe, but if made into an eyeshadow it might be called "apricot and gingerbread". Tall, I noted, with a graceful posture and very long legs. Then I saw your exquisite, heart-shaped face. As I approached, I had no idea what I would say to you. You laughed at something your Aunt said; the sound of your laughter seemed to tickle me all over. Infectious.

Displaying unprecedented nerve, I sat down right beside you. I don't remember what I said, only that you did not rebuff me. You fixed the light of your countenance directly upon me, knocked the breath from me with a dazzling smile, and that was it. You had a new slave.

Eventually I would learn that countless people lost breath and brains at the sight of you, falling immediately in love. You were inured to it by then, weary of it, poor baby. Love meant nothing to you, it was not what you wanted. People who love you make tiresome demands, think they have a right to a piece of you, some love in return. You could not begin to meet your obligations. You had more love than you knew what to do with. Your gemstone heart, imperial jade clasped in gold and set with rubies, pearls, and jasper, remained unmoved.

I decided that the next time I saw you, I'd ask you out. I asked your Aunt about you, but she didn't warm to the subject, and therefore wasn't much help. She said you were an art student, and you paid for this by working as a fashion model. It seemed she held you in low regard. "That girl's crazy," she complained, "off in her own little world." She was right yet again!

I was twelve when I knew. I found a windblown magazine in the woods near my house. Pictures of women, fairly straightforward pornography. As I looked, I was overcome by a new feeling, one I would someday call arousal. I pulled out a few of the least weather beaten pages, took them home, and carefully cut them out. Kind of like paper dolls.

I hid them from my mother. I knew she'd be shocked, as the subject of lesbians upset her terribly. Oral sex, too. I wasn't exactly sure what those things involved, or what the connection was between them, but I had a rough idea from hearing her vilify them. I didn't know what might happen with a girl if the situation arose, only that I now wanted it to.

My grandmother had a housekeeper, an amiable black woman about the same age as mother, and once in a while she'd come to clean our chronically unkempt house. Mother was usually too stoned to clean, or cook, but that's another story. I don't remember the maid's name, only her face, and the acute terror I felt when I came home from school one day just as she was leaving. She'd cleaned my room, no small job. My pictures were gone! Had she shown my mother? I lived in fear all afternoon, until it was clear she hadn't. Was it an act of discretion or simple disinterest? Whichever, I was grateful.

Despite mother's unexplained attitude, I grew up without feeling confusion or guilt about desiring women. It felt so natural. But I ran into difficulty when I found that I was also sometimes attracted to men. That distanced me from nearly all of the socially unconcealed lesbians I met. There seemed to be scant patience with ambiguity, a closed club with ironclad rules.

The 'hetero' scene in my age group also had rules, foremost of which was 'don't get serious.' I was often chided by well-meaning friends for feeling hurt, taking seriously what every one else was so casual about. Few were worried about AIDS yet. That nightmare was only just dawning, so that wasn't the problem. I just always took it personally. The shedding of clothes, of being physically naked, has always left me feeling emotionally exposed as well. Worse, I sometimes feel as if I don't even have the protection of my skin, as if a walk across the room might cause injury. Intolerably vulnerable, and thus wary of sex with someone who didn't care about me, or someone I didn't care about. Isolated as a consequence, my lovers were few and far between. Still, I'm not complaining. Most of them were worth the wait.

I saw you again a few days later, and you scattered my wits as before. You were enchanting. I must have looked a complete idiot, but you seemed to like me anyway. You had experience with zombie-like adoration.

I recovered sufficiently to suggest going to a   nightclub. "When?," you asked. "What are you doing this evening?" I rejoindered, emboldened. "I'm going out with you!" I couldn't believe my luck.

I flew straight home to make myself beautiful. Not like you, of course; you did magical things with make-up: Japanese rice powder, precise eyeliner, bright lipstick, blush, even glitter. You knew what looked good on you.

What looked good on you would look clownish on me. I'm not an unattractive woman, but for me less is more. A white shirt, dark slacks or jeans, a bomber jacket, thick dark hair kept short. Not a deliberately butch sort of look, just kind of androgynous. Kohl and mascara applied with a conservative hand. As far as I could foresee, my style of streamlined simplicity would be the ideal foil for your bird-of-paradise pageantry.

Out we went. You met me with a kiss. Those lips were as exceptional as they looked. Later, you concluded the evening with another, longer kiss. You flirted and teased, and that was all.

We went out many more times. More kisses, kisses that made me melt inside, kisses that promised so much more, but you seemed to dart out of reach anytime it looked like the game might turn into something real. It was never more than that to you, a game you were extremely good at playing. You always left me feeling that next time you'd offer more than a kiss, always next time.

Then one night you met him: tall, arrogant, great hair, white boy. Uncanny resemblance to a young J.F.K. and not only visually. As it happened, he too was a walking libido, mendacity made flesh, and heir to considerable wealth. Like you, he was accustomed to being worshipped. You recognised each other as equals. I ducked for cover as the sparks flew from the resultant electrical storm, great arcs of blue lightning.

In the spring I needed to find a flatmate, and surprisingly, you wanted to move in. Once again I couldn't believe my luck. I was so happy to have you near me, on whatever terms. The terms were supposed to be that we were 'just friends,' but you continued to kiss and tease, blurring the lines and mixing the signals. I didn't care. I'd take whatever you offered.

The flat was instantly yours. You changed everything. You decorated it like an opium den; little low-set tables, huge paisley cushions, secondhand velvet drapes, mirrors, bits of lace, swags of scarves, peacock feathers, and candles everywhere. Your technicolour wardrobe tended to end up on the floor, all trails leading to your net-draped bed. I loved being surrounded by your things. The place even began to smell of you, the fragrance of your hair. You also cluttered the flat with people, which I didn't like quite as much. You loved to hold court, encircled by adoring, textbook misfits: frilly dolls, poseurs, the occasional psychotic. Your new boyfriend pissed them off, though, one by one. Your old friends would leave, hurt and insulted, never to return. He said he couldn't stand being in the company of obvious weirdos. You said nothing.

I got to know your mother, and sometimes we would talk about you. She told me that he was the unstated reason that you'd moved in, because she flatly refused to allow 'that boy,' as she called him, to sleep with you in her house. She had said no, which made you furious.

One day she talked about when your father had suicided, hanging himself from a joist under the house. You, only four, had found him. Your mother spoke as if I already knew, as we were such close friends. I didn't admit my ignorance. She said she worried that it had harmed you psychologically.

I noticed things after that. How you avoided black guys. How you bleached and peeled your blemish-free skin, to lighten it. How you scrubbed your body daily with a scratchy loofah, which left you sort of pink. How you'd never be seen without your layers of make-up, the pale rice powder that might have looked odd if the embalmed look were not high fashion at the time.

One night I caught you, by accident, vomiting after dinner. You said you were ill, but I observed more closely, and you disappeared without fail after every meal. You were looking sallow, your hair was losing its gloss, becoming brittle, and you were losing your lovely ripe peach curviness. I worked up the courage to confront you. "Why?" Your eyes narrowed, and sweet lovey-voice contracted to a strangled hiss warning me to mind my own business. "But I'm concerned about you," I pleaded, "you're precious to me." You softened, smiling again, letting me hold you. "Don't worry," you said, "I can stop if I want to."

I grew frustrated and increasingly incensed at having to share you with him. I still can't think of him without feeling angry. He was using you, and me, by living in our place, making messes, eating the food, but never paying a share of the expenses. It was infuriating. He had plenty of money.

"I don't have my own room," he'd say when I pointed this out to him, "so I shouldn't be expected to pay rent."

"You wouldn't use it if you did," I'd argue, "and you live here, seven days a week."

"You're just jealous," he'd sneer, "because you can't get a man."

You'd stand mute while he said things like that, and so would I. I wore his smug, fatuous presence for the warmth you'd reward me with when he wasn't around. Those rare times you let me prove my love to you. For a while, that was enough.

Considering his attitude, imagine my surprise when you both met me at the door late one night, smashed, and dressed only in towels. The message was transparent. His hands were on me, your arms reached out, both of you kissing me. Somehow I untangled myself and politely declined the invitation. By then I genuinely hated him, and didn't want him touching me. What's more, I wouldn't have my feelings for you reduced to a performance for the entertainment of an overgrown schoolboy. I spoiled his fun, and it felt great. It was a turning point for me, the first time I didn't do exactly what you wanted me to.

A short time later, a mutual friend hosted his annual solstice party. He threw open his enormous old mansion, crammed with priceless carpets and antiques, and put it, and the lush gardens, at the mercy of three hundred revellers. He'd never divulge the cost, but it would have been well into four figures, if not five. There were alternating bands, providing uninterrupted music. The catering was lavish, with a continuously replenished buffet. If moving around became troublesome, there were delicacies and drinks circulated by waiters bearing silver trays. The bar attendants, instructed to pour generously, wore summer livery: white jackets with gold buttons, black trousers sharply creased.

A hush fell when the midnight toast was ordered: little glasses of aquavit meant to be swallowed in one gulp. All eyes glistened with tears - aquavit burns all the way down. Our host had just finished a charmingly slurred and emotive tribute to the solstice, and the virtues of hedonism, when you commanded attention with a piercing shriek.

As it wasn't your party, this was considered rude, but you'd never have done it had you been sober. All eyes were upon you when you shouted out that you were engaged!

Questions came at you from the stunned herd: "When's the date?" "Where's the ring?" You didn't notice the sheepish look of your 'fiance' when you could produce neither.

I remembered your Aunt's blunt boat metaphor. I wasn't aboard the same class of ship, but I was familiar enough with his world and how it worked to understand that he'd never marry you. I knew it before I asked him point-blank, and he mumbled something lame about his dad not approving. In other words, no.

His parents had his life meticulously planned, and he intended to follow their wishes. There was no option in the program for marriage to a black girl, no matter how pretty. They thought themselves broadminded to have endured his dalliance with you for as long as they had. They'd have used a word like that: dalliance. I could hear the condescension when his mother rang, her distaste audible, as if she'd found herself obliged to ring a brothel. Fair enough - for him it basically was. Sooner or later he'd quit fooling around and find himself a bride acceptable to them.

When I saw him at another party, nuzzling a stunner of a suitable young lady, he leered at me with shameless self-assurance. He knew I wouldn't tell you, or if I did that you'd never believe me.

When a diamond graced your hand I congratulated you, and was honestly relieved I'd misjudged him. Your mother told me the truth. You'd bought it yourself, spent all your tuition money on it. I felt sick. He was completely unworthy of you, of you covering for his deceitfulness for the sake of appearances. Then you really started to slide, drinking way too much, eating far too little. Did you hope you'd impress him with your wretchedness?

Finally, I confronted him with an ultimatum: start paying your share of the bills, or get out. Angry words were exchanged. You joined in, on his side. I thought I'd won, but actually he had. I'd done precisely what he hoped I'd do.

I came home one day the following week to find all of your things gone. The place was more than empty, it was cavernous, echoing.

You'd gone home to mother, where he was unwelcome, giving him an excuse to slither out of your life. You saw him much less often, and you blamed me. It was my fault you had to leave, and because of that, your relationship was strained. I was hearing it from others, and seeing it in evil, near smoking, notes shoved under my door.

Reality body-slammed you the day you discovered he'd gone. He didn't even have enough character to face you; he never said good-bye. His parents had sent him where they were certain you could not follow, a school as far away as they could send him without the aid of a spacecraft.

The last time I saw you, you were in my bed; naked, drunk, and hysterical. You still had a key. I tried to comfort you, rocking you in my arms as you screamed and wailed. I was telling you how I treasured you, loved you, precious....but you couldn't hear me over the sound of your despair.

Confused, you seemed unable to decide between making love or fighting. We'd be embracing, then I'd be fending off a punch to the head. You raved something like, "you might as well have me," as if you were so much refuse. It was horrible to see you so hurt and degraded. You struck at me again. Fed up, I restrained you, holding you with all my strength. "No more," I said.

You stared at me, eyes wide with astonishment as I tried to explain that I wanted you to be there because you wanted me. I wanted you to remember it when you woke up. And, yes, I loved you, but I wasn't going to lie there and let you hit me.

All you heard was "no." The hateful word. You broke free, and ran away.

Then the vengeance began in earnest: malicious phone calls, accusing letters, a rock through a window. You told some ugly lies, lies that hurt other people and took me months to straighten out. You betrayed confidences, which was even harder to deal with. It was vicious and methodic, the fury directed at me in the absence of the rightful target.

And then it just stopped. I wanted to know why, but I didn't dare approach you, for fear of provoking renewed wrath. I resolved to wait until I heard from you.

Today I opened the door to find your sweet mother, red-eyed and alone. I took her hands, colder than death, and brought her inside. With great effort, she explained she'd come to tell me that you had drowned, some swimming accident. I put my arms around her. She was trembling, struggling to hold on to her fragile composure. She seemed about to explode, all her feelings for you dammed up, left with no outlet, the circuit fractured. She broke down suddenly with a sharp cry, and then both of us dissolved. We mourned together in the face of a common tragedy: our final words with you had been angry ones.

She gave me an envelope with my name on it, found among your things. I took it from her, and put it gently aside. Perhaps she was hoping I'd open it, so she could know what it said. If so, she went away disappointed.

I wondered how, raised by a mother like that, you could grow up unable to recognise love. She'd come to comfort me in the loss of you, to prevent me from finding out from anyone else. Such was her affection for me, and her love for you was without limits. And like mine, unreturned in kind. You couldn't respond to something you couldn't feel. Love looked you in your angelic face time and again, but you could not see it.

Later it occurred to me that I'd never known you to swim. I couldn't even imagine it. Immersion in water would have been entirely at odds with your complicated grooming habits. A rainbow slick of make-up, waterproof mascara notwithstanding....a shower of rain was anathema to you

The envelope your mother brought is still sealed. I don't expect words of reconciliation. On the contrary, instinct warns me to beware the arc of a stab to the heart. What purpose would be served inflicting that on myself?

Do you want to hurt me even now? Do you think I'll do it for you? No. Do you hear me, precious? No!

Two more letters for the fire, now, with this one I've just written. Then I'll wait for the gentle breath of your ghost, the fingers of a soft breeze through my hair, caressing the back of my neck.

I WAS A GAY GARDENER

Ian Rohr

I WAS ABOUT TO BECOME A GARDENER and I was already gay and logic told me that one had little to do with the other. That sexuality and planting flowers, hoeing weeds, fucking men, picking up papers and picking up poofs were linked with slender threads. "I am a gay gardener" sounded more like a bad confession than a self-description but over the years I'd done enough different jobs with enough different people to know that sooner or later, one way or another, homosexuality always came up. Once upon a time, when it did, I would have kept quiet and low, laughed along with poofter jokes and felt bad for it or, if pressed, made up some vague, shadowy girlfriend. I was older now and hoped I'd put all that behind me but even so I wondered. I decided not to think about it. I already had a gutful of first day in a new job feelings, my nerves were fertile enough without watering them.

It was the summer of 1991 and I'd landed a job in Hyde Park in London, one of about 20 casual 'parkies' employed each summer to mow the more abundant grass and pick up the more abundant papers that the warmer weather brings. I walked across the park paying little attention to the other early inhabitants around me. In

---

Ian Rohr was born in Lithgow in 1959. He has had a variety of occupations with bouts of travelling and unemployment.

Currently he is Production/Editorial Assistant for a printer. Apart from being published in a University (ANU) newspaper and a small local newspaper on the NSW coast he is a publishing virgin.

He shares a house in Newtown and enjoys a schooner, a game of pool, touch footy, museums, good country music, bombastic opera, a catchy pop tune and the occassional flutter at the races.

time I got to be familiar with the puffing joggers, the dogs chasing the squirrels, ignoring their owners shouts and bluster, the homeless, but for now I was pre-occupied with the next eight hours.

I got to the main yard, hung around, and eventually got given to a 'gang' and with them about a third of Hyde Park. Another new starter was going on that gang, a Londoner called Pete, and after a bit of paperwork we got taken over to another yard, arriving just in time for breakfast.

The lunch room was part of a building known as the Magazine from it's one-time use as a munitions store. Stored bombs and bullets don't make any noise, they just lie there waiting but on that first morning it seemed the Magazine was exploding. Bangs and shouts and laughter and curses, snatches of conversations in a barrage of British accents came from the tables, sinks and kitchen. Smoke filled the air. People were chucking stuff down on tables, opening lunch-boxes, making cups of tea, grilling, toasting and frying things, smoking fags and reading the tabloids. One group was playing cards while another were making a lot of noise. Me and Pete sat there, both smoking, me wishing for a cup of tea, him probably doing the same and I sneaked glances around the table and room at these new faces and thought no, I don't think I'll tell them. Ever.

I looked around at my gang. A spiky-haired, bleached blonde who looked like Fagin was huddled in the corner near the radiator, eating what looked like devon sandwiches, holding his cup of tea with grubby chewed fingers encased in fingerless mittens. He's been out digging already I thought. A massive young black bloke whose bright yellow jumper offset any look of real menace was half-heartedly arguing with the fit, dark haired middle-aged man sitting next to him. The bloke opposite me sat quietly eating. There were another couple of men, me and Pete and finally, a little man with a big moustache who'd been introduced as Mark, the 'boss'. I sat there wishing I'd thought to bring tea-bags and finally asked the quiet bloke opposite. "Is there any chance of getting a cup of tea around here mate?" As he started to explain the situation the spiky little blonde and the middle-aged bloke pounced. "Want a cup of tea do ya? Well you're s'posed to bring your own, ya know," "Yeah, everyone brings their own stuff." "Probably be wanting some milk too, won't he Perce?" "Yeah these poxy casuals never bring their own stuff." I sat there. They carried on. One of the young blokes sitting near me butted in. " Shut up Percy and give him a tea-bag. There's milk in the fridge, the sugar's mine, help yourself." The spiky blonde muttered a bit then delved into a crumpled paper bag and pulled out a Tetley's which he dangled before me. "Thanks mate. I'll pay you back tomorrow." He just muttered a bit more. "Well, you're doing alright for yourself aren't you?" said the other one. "Shut up Ted," said the bloke opposite me in a weary, soft, don't start sort of voice and the table settled down.

Suddenly one of the blokes from the noisy mob shouted out, "Hey Ted, who was that young lad I saw your husband with down Earls Court the other night?" "You leave my husband out of this," the cup of tea stirrer called back, "he don't go anywhere without me."

They hassled each other from opposing ends of the room, the other blokes laughing or groaning when particularly good or bad barbs were released. Ted's opponent looked interesting. He was a big, solid man, lots of tattoos and cropped hair. He was loud and he laughed a lot, more at his own jokes than Ted's but that seemed fair enough since most of his were funnier. "The Boy's crazy, ain't he?" said one of the blokes on our gang. "That's Dave the Boy." Ted turned to me conspiratorially. "I've known him since he was sixteen. They're the tree gang that lot." "Out of their tree gang more like," someone said. "Don't but in sonny, it's bad manners," reproached Ted, before turning back to me, "I've been in this park for thirty years. There's nothin' I don't know about it or anyone working here son," he said. "I'll bet," I thought as I smiled and nodded and said, "Right." I also thought, "this Ted seems like a bit of a dick but at least I'm not the only poof here."

Presently the bloke with the mo stood up and said something like, "Wey ee mun, let's get crackin'," in a thick Northern accent and the gang began to stir. Flasks went back into bags, newspapers were folded, cigarettes were put out or lit up, and out we wandered. I went into the toilet and while I was in there the quiet bloke came in. "My name's Jim mate. Don't worry about mad Ted. He's a poof but he's alright, just carries on a bit sometimes. Mark can't stand him but he's a little bastard anyway." "Right," I said, nodded and followed him out into the yard and over to a shed in the corner.

Most of the gang seemed to know what was expected of them. "I still got a bit of paper picking to do Mark." "Right-o Perce. You carry on wi' that, then meet us up the Border. Ted you get a barrow and hoe and rake and start on that shrubbery on the other side of the bridge. And make sure you get all the fuckin' crap out." Ted got his gear together with a lot of banging and muttering. Mark turned to us. "Right. You two. Grab a couple of hoes and a rake each and a beezum, put 'em on the back of the van and hop in." We grabbed a hoe and a rake and looked at each other. "What the fuck's a beezum ?" I said. "Maybe it's one of those broom things," whispered Pete. I grabbed one from the pile in the corner and held it forward gingerly. "Is this a beezum?" "Way aye man it is," he replied and on the back it went and in we got. As we drove slowly across the park Mark explained our job in some detail. It seemed that some noxious weed had grown to a massive size and density around the perimeter of a shrubbery and we were to hoe it down, rake it up, and chuck it over the fence. They drove off. Pete turned to me, " Fancy a joint?"

Two and a half years later I was still working in the park, refining the bad habit I'd picked up of smoking joints in shrubberies but time was running out. Thatcherism had crept up on horticulture, the Royal Parks were being privatised. I was taking the redundancy money and running, jamming as many future memories as I could into a tea-chest and shipping them back to Australia. I was pleased to be going home, I'd been gone for a long time, but there was also a big emptiness looming. I had gotten to know this big green space and many of the people in it. It had all been a big part of my life for the last few years. At times the shrubberies, the hut, the van, the gang had been like sanctuaries and I'd soon be without them.

Seasons had rolled around. Swans had been born, learnt to fly and died prematurely when a heat wave caused an outbreak of botulism in the waters of the Serpentine. I'd dug a lot of holes, raked mountains of leaves, smoked lots of joints with Pete and others, huddled in dense shrubberies in winter, wandered around in shorts and singlets in summer, as we picked up the papers and drink cans and condoms.

Pete only lasted about two months, he couldn't cope with picking up rubbish that would be back again tomorrow, and the early starts didn't suit him. I didn't like my alarm clock either but I liked how paper picking eased me into days that were pretty cruisy. Pete's attendance got more and more erratic, his excuses more fantastic and finally he just slipped away. On one of his last sickies he rang from Amsterdam, 500 hundred miles away and tripping, to say he was up at St Marys Hospital having his sudden blindness examined. His replacement, David, smoked even more joints than Pete and mornings quickly settled back into a routine that was becoming familiar; one skinning up in a shrubbery, the other keeping a bleary early morning eye out for the boss, sneaking a coffee from the Lido cafe, testing the limits of how early you could wander back for breakfast, picking up papers.

The first day fears I'd had of a dour hostile group, of pitch-fork shaking, burning beezum waving homosexual haters was a romantic fancy. Ted's treatment had shown me I wasn't likely to be lynched; most of them didn't seem to give a fuck. Even so, my coming out was a slow process. I told people when I wanted to, when I trusted them or felt it was the right time. Like the day Jim asked had I gotten my leg over with any English lasses yet.

I'd decided pretty early on to keep Mark and Ted ignorant. Mark was every 'ist' and 'ic' imaginable; racist, sexist, homophobic, melancholic, at times idiotic, and he was the boss. As chargehand he assigned the jobs and I noticed early on that Richard and Ted got more of the poxy ones. I preferred pruning roses to clearing out the rat-riddled shrubberies along the murky Serpentine, and whereas Richard couldn't hide being black and Ted wouldn't shut up about being gay, I was a white male and Mark didn't need or want to know any more than that. If anything about me ever struck him as odd he probably explained it by my being from the upside-down half of the world.

With Ted, my reasons were more complex and just as selfish. Ted had chosen to be the gay in the public gallery. He seemed happy to play up to the carry on Mister Humphries image that a lot of the others had. I think that years of bunging this on had blurred the lines between the public and private Ted. Like an actor who can't always stop just because the camera has, Ted had in part become what his audience expected.

He was good in the part. He had the gestures, the language and the attitude down pat but even so the part didn't really suit him. He was a big dark man, in his mid-to-late forties and though there was a certain amount of stomach that no amount of shovelling was going to move, he was fit and strong and healthy. Ted had gone a long way towards becoming an unwitting embodiment of other people's creation.

I soon decided Ted was the last person I wanted to know that I too was a poof. He had set himself up as the guru of gay to a bunch of blokes who could have done with an alternative. I could have provided one and maybe I should have but I chose not to. I didn't want to get that intimate with Ted. I had no desire to be his new friend and second fiddle so I shut up.

Ted's problem, if he had one, wasn't being gay, it was being a not very bright shit-stirrer. He spread rumours, started rumours, took both sides in every argument and then the winds would change and all the crap he'd stirred up would blow back at him.

He'd walk into verbal traps from Dave the Boy and make Mark's dislike worse by always getting caught coming back early, having coffees in the cafe, deserting his shrubbery. He thought he knew it all but, like everyone else, he didn't. If you didn't point this out to him you got on OK.

Ted was full of words like gay rights and discrimination but he had trouble working out what they meant. If he got into trouble he was being discriminated against. Not looking where he was going he would run over a tree or he'd lose a spade and when he got a bollocking it was because he was homosexual. Ted's gayness was at the core of everything that happened to him; sometimes in reality but often only in Ted's head.

Telling Ted would have meant involving myself in his world more than I wanted. I did come out once, to a bunch of the older, seasoned workers who were going on about him and poofs at the pub one night. I did it to say. "Look we're not all like Ted. No-one is really like Ted." If he heard about this, and he probably did, he never mentioned it; perhaps he didn't want to be associated with me either.

Days in the park were a routine that always differed. Like most jobs it was a constant cycle of repeated tasks, but the park and its users made it interesting. The park would change and we'd follow, cleaning up after it, helping the bits we wanted to and through it all wandered the Western world. Pavarotti and Madonna. The Queen and Rolf Harris. A dog with no hind legs that got around with it's back-end strapped into a little two-wheeled chariot. He was always worth a second look. The lonely and the contented and the poor sat on benches and read the newspapers. The really poor read the day before's. In broken English tourists would ask how to find Peter Pan. There was a lot of rubbish and dog-shit around. It was interesting.

We worked away and around us things would happen. They differed in magnitude and frequency but there was always something to report at smoko or lunchtime. Sometimes the incidents happened to the outside world and we witnessed car crashes, bolting horses and even drug busts. Other times the incidents happened to us. Accidents, upsets, arguments, laughter and drug busts. Our gang had become a tight little bunch. Mark's bigotry, bastardry and boss status kept him on the outer and Ted had become a tractor driver and been let loose on the whole park. The others on the gang knew I was gay, just like we knew about Jim's marriage and David's ex- addiction, all except for Percy. I'd never told him.

Despite the tea-bag incident that had started our relationship so poorly, me and Perce had grown to a mutual liking and trust. He was an eccentric little bloke. His full name was Perceval Douras, which I liked because it sounded distinguished but he hated cause it sounded foreign. The dirt and grime that I'd mistaken for some early morning hard work turned out to always be there. He was about thirty-eight years old and he looked as if all the dirt he'd ever encountered had stuck and then slowly ground its way into the creases of his skin, the lines around his eyes, his wayward spiky bottle-blond hair.

It was obvious from the start that Percy didn't like poofs. He said so a lot, usually to Ted. He'd sit there, eating the Spam sandwiches that he ate every single day and slag Northerners or foreigners or blacks or farmers. He didn't like anyone. He'd argue with Richard and if he was losing he'd come out with. "Why don't you go back where you bleedin' well come from." Richard would frown and say. "Wot? Peckham?"

I told him one day, when the two of us were shovelling soil on to the back of the van. Ted's tractor mishaps kept him a source of conversation long after he'd left our gang and Percy was enjoying himself. "Wot a wally...he ought'nt be a driver, he can't bleedin well drive, and 'e's a poof."

"Well, you know Perce, I'm a poof too." There was a bit of silent shovelling and then, "no Ian, I don't think you are." We stopped, looked at each other, hot and sweaty, breathing hard and I said. "Yeah, I am Perce, I've just told you." "No. No you're not. You just think you are." There was no way I was kissing him to prove it so I just re-stated it. "I am Perce. I know. I'm just telling you cause we get on and work together well and you might as well know. The others all do." " Wot, even Mark?" "Well no, not him." A bit more shovelling. "We're not all like Ted you know." Percy cackled a bit. "Wot 'im? He's just a wally 'e is. Poor ol' sod, he can't drive a poxy tractor." He paused, shook his head and said, "but you.... no I don't think you are."

I put down my shovel and took out my fags. Perce bummed one off me, work ceased, and we talked about it. "Well you're not like them ones that put on make-up and go to pubs and kiss one and other and stuff like that. One of me mates is a poof and he took me to this pub and they were all there. Dancin' together and kissin' one and other like a bunch of wallies. You should'a seen 'em. One of them came up and asked me to dance." He chuckled a bit at the recollection, I shuddered slightly at the thought and asked, "so what did you say?" "Fuck off I said," "I'm not a poof." "And what did he say?" "He said, "well what are you doing here then?" "Good question Perce," I said. "Yeah, well I just said I'm here with a mate of mine. He's one of you lot, E's alright, but ...."

A few fags later, my shout, I'd half convinced him that it takes all sorts, that me and Ted and the men who wore make-up to pubs were just a few examples of a group of millions who have no 'norm'. That it really didn't matter.

The next day a few of the others said to me, "hey you really sat Percy on his arse yesterday. When we came in this morning he was muttering about what you'd told him. How he couldn't believe it but knew it was true. We told him to stop being stupid, stop worrying about it."

I don't know if he did. He sure didn't stop going on about poofs or blacks or whoever but it was his right to talk shit if he wanted to. Perce liked animals a lot more than people and with good reason. They had probably given him a lot more respect and affection than most people had. But in spite of himself Perce couldn't help liking some people. If he was ever talking about his gay friend who had taken him dancing he'd conclude with, "but I don't like him." He had a black mate as well. "Don't like him either. Don't like 'em." But he did. He liked them and he liked me and he liked Richard. "I don't like them lots," was Percy's way of having his final say.

I don't think he really meant it. Fuck the smelly little bastard if he did.

There is a part of Kensington Gardens known as Buck Hill, a long, gently sloping tree-studded swathe of green that runs down to the willow-fringed Long Water and the fountains and balustrades of the Italian Gardens. It is a nice place and a popular sunning and cruising spot, well known to local gays and park workers. We drove around its outskirts a couple of times a day and I used to walk across it in the afternoons. I had to. Buck Hill lay right between me and home so every day my path led me into temptation. On hot summer afternoons we'd weave our way across. A gauntlet I guess for my work-mates but a maze of eyes and bodies for me. Sometimes Percy would mutter something about poofs and sometimes poofs would mutter something about Percy, wandering along, sweltering and sweating in the grimy once-was-blue Parka he rarely removed.

This afternoon walk home had an edge for me, nice faces, good bodies, a summer afternoon, a few looks. In winter you'd hurry across the bleak, abandoned hill but on warm afternoons it was a place to linger. I only lived a ten minute walk away. I could go home, grab a towel and a book and be back while the others were still waiting for the tube. Sometimes I did. It had an aesthetic appeal, a sexual edge and danger. Work might have finished for the day but there were often still workers around. Being seen sunning on Buck Hill had only one interpretation. It would have been the way to do it, a grand gesture of shameless pride and defiance played out on an emerald stage with an all-male chorus. I chose to bury my head under my arm and pretend I was asleep when green trucks or yellow tractors loomed. It was an ostrich attitude. I thought I was undetected. I couldn't see them.

It was raining, we weren't working. Sitting around in the Magazine, drinking hot drinks, talking, reading, smoking, getting bored. Driving to the shops, having a joint, coming back and sitting down again. Now and again Mark asked "Is it still raining?' and Percy rubbed the window, looked out, and said, "yeah."

All topics had been exhausted, all arguments had, and everyone, even the tree gang, was sitting quietly in a sort of shared reverie. Dave the Boy caught my eye from down the other end of the room and slowly probed his cheek with his tongue. In and out, in and out. Over and over again. There was no mistaking it. Jim was the only other person who saw and he whispered to me, "I think the Boy's got you sussed." "I think you might be right Jim," I replied.

"So how did you know Dave ?"

"Know what Oz ?"

"That I was gay."

"Wot! You're gay? Fuckin' hell. Are you sure ?"

"Yeah, right Dave. C'mon, how'd you know?"

He laughed, "Seen you over on Buck Hill didn't I, having a kip"

We both laughed, " I thought no-one could see me."

"Don't ever think that mate, it's dodgy. So your mob all know?"

"Yeah, except for Mark."

"Mark! Bloody hell don't tell him, at least Ted's gone. He don't know does he?"

"Fuck no," I said

"Smart," said Dave, "anyway we'd all know if he did. So why'd ya tell Perce, what did he say?"

"Well he was goin' on about Ted, you know and he's not the best ambassador. Anyway, we get on OK. He might as well know. Hasn't changed him anyway."

"Yeah, can't say I've noticed any differences. He hasn't had a bath. So would you have told me?"

"Probably, if it had come up or you'd asked me."

"Ha. I'll ask you in front of Ted."

"I'll lie, Dave. I'll lie."

I wouldn't now, except to piss Dave off. Maybe I would not have then. By the time I left I didn't really care who knew or what they thought. They were all wondering whether they'd get their old jobs back with the new regime. Their own sex lives were probably suffering so they wouldn't have given a toss about mine.

I know what I was like at twenty, what I would have done. Coming out at work was something I just didn't consider back then. Those were the days of the mysterious women, the 'oh, sort of' girlfriends, the lies and the evasions.

Everyone's life follows a path and it takes them from where they're born to who knows until you get there. Sometimes you don't really know you have been somewhere until after you have gone. For a few years my path wandered through a park and during that time I gave and got a few lessons.

I learned how to lay turf, and drive a tractor and prune a rose-bush but I also learned a bit about other people and a lot about myself. Mark had shown me that I was still capable of selling myself out in order to have an easier ride. From Ted I learned that there can come a certain sadness from living up to other's expectations, that you can become a servant to your sexuality if you aren't careful.

I hope I taught Percy that you can't tar people with wide, convenient brushes, that it didn't follow that you carried your make-up around in a handbag just because you were gay. From Dave I learned that tattooed, skinhead yobbos can have big hearts and good attitudes. After our rainy day conversation he used to give me advice on my love-life. We'd be leaning up against a truck, me moaning about some affair going wrong and Dave telling me, "Well mate, the way I see it is you get on the blower and tell this geezer....." It was usually good advice. And touching, coming from this big, hard man.

On foggy Winter days the park would remain shrouded in mist while the roads that encircled and divided it would clear early in the morning. Sometimes this would last until lunchtime, behind the iron railings a peaceful white world, close to the hard and noisy lines of bitumen but silent and ghostly. Life isn't so easily demarcated as this, our forward vision clear and only the periphery blurred. Often our paths are as shrouded as the park was and we aren't sure what will loom up in front of us. For most gay men and women coming out to workmates is something that will arise for them, usually not just the once. No one can tell you when to do it or how others will react. There won't ever be a guide-book written to get you through it, you just have to make your own decisions, trust in your instincts and have some faith and hope about the attitudes of others. Working in the park taught me that more than any job I've had before or since. I think I learned a lot about being gay in a straight world during those steel-toe capped days.

QUEEN

William Phillips

MY LOVER WAS TWICE MY AGE. At sixteen, at school, I was proud of that, in a smart sort of way. Having survived the brutal scorn of other children from my earliest, tottering, sissy-boy steps, appearing at school late on Monday morning, smelling of sex and scored by love bites finally gave me some status and notoriety.

In Brisbane, in 1971, Stonewall was a recent glimmer of hope. We were still camp, and society was dominated by a small flock of *grand-dame* queens whose style owed much to the films of Bette Davis and excessive amounts of gin.

Into this tight, noisy world I stepped shyly, through a door that had opened with a bang: the theatre. Amateur and professional, theatre people stunned me: here were men and women just like me, or what I'd like to be; here they talked aloud of things

---

William Phillips has been an actor, a dancer, a farm hand, a Dominican friar, an Oxford student, a lush, an editor, a cook, a toilet cleaner and a teacher of Temple Dancing. These adventures took him to many places on three continents. He came from Brisbane, survived Thatcher's Britain, Reagan's America, and found refuge in Adelaide, where he now works in retail bookselling.

He is also a regular contributor to Adelaide Gay Times as a theatre reviewer and feature writer, and has written for 'Opera Australasia, Theatre Australasia,' 'Campaign Australia' and 'The Sydney Star Observer.'

He'd like to live by his writing but is holding on to his day job, so far. He lives alone but is willing to receive gentlemen callers.

His plans involve relocation to Sydney in 1995, more stories, a play, a novel and a scheme to finance an Australian Opera subscription.

"I am a philosophical rather than political creature. I continue to be delighted by the depth and strength of our community and our culture."

I'd barely imagined; they gave me a place and a history and a sort of pride too, though often enough it was washed in self-pity.

At least they had fun. Behind closed doors, among their own, these queens could girl it up something fierce. The contents of their lives were under pressure, and when released, condensed wit and venom poured out: there were screams and tears and great friendships.

Onto this strange stage I stepped. I shall be immodest and say I was gorgeous – tall and lean and long-haired, gazelle-eyed and eager and just sixteen, so before you could say seduction I'd acquired a man. I was what Genet referred to as a girl-queen, fairly feminine in nature (it was watching all those midday movies with Mum), as opposed to boy-queens, who played football, walked butch and worked in factories. It was considered highly desirable to have a man of a certain kind, either a hunky boy-queen to decorate your forays into society, or an older man of means to show you the way through treacherous dinner parties, opening nights and other atrocities.

It's like looking back at another planet.

James was a stage manager, early thirties, suitably studdish, who swooped on me like the eagle on Ganymede. He knew everybody I wanted to meet, he loved opera and theatre, he took me in hand. Everything had an air of excitement: discovering theatre, music, men, the city. At any moment something wonderful could happen, you could end up anywhere, an electrifying idea could strike, a sexy man could appear, a party would explode – anything was possible.

Thank God it's still the same planet.

One of James' friends was a reigning *grand-dame*, Ivor (known as Ivy), a man of middle years, of tremendous erudition and class; a huge queen whose personal style was pure 1950's slick, whose eyebrows arched, whose hair sat in careful waves, whose pastel shirts were shiny silk. Ivy lived in a big old Queenslander halfway up a hill in Bardon, furnished in an expensive clutter of crystal, silver and red velvet; lit by lots of little lamps. I remember that, at the time, indirect lighting struck me as awfully stylish and wicked.

Ivy shared this exotic nest with Rolphie, who owned an entire, authentic and lush set of ecclesiastical vestments. A spare room had been equipped with a splendid altar, with all the requisite apparatus, upon which Rolphie would celebrate Solemn High Mass on Sundays, Feastdays and Solemnities of the Universal Church. Ivy would occasionally assist in lace surplice. In his youth, Rolphie had attended St Francis' Seminary until a few weeks before his ordination, when an excruciating event involving another seminarian resulted in his prompt expulsion from this institution and a death-blow to his dream. He'd never really wanted to do anything else but be a priest, and now thought of himself as one. "But only in private, dear. I wouldn't want to scandalise the faithful."

At home, he'd lounge about in rubber thongs and a very smart scarlet silk soutane. By day, Ivy was a public servant, Rolphie worked in a bank.

On the Friday evening after my final exams at high school, I met James in the city well away from where he worked, so as not to arouse suspicion. Back then I thought him paranoid, and so it would appear today - of course, from his point of view, I was jailbait, and he could have gone to prison for a considerable stretch. We were to dine at Ivy's, then join a small party for a country picnic early the next morning. We went back to James's house in Spring Hill (a ghetto of dags and drunks and inner-city arty types), where we made sticky love in the Brisbane heat before dressing up and driving off to Ivy's for "cocktails and tea". Society revolved around *salons* - where queen bees entertained and dispensed wisdom to those dependent on their largesse, their cunning, their camp.

A dozen or so men, of all ages, some fey, some sporty, sat around Ivy's *drawing-room* (as he insisted it be called), dishing gossip and heaping shit on each other in a time-honoured way. Ivy was drunk by the time we arrived which interfered not a bit with his ability to produce a fussy, French, extravagant three-course meal precisely at 8pm. There were standards to be preserved. Afterwards, Ivy did a beautiful thing for me. The talk turned to opera. Ivy had insisted I sit at his right - pretty young things were to be protected and *trained up* properly to face the world of men.

Ivy took his music seriously.

"So, darling, what's the gorgeous James been making you listen to, assuming that you have a few spare moments when he's not ramming your bum with that lovely huge penis."

I assumed a high colour and looked embarrassed, which was no doubt the point. As for the question, I was tempted to say *Jesus Christ Superstar*, but somehow felt that wouldn't have raised my stakes much in this company. My taste ran to Janis Joplin at the time.

"Penderecki: Die Teufel von Loudun," I replied coolly, watching for James's reaction. He was pleased. High school German came in handy.

Ivy screamed. "James, you big-dicked, stupid bitch! You'll *ruin* this boy's chance of *ever* loving opera if you play him that shit!" He turned to me and became maternal, pouring more gin. The wine had been left way behind. "I can see I'm going to have to take your musical education *firmly* in hand! What instrument do you play?"

Rolphie giggled, worse for drink.

Ivy gave him the Imperial stare: "Shut up, bitch. Let the girl talk."

I hated being called a girl, it reminded me of school.

"Do you play a musical instrument?" he repeated.

"No, I don't," I said, and felt defeated somehow. I tried to look at James for rescue." I don't think I'm very musical."

Ivy's eyebrows ascended.

"Oscar Wilde may well have found that statement amusing. However, it's not your fault, my dear. I blame the modern education system. In my day, a young lady wasn't fit for society until she could knock off a Rondo on the virginals. Standards have sadly slipped. However, at least you can start *listening* properly. What you need is to study some *decent* music." He gave another poisonous stare in James's direction. "Penderecki, indeed! Come with me, darling. You too, Rolphie. We may require manual assistance."

At this command, I was hoisted from my chair and propelled into the drawing room, really rather pleased at being singled out like this. Having ushered me to a sofa covered in frou-frou cushions, Ivy took to pacing the floor dramatically.

"Think, Rolphie! What is the appropriate music for this delicious young thing about to be raked by the talons of a Grand Passion?" (He got that one right.)

"Now show some mercy, Ivy." Rolphie was on his knees, not in prayer, but searching through the largest record collection I'd seen. "Here we are. Smetana!"

Ivy staggered, then lunged: "Are you *insane*?!" He swept Rolphie into a heap on the shag-pile. "Out of my way, you drunken old slut. Let a civilised woman at that collection!"

On all fours, he squinted at titles and rifled through the records muttering, "Wagner, Wagner, Wagner... the *Liebestod*! That's it! Of course!" He peered rather oddly over his chubby shoulder at me: "This will open up that budding heart. The question is which soprano and which recording."

He sat back on his heels, tummy straining the mauve body shirt tight, and studied me, hard.

"Nilsson. Solti conducting. The Proms, 1963." He dived back to the ranks of records and pulled an LP from the shelving. "Rolphie, put this on while I organize our little friend."

Ivy heaved himself to his feet, assumed an awed expression and moved to the centre of the room. "It was a *transcendent* performance, at which I was fortunate to be present, having made the acquaintance that very afternoon of a divine guardsman, a creature of truly Olympian prowess. Birgit nearly got short shrift. However, the Muses led me on, in an intoxicated sexual haze, to this epiphany."

"The hysterical queen you will hear as the orchestra finishes is my old, late friend Frieda, the guardsman's *patrone*, whose frenzied shriek of 'Brava' almost before the last chord sounded, sent Miss Nilsson about two feet into the air in shock. And Birgit was a big girl. Now come along, my dear."

I was led to the centre of what small free space there was and asked to lie on the floor.

"Make yourself comfortable, darling. A little pillow for the head."

A frilled article was offered. "Now, just breathe in a relaxed fashion and give yourself to the *feeling* of the music."

Ivy and Rolphie fussed, clucked and manhandled the huge speakers into the space, placing one on either side of me. They then left the room, turning off most of the lamps and closing the door after them.

At first I felt silly, lying on a floor while this lush, massive music moved around me, then I started listening to how this woman sounded, how the power of her voice was a part of how she felt, how the voice spun in space, hovering in the music; and how horribly sad it was. Tears rolled down the sides of my face, and made tickling pools in my ears. By the end I was sobbing like a hurt child.

They left me alone for quite a while. Ivy came back in quietly and enthroned himself in a florid armchair. The rest of the troupe straggled in splashing more gin about, so I went and sat on the floor by Ivy's chair and just said "Thank you."

"That's all right, dear," he said and patted my shoulder. He smirked at James, who came and sat beside me on the floor. "Wagner isn't for everyone, but he has his moments. At least that should put Mr Penderecki in his place."

By nine the next morning James and I were back at Ivy's, helping store vast quantities of food and liquor in the big Volvo. We were off to the country, somewhere in the hills out west of Samford, for a picnic. Provisions had been assembled, hardware and necessities acquired, blankets packed, champagne chilled, petrol tanked, and a manic festivity, fuelled by much coffee and the hair of the dog, took over as Ivy bossed everyone about. Rolphie looked awful and was to return to his couch as soon as we waved goodbye. Ivy had carefully selected the best looking men he knew: James, and therefore me as the boy of the month; Scott, a beautiful young man making his way as an opera singer (a tenor), and his boyfriend Mark, a very butch bloke who worked as a plumber's mate. Even I was aware, in my emerging consciousness, that we made a strange party.

Finally in the front passenger seat, Ivy threw a long scarf around his throat and shrieked: "Goodbye, my darlings! I'm off to glory!" then mugged choking on the scarf as it strangled him. I giggled. He turned to me in the back seat and said, "*Such a sad death for poor Isadora. I shall dance her spirit for you when we reach an* appropriately sylvan setting."

He noticed Rolphie hovering at the car door. "What do you want, you sad old queen? Christ you look bloody awful. Go back to bed!"

"Ivor, don't joke about car accidents. It could be an omen." He actually looked worried, which wouldn't have been difficult with a hangover like that.

"Oh fuck off, you depressing old pisspot. We're off to have fun! Now are all those gorgeous men in my car? Then let's crack a bottle and get this show on the road," and he fished about in his front seat hamper ("emergency supplies, darling") for the first bottle of champagne and four glasses (Scott was driving and forbidden strong spirits until we reached the picnic spot). Mark, James and I were handed our glasses in the back, Rolphie closed the door on Ivy and waved limply, Scott revved the Volvo hard and we shot off uphill. Champagne splashed everywhere, our heads jolted back, Ivy flashed the scarf out the window as a banner and launched into dazzling falsetto rendition of *Visi d'Arte*. Scott joined in. James put his hand on my thigh and I relaxed. He then put his other hand on Mark's thigh and I went a bit tense. "Nice tight fit back here, hey?" he said and smiled. Mark knocked back what was left of his drink and smiled back. We were on our way.

We got lost. After a few minutes of several aria, Scott finally asked directions. Ivy was not particularly helpful. "Oh darling, just sort of head west for an hour or so, then there's a fork in the road with a gum tree and a sign. I think it's called Fontainbleu, or something with F anyway. More champers, you filthy sexpots in the back? Scott dear, Jamie's trying it on with your plumber." Scott was tense already, the sparks flying between James and Mark didn't make driving easier. I wasn't entirely reassured either.

After whipping up mountainsides for a while, Scott pulled up at a tiny shop in the middle of nowhere to ask directions for Fontainbleu. He got back into the car in a temper.

"Fontain-fucking-bleu. No-one's bloody heard of a Fontain-fucking-bleu around here. Where do you think you'd like to go next, Ivy?"

"Oh, calm down, darling. Have a drink. This humble grocery looks familiar. I think if we go another mile or two, we'll find that turn-off."

He was right. Another mile down the mountain road was a tatty little sign with *Fernvale* crudely scratched on it, pointing off to the left.

We shuddered to a halt by the sign, and there was a chorus of *Fern-fucking-vale*.

"How the hell did you get Fontainbleu out of Fernvale?" asked Scott.

"Menopausal delusions. I was Louis XIV's bumboy in a former life. *Nobody's fucking perfect!* Just drive, you overrated music-hall crooner. About a mile down that goatpath there's a creek and a swimming hole, and mother will feel so self-righteous when you all swoon for the beauty I'll have set before you. Step on it, I need to get at that gin in the boot."

It was lovely indeed. Soft green grass down to a creek and deep swimming hole, well away from any roads, shielded by great boulders and bush. James stripped off and dived in while the rest of us settled Ivy on mats and blankets, opened bottles, dispensed ice, cold chicken, damask napkins. Ivy was drinking very heavily - large gins with a dash of tonic. I wouldn't keep up; drink made me ill at that age. James alone attempted to go drink for drink. We ate everything. Ivy got abusive when told he'd had enough gin, then lay down for a nap. I wandered off with James along the creek until we found a good place to make love, which we did with much energy, up against a gum tree. Leaning against the trunk while James went at it behind me, I straightened up to kiss his mouth. As I turned my head, I saw Mark perched on a rock about 50 metres behind us, pants down, jerking off. I wanted to ask him to join us. James followed my eyes with his and smiled at me, licked my lips, pinched at a nipple.

"Let's make him watch. I like an audience. It makes a better fuck." He was right.

When we got back to the picnic site, Scott was making tea, Ivy had revived and it was late afternoon. "No prizes for guessing what you two have been doing. Where's Scott's friend?"

Ivy could be a real bitch when disturbed. He poured tea, and then opened a fresh bottle of White Horse whiskey. "Drinks all round, dears." Scott took a big one. Mark appeared a few minutes later, and Ivy intervened. "If there's so much as a hint of a big domestic, I'll make you *all* walk home Now, sit down Mark darling. You tell me about drains, and I'll tell you the plot of *La Sonnambula*. Scott, pass the scotch."

We all got drunker.

When dusk came, we had to help Ivy to the car. James and Mark weren't much better. Scott was weaving about on his feet, but feigning sobriety. I was staggering. We loaded up the remains and set off down the mountains. Scott found an opera recital on the radio and turned it up, which got Ivy singing along.

In the cramped back seat, hot, squashed and horny, James and I started touching each other's body. The invitation to Mark was explicit. He joined us. Tongues explored mouths, hands groped crotch and arse. Lack of space made us more inventive. Ivy kept peeking at us, alternately muttering "Filthy beasts," or feeling someone's cock. It was very sexy. Even Scott kept turning to look at what his boyfriend was up to. It was very quiet and intense and we sped downhill. We had actually stopped, realizing that a three-way fuck in the back seat of a car hurtling down a mountain in the hands of a drunk driver was not a good idea, when it happened.

Ivy turned around to say, "Darlings, I had each hand up somebody's arse..." as we took a corner.

The front left fender met the cliff-face on the roadside, and the car screeched and bashed into the rockwall, again and again and again. Ivy was screaming maniacally. James and Mark and I held each other as we bounced high enough to bang our skulls on the roof of the car. Scott hung on to the steering wheel and bravely, brilliantly brought the car back under control. It was only a few seconds, but oh so slow, each swerve and howl of metal clear in my mind, all enlarged as if on a screen.

We sat still in the ruined car, silent. Scott took over. "Everyone out. Someone help me with Ivy." None of us were hurt, apart from minor bruises and shock. We'd come to rest in the middle of the road on another tight bend. Christ knows how Scott had prevented us going over the side into the bush that fell away into the night at the edge of the road. The adrenalin rush that hit me made me shake with the sheer ecstasy of being alive. It took Ivy differently; he went wild, screaming and flailing in a drunken fit. Scott and James wrestled him out of the car and away from the wreck onto the roadside. Mark and I just stood beside each other and trembled.

Scott and James crouched over Ivy lying in the roadside gravel, whimpering like a dog in pain. He'd started vomiting. A dark stain spread over his trousers where he'd wet himself. I went into a different sort of shock, where you hate what you see but can't turn away. Scott turned and snapped at us, "Someone get a blanket out of the car, and see if you can find if there's any water left. Don't hang about the car in case there's a fire."

Both Mark and I went. While we searched, car headlights shone over us from up the mountain. Someone was coming down after us. God hope they were slow enough to pull up before hitting the Volvo slewed across the road. Of course they were, they were sober.

Headlights on full beam came around the corner, pinning Mark and me like white-faced bunnies in a hunter's spot. The car pulled up, the lights dipped, and for a few beats nothing happened. A dark figure, very still, sat at the wheel. The door opened and a big bloke got out, walked straight into the lights and toward us. We broke and headed for James, Scott and the fallen Ivy. The big man was just a normal country type. He joined us peering over Ivy.

"Anyone hurt bad?" he asked.

Scott answered, "Well, he's in shock and pretty pissed but nothing's broken. I reckon he'll be OK."

"Fair enough. I'll go down and call the tow-truck from the store down the hill.

Shouldn't be too long. The bloke lives just down the mountain," and he ambled off to his ute, manoeuvred around the hissing hulk of the Volvo, and drove off.

Mark and I were amazed, Ivy needed help surely. Scott didn't want any cops around.

Apart from Ivy's flaming queendom, a big drawback in darkest Queensland back then, I later learned that Scott's dad was an Assistant Police Commissioner. We were not an ensemble that wanted attention. Jailbait, loud queens, aspiring well-connected man from 'good' family - we were a disaster looking for a home.

It was very quiet after that, and the shock made us cold. Mark and I sat huddled, cuddling. James and Scott soothed Ivy, now wrapped in blankets, propped against a tree and reasonably sane again. He was still rambling in drink and kept moaning about the car.

Scott sang to distract him. We sat still, cold, wrapped in each other's arms for warmth, staring at the stars, listening to the nocturnal noises in the bush, while Scott sang lilting English folksongs into the night.

After a while, perhaps an hour, an old-fashioned tow-truck arrived, driven by a sexy, chunky country boy in denim and rough flannel. Ivy perked right up. He insisted on thanking the man personally in the most courtly terms. The driver looked quite bemused, standing on a mountainside while this staggering, stinking, slurring queen addressed him with all the pomp and hauteur of a duchess.

"No worries, mate - all part of the job, hey," he mumbled.

"I want to thank you so much, my good man," Ivy reeled off, and extended a hand (to be kissed?), slipped on his huge clogs and went down again with a soft "Oh dear!"

We bundled him into the cab of the truck, salvaged the necessaries from the Volvo and waited while Ken, as our rescuer turned out to be, did his stuff and hoisted the car up onto its back wheels. Scott sat with Ivy, to keep him upright and make sure he didn't grope Ken. James, Mark and I got to ride on the tray-back of the truck, perched on chains and boxes, clinging to bits of crane.

We moved slowly down the mountain, and from the back, through the little rear window, we could hear Ivy chatting up the driver.

"Tell me, Ken, do you enjoy fine music? Perhaps I could fiddle one of your knobs here and find something to amuse us." Ivy waved a hand in the general direction of Ken's car radio - or his crotch.

"Leave that to me, Ivy, er.. Ivor. I'll find some music," said Scott. "Do you mind, mate?" he asked Ken.

"Go for it, mate."

"You must call me Ivy, Ken, my dear, everyone does."

Scott fumbled at the radio to drown Ivy out. Ken was enjoying every minute of this.

"Try and find Auntie ABC, Scott darling. I feel a song coming on. I sing, you know, Ken, my dear..."

Scott found it right on cue. "Oh, turn it up loud, darling. This will be glorious!"

And indeed it was. Clinging on to the back of a truck, moving down a mountain, the cold night wind rolling over our faces, stars bright, the smell of the bush, and a sensational mezzo-soprano ripping into what I now know to be Cherubino's aria.

I looked into the cabin through the grimy little window at Ivy, dirty and bedraggled, slumped against Scott's shoulder.

I looked at James and Mark, leaning against each other, pale faces and huge dark eyes against the night. James smiled and kissed Mark, then offered me his hand and drew me close.

I flew down that mountain that night. The music and the cold air forced tears from my eyes, the trees drifted back into the dark as our headlights passed; Mozart spilled across the hills.

LOINCLOTH

Rob Cover

S UNDAY: "DAMN," ADRIAN MUTTERED, climbing out of the Mercedes front passenger door. He was now wishing he had the sense to wear button-fly 501s. These 501s were too tight and he had just torn out a pube caught in the zip. He knew he would feel a little more confidence in 501s. Feel protected.

"We're late," mother told him as she locked the car. "The singing's started."

So sad, Adrian thought. So tired. So hung over.

The choir ended their first song/moment of fame, only two or three off pitch in the final chord.

Mother hurried to the usual pew. The one with Janie and Janie's mother. Adrian sauntered, genuflected, sat on the end. Two mothers in the middle. Janie now sat so far away.

She leaned forward as the first reading began, looking past her mother and her mother's best friend and smiled at Adrian.

Adrian squinted at her. How white her teeth are, he thought, much better now

---

Rob Cover is twenty-two, a student of Renaissance History at the University of Western Australia. He has had short stories published in Gary Dunne's anthology, 'Fruit,' and in the 'OutRage 1994 Short Story Anthology.' He works for Perth's gay and lesbian newspaper, Westside Observer, writing feature articles and reviews. Rob supports coalitionist gay and lesbian politics, while still respecting the diversity and individuality of human and animal life, and admits that while the queer community has come a long way in recent decades, there are many areas for improvement in the way we interact. He lives with his partner, David, and cat, Andy, and often has a brandy in one hand and a cigarette in the other.

that the braces are gone. My, God, that blouse-thing. How awful. Looks like she's off to church or something. Oh, yeah, hey.

"His word is a rod that strikes the ruthless, his sentences bring death to the wicked. Integrity is the loincloth round his waist, faithfulness the belt about his hips. The wolf lives with the lamb..."

Adrian thought about that kiss last night. So sweet the lips had felt. So soft. Unexpected. The tongue winding and winding around the other tongue, feeling teeth, biting. Stubble hurting.

"The cow and the bear make friends, their young lie down together..."

It would be nice to go for a walk with Janie after mass. Leave mother and her mother to talk mother-talk. Mother talk and marriage.

It would be nice to...

"The infant plays over the cobra's hole, into the viper's lair the young child puts his hand..."

The hands, last night. How drunk had he been? Who would have thought he would go that far? Everything else was nice, normal, usual. Lips and tongues and mouth and cocks. But he never thought he would have touched there, felt there, fucked there.

"...for the country is filled with the knowledge of the Lord as the waters swell the sea."

And all in the back of that nightclub. Paul was so beautiful. Older but cute. But then he was younger than the others. Than the past ones. How old was he? Eighteen? Nineteen? Something.

All these words. So many words. Wasn't it the word that became flesh? Too many words. Those biceps. Tight singlet of Paul's. Show-off. How can a fifteen-year-old compete? Adrian moved his hands out of prayer-position, felt his upper arm. Well, not too far off. Not too bad at all.

Standing.

Sitting.

Love that altar boy outfit. Must get one.

Standing.

Kneeling.

Transubstantiation. Never looks like it. No, hey, must have faith. Or imagination. Don't know which.

Standing.

"Peace be with you," Adrian replied to Mother's gesture. Routine. "Peace," he smiled at Janie's mother. A nod for Janie herself. One for the old man a pew in front. And the fat Italian lady behind, with all her children and the ugly husband. Such Catholicism.

Glance at Janie's skirt. So...floral. Shows off those hips. So curved, these days. Well, she's growing up.

In line for the daily bread-made-flesh.

Paul's hips and arse. So firm. Whole body so hard.

"The body of Christ."

"Amen," whispered Adrian, taking the host. Reverence in placing it on his tongue. Dissolves so quickly. Swallow, swallow. Not so smooth as it goes down his throat. Not smooth enough at all.

He recalled the surprise when Paul shot in his mouth. Unexpected. So unreal. So much to swallow. But smooth. Sorta like phlegm. But good.

Everything's good when you're drunk. And that was on only a bit of wine. Well, a lot of wine.

"Go in peace, to love and serve..."

"I love you," Paul had told him. "You can fuck me up against the wall, if you want," he had said too.

Adrian didn't want to. But he did anyway.

Outside church. Clouds in the sky, a little drizzle. Storm coming.

"Hi, baby," Janie said, clasping his hand. "You look tired."

"Hard night."

"What did you do? I went to Marg's and we went dancing at Havana's. Took ages to get in."

"I went to...a pub. With some guys."

"Oh. Have you done your History assignment yet?"

"Yeah," Adrian lied. "But I've got to add some stuff to it. You know, correct it." He knew the history; it would not take long to do the essay. There were more pressing matters. "Janie?"

"Mm?" she smiled.

"What are you doing the rest of this morning?"

"Not much. Are you and your mum coming to lunch?"

"Don't we always?" Irritation. "Have we ever missed even one Sunday lunch?"

"No. Dumb question."

"Janie, let's walk back to your place."

"Why? It's going to rain."

"Don't care."

"Okay."

They made their goodbyes to the mothers, promises to be back in time for lunch. Janie and Adrian walked. Keeping step. Silent.

Interruption of thought. Janie spoke. "You know, my mum asked me if you and I have had sex. Can you believe it?" Laughter.

"No," Adrian said quietly. "What did you say?"

"I said we were a bit young."

"Did she say why she asked?"

"No."

"Didn't you try to find out?" Adrian was annoyed. Why would Janie's mother ask this? Old bitch.

"I didn't really wonder why. I think she just wanted something to laugh about."

Silence. They walked past the old school. Their primary school. Both remembered lunch hours. Quiet hours. Hours of Adrian alone and Janie and Marg together. Hours of the three fighting. Bitching, really. Hours of the three lying on the grass, feeling the sun. The heat, the power. But Adrian knew there was no power. Not then. Only a little now.

They crossed through the park. Janie looked at the flowery bushes at the far border. Adrian glanced quickly at the toilet block, the smell of shit and piss in his mind. And the smell of Paul. The new smell, because they had only just met. Too small a cubicle. No paper on the roll.

"Come out to Connections tonight," Paul had said. "I'll pick you up."

"I think you already did that," Adrian told him. They laughed as they hugged. Paul's stubble so scratchy.

It wasn't his first time at Connections. He didn't tell Paul though. He wanted Paul to think him younger. Simpler.

Adrian remembered his first time in the nightclub. He had gone too early. Much too early. For cruising, anyway.

The barman had talked to him. The barman in the lycra shorts and the too-small T-shirt. "I've never seen you here before."

"I've never been here before. It's my first time here," Adrian told him, accepting the free drink.

"Oh," the barman smiled. "That means you're a new piece of furniture in town. And if you keep that smile, I guess you're gonna get French polished."

"I hope so," Adrian laughed - a pretend grownup's laugh - as he walked away to a corner.

"You're being very quiet," Janie told him.

"I know." He wanted to tell her about Paul. He wanted to spill it all. But...no.

They arrived at Janie's house. The garden needed weeding again. Spring weather makes the weeds grow. Adrian lamented the lack of spring feeling this morning...whoops, afternoon now.

Janie led Adrian into the kitchen where mother and the other mother busily chatted and prepared food. Such Dalkeith hospitality. They might be unwed outcasts, but they knew how to behave as society women. To dress as their address would have them.

Janie's mother and mother met first at the church's women's group. At a counselling day. Janie's mother's husband was dead two weeks, and father had been gone for four. The newly widowed and the divorcee knew their children were at school together. Primary school was small enough for Catholic society parents to recognise each other.

Adrian was five and Janie just six. And then they were together so much. Except when Marg made them fight. Marg had always been a bitch. At age seven she knew enough to be jealous of the Mercs owned by mother and by Janie's mother. Never realising what life assurance and alimony can do for a single parent.

Mercs aside, it was never easy for the women. Or for Adrian and Janie. It hurt them both to see their mothers cry in each other's arms. So often. Witnesses to a common display of pain. But that stopped after a while. Adrian knew, even then, that the warmth of a husband-father was missing.

Luncheon. Cold meats. Hot ones as well. So much animal on a plate.

"Adrian ... Janie's mother and I were thinking of going down to the beach house next weekend. If you and Janie don't have too much homework. We don't want to drag you away from study."

"We could stay behind," Janie suggested, though it sounded more like a question.

"I don't know if that's a good idea," mother said, looking to Janie's mother, waiting for the ever-needed advice.

"Well, would you two behave if we went away for the weekend?"

Janie complained. "It's not like we've never had to cope alone before. Adrian can come and stay over here for the weekend. And we'll get Marg to come and chaperone if you're going to be worried."

It only took two hours to convince the parents to go. Lunch over, Adrian went

175

to Janie's room to help her begin her history assignment, knowing he had to go and do his own.

"Can I bring someone next weekend? To stay?"

"Who? Not that dag friend of yours from school. Mark something."

"No, not him. I haven't even spoken to Mark for about six months. He was never really my friend."

"Who then?"

"Just a guy I ... was introduced to. At the pub."

"Who is he?" Janie asked, not really interested.

"Oh, you'll meet him."

"Okay. Marg's coming too, so we can play Trivial Pursuit or something."

"Mm."

★

Paul was reluctant. Nervous. "Why can't we just stay at your place?" he asked, squeezing Adrian's cock, both cramped in the tiny cubicle with no paper.

"Can't. Mother will probably ring about ten times at Janie's. She would never trust me on my own. Thinks I'll become a heroin junkie if I'm alone. Besides, Janie's got a pool, and I don't. C'mon, please. Or I'll die. I'll kill you if you don't."

"Okay, babe." Paul, standing taller than Adrian, held him tight to his body.

Adrian kissed him on the chest - shirt undone - and pulled closer. A body in his arms. A great, sorta powerful, beautiful body. The creation of God and the best thing God had created. The proof of God's existence. Can't it just be any body though? Adrian wondered, arms slackening a little.

Would this feeling be different if it was another body and not Paul's? Not Paul? Perhaps. There are other bodies. Equally beautiful. Sometimes more. Many who dress well. Paul dresses well. Others do too. Many. But the spirit is in this body. Paul's spirit. His soul. That is why it would be different. Adrian decided this was love as their lips joined again in that embrace that felt so ... eternal.

FRIDAY:

It was still early. Paul will show. No fear.

Adrian looked around Janie's mother's lounge room as if it was his first time there. He had known this room since he was five and half, but it seemed different this day. He looked at the fire place - cleaned out now for the approaching summer - and above it at the tapestry of the Last Supper.

"Da Vinci, isn't it?" Never really looked before.

176

Janie came in from the kitchen, bottle of Coke in one hand and bourbon in the other. "You really should change, Ade," she said, eyeing his grey trousers, white shirt and school-colour tie. "Uniform makes you look so young."

Adrian thought about changing. Into 501s, a cool t-shirt and maybe a Daniel Hechter shirt thrown casually on. But he didn't want to. Didn't want to show his usual identity, his club membership pass, his gay ID clothes. Does it matter anymore? Marg came in now. Holding three glasses, and wearing a black bikini. Her hair was wet. Adrian examined her breasts. Nipples poking through the tight material. So ... full. So ... woman. Pretty, really. No, pretty means little girl, and she was not that. Adult woman. He looked away.

The girls began drinking, despite Adrian's refusal ("I'll wait till Paul arrives.") He sat, planning the night. Wishing these women-bodies would leave. He thought how it would be to have Paul in his arms in the pool, beside him at dinner, in bed together. Doing lovely things in private. Such a change that would be from their 'public' sex. To the cubicle with no paper, from the back corner of Connections.

"You look really out of it, Ade," Marg told him. "What's your problem?"

"Nothing. I'm just sorta tired."

Just before the girls' ninth drink each, and slightly after 'Home and Away' finished, Paul knocked at the door. Adrian rushed there, knocking a pile of magazines off the oak coffee table. He opened, smiled, and grasped Paul's hand for a second as he led him into the lounge room.

Introductions.

"We're going for a swim," Marg announced, feeling an apprehension in new company. Janie, obediently, followed her outside. Paul stood, took Adrian's arm and pulled him to the ground. They kissed, rolling their bodies together as if into one.

"I still don't want the girls to know," Adrian said, breaking away momentarily. "We'll have to be fairly quiet."

"That's cool. But they already suspect. At least the girl in the bikini - Marg - does. She looks like she's been around a bit. How old is she?"

"Sixteen."

"Sweet."

★

Skipping dinner, the boys went to the guestroom; Paul not caring to make excuses to the other gender and Adrian too embarrassed and confused to say anything. Paul threw off his t-shirt and jeans hurriedly, then began to undress Adrian. The boy slowed down the process, pulling away to unbutton his shirt. He unlaced his shoes, socks sticking to the hairs on his ankles. With Paul nude and Adrian feeling strangely naked, they began their act. Paul's act. A heated and rushed performance. Not amateur: too experienced, too rehearsed. Adrian felt he wanted something slower. Something not about their two bodies. Not anymore. They were here, together, in a bed, in a house, in Dalkeith. It was meant to be different. Not like in the cubicle with no paper or the corner of some sleazy club. Not like it was with 501s around the knees, Calvins just pulled down, Unionbay shirts, B.U.M. tope or Mossimo singlets casually hanging off the body, fashions and labels to hide behind. Could they ever be genuine, even with the fig leaves gone? But Adrian said nothing. He could not complain and come at the same time.

SATURDAY:

A morning swim. In the small but stylish Dalkeith-style pool. Beginning not far from the house, water to the rocks and shrubs that make the far edge of the pool seem no different from a natural pond. Man-made at one end, merging into the earth at the other. Very stylish. The spring sunlight caused Marg to warm a little to the boys. Chatting and drinking. Snacks poolside. Laughter from them all. Paul's hand sneakily in Adrian's shorts, underwater. That was when the cloud blocked the light.

"Ade, can you come and help me inside for a minute?" Janie asked, not looking at him, walking to the glass door.

"What is it?" he asked as they stood in the kitchen, he pouring another bourbon, she tying back her hair.

"Why didn't you tell me? You could have told me, I'd have understood."

"What? About Paul and me?" It was so easy, so casual.

"Obviously."

"How'd you know?"

"I'm hardly blind. Or deaf for that matter," she said, looking towards the guestroom.

They'd been quiet but not quiet enough. It's hard when you're getting fucked. "Sorry," Adrian smiled. This was too easy.

Janie slid herself down the oak cupboard as she moved to the floor. Tears.

Oh no, this isn't so easy. "Why are you crying?"

"I don't know. You're a homosexual. I thought I would have known. You could have told me, couldn't you?"

"I suppose. I wanted to. But I just didn't." He looked out the window, watching Paul and Marg laughing together. Marg moving her chair closer to Paul.

"Go away," Janie mumbled quietly, her head in her hands.

"Do you want me to go home?"

"No. You can't. Our mothers agreed about this weekend. You can't go."

"I'm not sending Paul away." Defiance?

"You don't have to. Just leave me alone." She pulled herself up, reaching for the Bourbon.

*

"I've got to make a phone call, is that okay?" Paul asked. He left the three at the dinner table and his half eaten taco. Marg adjusted her t-shirt while Janie drank some more and Adrian ate.

"He's really cute," Marg said to Adrian. "Are you two actually boyfriends or just, like, casual. Dating."

"Don't know." Adrian said. And he didn't. What were they? What names and labels?

Paul had been so quiet towards Adrian as the afternoon continued. By sunset he and Marg were sitting close together inside, away from the others. Those two, with their bodies almost touching as they constantly clinked glasses in toast of each other Adrian was not really disturbed by this. He felt he didn't want Paul with him then. Not someone else, either. Well, someone, but who? Don't know. He wanted no explanations from Paul. Paul could be mean. Did it matter? No. Well, a little. Adrian wondered, then, how well he knew Paul. Or knew himself. He was feeling....different. Unusual. Up in the air. Not a love-like feeling now. So he went to the guestroom, changing out of his boardies and into 501s and a t-shirt. Knowing the usual feelings were still not there. He should feel the strength he usually did. The confidence, the belonging. It should all be there. But it's not. He returned to Janie and Marg in the dining-room.

Paul came back, too. "I've asked a friend over. Is that alright?" He directed this to Janie.

"Yeah, fine. The more the merrier," she quoted her mother, with her mother's deep-voiced intonations, but with no real meaning.

*

Gary arrived at half past eight. They all moved into the lounge room, lights dimmed, music going, Janie and Adrian sitting under the 'Last Supper,' Marg, Paul and Gary slumped back on the suite. Adrian watched Gary as this new person and Paul spoke and laughed loudly. He looked about twenty-eight, thin but muscular, and fashionably dressed. One of ours, Adrian knew. The endless Bourbon ran freely for all. Gary and Paul laughed and became more and more camp as the minutes ticked. Adrian listened as their voices were transformed into women's voices, as they laughed about hair and hair spray and clothes and ugly people and more. Janie was horrified. They could tell and camped it up a notch further.

"Stop! Just stop it," she cried out suddenly, grabbing the bourbon and half-running from the room.

They laughed. Even Adrian laughed. It was sorta funny, after all. Marg saw the humour too. She was almost joining in with the boys.

"Ade, can you go and get the cask of wine from my car?" Paul asked; ordered, throwing the keys at the mostly ignored Adrian. He picked up the keys and stumbled out. When he returned, he found Gary sitting on the floor, and Paul with an arm around Marg. He put the wine down, avoided making a comment. Nothing came to mind to say. Nothing really mattered. He poured wine for them all, silently handing Paul his glass. Paul smiled as he accepted it. He turned back to Marg, as they touched glasses, she drunkenly spilling a little red on her top. The radio played. Adrian watched as Paul's slender hand moved onto Marg's exposed thigh. Slowly, casually running his palm up and down. He kept talking to Gary who seemed not to notice. In the dimness, the palm moved up and down, eventually up and up. Into the viper's lair. The corners of Marg's lips twitched as the hiding place was breached.

Adrian stood up. "I'm going to check on Janie," he said, more to Gary than the others.

He found the girl in the kitchen, lying on the floor, a half-eaten bag of chips next to her. Chips on the floor. Coke spilled. Bourbon at her lips.

"Are you okay?"

"Fine," she said monotone. Moving her eyes slowly, she looked up at Adrian, her expression changing. She started laughing, strangely. She picked up the bag of chips and flung them across the room at the boy, chips flying to all corners, then became serious. "Get out of my kitchen you fuckin' fag!" Adrian turned and left as Janie started up her laugh once more. Back in the lounge room he found Gary alone.

"Paul and Marg have gone to one of the rooms," Gary informed him.

Adrian threw himself down next to the man. He lay on his stomach, head in the plush pile, and started sobbing. He had thought it didn't matter, but now it did. There was chaos all around, as if the furniture itself was flying around the room, manipulated by ghosts who were born of an ache inside him. How could Paul? They were supposed to be here together. He was supposed to be gay. A fag. Well,

180

he never said so. What did it all mean? Nothing meant what it had before. Adrian cried more loudly.

"Don't," Gary said softly. "There's no point."

Adrian looked up. "Why did he go off like that? With a girl?"

"Because he's a fuckwit. A nice one, though. He's proving himself. I guess he likes dominance. With a woman he thinks he can find it, but he probably won't enjoy it. He used to do it a lot." Gary paused for several seconds. "Actually, he asked me here to distract you. I was supposed to seduce you. But I'm not going to."

Adrian moved quickly into Gary's surprised arms. He buried his head quietly in Gary's chest.

"How do you know Paul?" came the muffled sounds.

Gary told him the story of a doomed relationship, of a boy young and insecure, fashionable and pretty, of needs to be with others, and of an affair turned to friendship.

"You have to be careful if you get attached to someone," Gary taught. "You mustn't feel hurt when you're let down. It will happen, always. You have to remember you have yourself. It's important to be strong for yourself, otherwise the people who come and go in your life will hurt you. You're only young. You'll be even stronger as you grow older."

"I know. I will."

Adrian pulled away, pouring more wine for each, and then returned to the warmth of arms and body. They drank, then held each other tight, occasionally opening their mouths to talk, but saying nothing. Transforming, Adrian thought. He closed his eyes and saw these people. Changing, all of them. He saw masses of people, many he had known and so many that he might come to know. Their substance constantly transforming. Changes that could not be pictures, but some that were. Boys becoming girls. Girls being fucked, becoming boys. Lovers breaking apart and becoming friends. Paul and Gary in sixty-nine, becoming one, then becoming each other. Janie growing younger but wiser, then turning into her mother. So much change. He thought of the communion host at church. How maybe it does change without showing it. Maybe it's all true.

Lying down and pressed close to Gary, Adrian could feel himself drifting into sleep. In that embrace. He hugged more closely, and in that hug a million needs and emotions he had never before known were fulfilled.

The word "father" came quietly from his lips. Gary did not hear, for he too was asleep.

SUNDAY:

Brightness. Too much. Waking with a hangover. Not easy, but too achy to return to the joy of sleep. Adrian slowly pulled himself from Gary's arms. He struggled quietly to his feet and looked down on his new friend. Just a friend. Just a man and a maybe mentor. He walked into the kitchen, the sunlight streaming through the glass. Janie was still on the floor amid the chaos of chips, spilled Bourbon, and a hundred other disasters. Adrian watched her chest rise and fall slowly as she peacefully slept. They will talk later. Matters easily sorted out. Maybe a hug, too.

He quietly picked up the empty packet, binning it, and uprighted the Bourbon bottle. With his hands he swept the chips into a pile, picked them up awkwardly, and put them in the trash too. He looked at Janie's face. So calm. A little lamb, snoozing. Hard to see any trace of the wolfish bitch that spoke out last night. Adrian slowly opened the screen door, making as little noise as he could. He stepped into the sunlight, feeling the warmth press through his clothes, feeling the energy ebb into his every muscle. Feeling strength. Pulling his shirt over his head he took a step towards the pool. He brushed back a stray lock of his blondness, and stepped forward again. Belt undone, he lowered and stood out of his 501s, and then his Calvins; losing an identity, but knowing the imprint would always be in his mind if he ever needed it. It wasn't really him. He was not Adrian ... He was he.

Disrobed, he threw himself casually into the pool. Not too cold. Floating slowly to the surface, he noted how calm the water remained. The slightest concentric rippling, a little swell. Such peace. The sun in a blue sky, only a couple of stray clouds, and order all around. Order. Paul with Marg but not really with her, nor she with him. Both trying to be with themselves, and never realising which way to look. Gary knows – he understands. Janie will, too, one day. Adrian knew he knew. He turned and faced the rockery and shrubs at the far end of the pool, watching the waterfall pumped over the rocks and slowly streaming into the pool. The picture of nature at the edge of his world. He could hear birds chirping, imagining mother-birds carrying food, father-birds hovering overhead the nest. The babes know he's there.

Erect now, Adrian unashamedly touched his penis under the water, masturbating slowly as the sun-heat lit his face, thinking nothing erotic, just feeling sane. He came, surprising and quickly, and looked down to see his come dispersing into the water. No, it was merging with the water. He and the water. Together. Out of the pool now, he took a non-descript towel from the back of a chair and wrapped it around his waist, though he knew he needed no loincloth for respect or integrity.

Not now. Not anymore. The strength and protection came from the sun and world and from himself.

He sat, then, in the chair, leaning back, hands clasped behind his head, eyes closed, knowing he was grown. Knowing there were still a few waves to calm, a few bits of an unreal life to sort out. But first he wanted to enjoy these moments here alone.

SLEEPING ROUGH

David Johnston

I N YOUR TWENTIES, THE BODY IS A resource to mine. You drink till you stagger, you eat a big breakfast of eggs and bacon, and you don't even start to get fat till you're twenty six.

I looked at Simon. He jumped a little when I said goodbye too loudly. He moved, not sure what I was saying, not sure what I meant. He was still half asleep.

Later, in the tram, I stood up and felt the tiredness pull me back, down towards the green vinyl seat. It was like being buffeted by wind. I thought about Simon. He'd probably slipped back into sleep.

I fought to stay awake. Breakfast with Elise had brought me out. It was raining, slowly, Melbourne style. The neon signs down Brunswick Street were like squiggles of coloured pencil against the dark wet brick of the shop fronts. I found a table at Mario's and ordered breakfast. No use waiting for Elise, not with the hangover.

It was ten o'clock. At the bar several men were drinking. I was concerned with eating my scrambled eggs. I like plain tea, with milk and sugar, definitely not weak black. I hate weak, black, Earl Grey tea.

As for Elise, I knew she'd turn up late and have whatever was the special. Elise

David Johnston lives in Victoria and has been writing for some years. His work is often concerned in exploring the nuances of a meeting between friends, investigating the delicate nature of friendship.

"I generally avoid the big plot and rather direct my attention to the sense of place and time. Central themes in my work are the illusive nature of intimacy, the insularity of mainstream culture and the individuality of experience. These issues are most often of acute relevance to the gay and lesbian community."

often let the waiter run through the menu, and then she'd just say, "Give me the first special, but if it's going to take a while I'll have the fast special."

I felt an irritation run through my chest, like a current of electricity. It started somewhere in my spine and spread out in storm of referred pains. The restaurant was stale with dampness and the smell of wet clothes.

I thought of Simon asleep. The thought was on a loop in my mind. It started just as it finished. He was asleep, I could see the beard line and the dryness of his lips. I could smell the heaviness of his stale breath, see the crushed pillow on which he was sleeping.

Elise put her bag on the table.

"God, Elise."

"Sorry, I'm half asleep."

"So am I. You been out again?"

"No, it was one of those kids. I got a call at some shit of an hour last night from one of the kids at the shelter and I went out for him. Little bugger had some problem with the cops."

The waiter appeared and Elise ordered scrambled eggs and bacon, coffee and an orange juice.

"How's the new bit, the fresh flesh."

Elise leant forward, took a piece of my toast and ate it. Then she pushed herself back into the chair and yawned. I spoke slowly, to just make sure she understood.

"He is twenty five years old. He's lovely, although I feel a bit old beside him."

"Honey, my heart bleeds, getta load of it. God, I'm out at night looking after street kids sleeping rough at St Kilda, but do I complain? Tell you what, those cops can be bad news, but this one, last night, was okay."

The eggs arrived and Elise immediately began to eat. I had been picking steadily at mine. The hangover had made my appetite uncertain, still each mouthful made the food more interesting. I looked to my friend as she piled her fork with food, held it poised and talked at great speed about St Kilda at three in the morning.

I was back on the loop again, the dirty pillow case and the still face. The smell of the room, heavy with perspiration. The quietness of sleep filling the house that I had left.

"So I rolled over and told Johnno, 'I've gotta go honey'. He groaned. God he's wonderful. He never complains."

"Do you give him a chance?"

"Never."

She reached over and took the strip of red and white meat off my plate and chewed at it while she talked.

"This kid got picked up. He's fourteen, cute, but just so grubby. Very pretty face but so aggressive, anyway, the cops had noticed him around the entrance to this club, and they picked him up, and they asked him if wanted to phone his parents, and the little bugger phones me. Just as well."

Elise finished the bacon and ordered more toast and coffee.

"But the cops were sweet, they were. God, this kids lucky, he's got a pretty face. You know it comes down to that. The ugly ones can get a tough time. Seems brutal, but it goes like that. He'll scrub up and in court the magistrate will melt just a tad and he'll be OK."

I finally finished my breakfast and felt a tired satisfaction fill me. The loop began again as I got the waiters attention for another cup of tea.

"You in dreamland?"

"No, tell me, what will happen to the kid?"

"Well, you know, I'll place him in a shelter and he'll say all the right things for a while, then he'll tell someone, who will no doubt deserve it, to 'get fucked' and a row will start, and then he'll go underground and then I go to bed and snuggle up to Johnno and we'll have the first good night's sleep for a decade and then this angel faced kid'll get busted and call me at three in the morning. It kinda' goes like that. You in love?"

"Well, I'm too old for him Elise."

"Forget this convent guilt shit. You're worried that he'll wake up one day and say he's off. Enjoy it all before the inevitable flit happens. That's what I say. Christ, it's going to be more maudlin breakfasts isn't it? And regrets about not living in the present and God knows what other angle you'll work up on the case."

"Yep, you are a first class social worker."

"No, I'm almost jealous."

"Why, this one is trouble, trouble, trouble. It's the beautiful ones that hurt you in the end'. Prince said that."

Elise ran her toast across the greasy remains of her eggs.

"Yep."

"Believe me I'm worried, I feel old beside him."

"Guilt, it's ugly to see."

"Look, I got hair on my shoulders, and he's not bored doing weights, one day working on the iron, one off to let the bod' rebuild."

"Wax. I'll pull your hair off in sheets, virtually painless."

"Elise, that's really disgusting."

"Frankly I like a little downy dusting on the shoulder blades, but then again I'm not a poof. I got over smooth chested men in the court. Pretty boys, witless lads, bad breath and no underwear. Yep, revoltin' to touch and smell. Little dolls of disease and contagion. What else is troubling you?"

"He's from a nice Kew family, where they don't steal cars. His father is a specialist. He's got an Alfa, he's doing medicine."

"Yep, sounds truly revolting to me."

"And I got hair on my back, I'm too old and he's too young."

Elise drew a packet of cigarettes from her bag, then, after taking a match and lighting it, she looked a round in a casual gesture. She smiled and spoke softly, but aggressively.

"I'm on the 'Stop for life' committee. Sad isn't it. Sad, the hypocritical deceit of this sordid habit, but I love the tarbabies. It's truly a revolting habit, kills us in the thousands, but I'll quit before then. Truly-ruly."

I felt like a drink, maybe a Fanta, or a glass of Coke. Then I realised that I really wanted to go back to bed. It was a sweet cool pillow of white cotton, aromatic with hot sun and Surf washing powder that I thought about. I wanted to have Simon's heavy shoulder pushing me to the edge of the bed, the sourness of his breath mixing with the fresh draft from the window.

I just said, "Lord almighty, I've got to go back to bed."

Elise pulled out her purse. She put some money on the table.

"So do I, this cigarette is foul. I'm exhausted. I'll pay."

On the street, in front of the restaurant, we waited for our taxis. She put her arm in mine, like we were married. Her cab arrived first and she kissed me.

"Thanks, tell me what happens, every bloody detail."

She kissed me sharply, leaving a cold smear on my cheek.

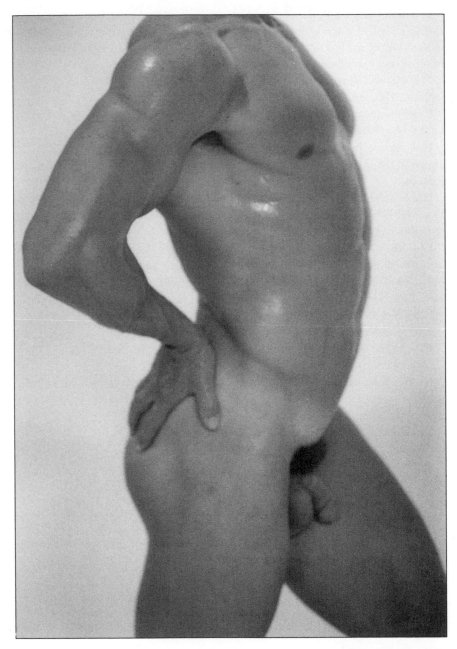

IDYLL

Victoria Carruthers

Long ago we made love in the evenings of the hot summer. You kicked away the sheet and lay heavily on top of me. You would stay there for ages; your full weight supported by my body; your breasts pressed against mine. I felt your breath burning on my throat. Your hips polished mine into two smooth fists of bone.

When you were finished, you rolled away, peeling your belly from mine - sliding your wetness away. Sometimes we slept immediately. More often you went downstairs to your kitchen and brought back a large bowl of chilled and glistening fruit. You carefully pared segments of ripe flesh from the whole and we ate them off that small bone-handled knife. It had belonged to your grandmother and, in my mind now, to those summer evenings.

Vicki Carruthers was born in New Zealand of very mixed parents but has spent more time living in England, Wales, Italy and Australia. She studied music for many years, has a Bachelor of Arts degree in medieval literature and philosophy, and recently completed a Master of Arts focussed on the late Romances of Shakespeare and contemporary socio-literary theory. She intends to undertake further study in the near future. Despite all of this, she has worked in the area of public health for some years and is currently involved in HIV/AIDS social research. Throughout her varied career she has belonged to, and written about, many subcultures but is still not sure which ones. She lives and works in Sydney where she is still hoping to discover a one-line definition of postmodernism and to conduct the Sydney Symphony Orchestra.
This story is dedicated to the memory of Tim Carrigan who died of AIDS in August 1994. It was obviously not written about him, but he always liked it. The story is actually for, and about, AD and TB.

One night we watched ourselves eating in the large mirror on your dressing table. We lounged on the bed, your white arm fed me pieces of apple from the blade of the knife. You said I was so beautiful that you wanted to live inside me. You said that if you had my flesh, bones and blood, that I would be yours forever. I agreed it was necessary that we should mix our blood together and I held my open palm out to you and you kissed me so tenderly that I never felt the shining blade on my skin. Then you lay on me and let your body sink into mine. You wanted to come closer and closer to me - inside me. You held my hand firmly while we made love and in the morning I saw the crimson stain where our blood had met and soaked into the sheet.

You dressed and bound my hand. You knew exactly what to do.

In the afternoon, naked to relieve that heat of summer, I sat reading on the couch in your sitting room. The clock silently ticking in the still air. You came in and smiled at me. You had been shopping for fruit. Peaches and mangoes brimmed out over the top of your basket. You peeled two mangoes and we each began to eat. The juice ran down my chin, onto my breasts, and you licked it away. You left most of the fruit on the seed and asked if you could put it inside me. You said that you wanted to see it there and eat what had been in my body. I spread my legs but you pushed them wider. I took that seed inside me and you sucked at its flesh each time it moved outside my body. Then you lay back on the floor and beckoned my mouth to your wetness. You held my head there until you had finished. When you slowly removed the seed from me it was slightly spotted with blood. I didn't mind - the small tear only makes more room for you.

You take pleasure from my body. It was, and still remains, yours to have; to keep. I gave it to you with love, and then, with need.

One night you woke up and wanted to make love. You lay on me with your arms around my head. You held my hair in your fists and pushed your cheek against mine. You told me not to move at all. Not even to breathe. You dribbled saliva over my skin and smeared it across my mouth with your chin. You repeated over and over that I was yours and always would be. That my desire was nothing without yours. You placed your hand tightly over my throat and I felt my breath become shallow. You pressed your pubic bone hard against mine. You rubbed and ground your body into me more and more quickly and, through a heartbeat throb in my eyes, I saw you, then, more clearly than ever. I knew that which dwells inside us both; knew its shape and form; its needs and boundaries.

Exhausted and breathless, your body convulsed. You removed your grip immediately and exchanged obscenities for words of love. And I had climaxed, too, deep in the stillness of my body – filled up with desire – knowing that I could never live without you.

In the morning the bruises were a testimony of your love. I brought you breakfast of fruit and coffee. You asked me to prepare a bath for you and I poured in jasmine oil. I heard you step into the water and I waited patiently on the bed for the invitation to come in with fruit and the small bone-handled knife to feed you and wash your back.

THE SUM OF US

David Stevens

I NTERVIEW WITH DAVID STEVENS BY
PETER CASTALDI.

When you wrote 'The Sum of Us' did you have an idea that it would end up on screen?

Oh no, no. When I wrote the play, part of my ambition was to write a play that was a completely theatrical experience and could not possibly be translated to the cinema. I was purist about it.

And when they said to me we want you to adapt it for the screen I said no, get somebody else, not me. But I do think doing it for the screen was a wonderful experience and I tried to approach it completely as a film.

And even though there are people who say that talking to the camera is a hangover from the play, in fact it's not. Talking to the camera is a device that I first used in a script, that never got made, in 1976. Where I had talking to the camera, I had scenes being run with different endings. It's a device I love to play with because I love to play with the form as well as the content.

David Stevens lives with his long term lover in Newburyport, USA. His latest work is a novel, 'Journey in the Desert.'

Peter Castaldi is a film critic for ABC television and radio.

David Stevens wrote the play 'The Sum of Us' and the screenplay for the Australian play of the same name. With skill and passion, his script illuminates the realities of being born homosexual and the need to love, embrace and accept life's rich diversity in sexual orientation.

So what sort of changes did you have to embrace when you were taking 'The Sum of Us' from the stage version to the screen version?

Well, first of all we had to sack the playwright. Ha, ha. He kept getting in the way. He kept saying you can't cut that speech. There are some very long and very, very beautiful speeches in the play version. I mean the woman on the train. I don't know whether you've seen the movie, but there's a reference to a woman on the train, which in the theatre is a page and half long speech at the end of Act 1, which is one of my better speeches, and that had to go. I tried to see how I could tell the story given that it is a wordy piece. How I could tell it in filmic terms.

Things like the sequence in the supermarket don't appear at all on stage, aren't even referred to on stage. That's a completely cinematic device that I used there. But the major changes, I guess, are to length and the fact that in the cinema - of course - show, don't tell. We can actually see people like Graham and Mary, we can see the woman on the train and we can see the scene in the supermarket.

What about location? Because it was originally written for the Western Suburbs of Melbourne and the film is transposed to the glorious city of Sydney with many recognisable, you know the Opera House, the Harbour, even Balmain - all instantly recognisable places?

Well, after me kicking and screaming about that, I wanted them to do this wonderful socio-realist document set in Footscray, which is the play's original location. But the poor producers, bless them, not only is this arguably the first film in which the act of want of the audience becomes the boy gets the boy, but all the producers are very straight and they're faced with this thing on their hands and they are desperately trying to think of ways to make it more appealing to an audience. And I don't think that they thought Footscray was one of those things. Nothing against Footscray.

So the decision was made to change it to Sydney and I now embrace that completely, as much as I fought against it before. Because I think the iconography of Sydney, the Harbour, the Opera House, the bridge, the ferry cat - all that adds to the reality of the location. And people accepting that, seeing these real people in recognisably real locations, helps enormously.

So does that recognisable reality of Sydney turn and act upon the relationships that play in the film and shift them from an ideal to a reality?

Well, I don't think they were ever an ideal. In my mind they were always a reality. People have said that Harry couldn't possibly exist. That there is no Ocker as tolerant as this. But, you know, that is an astonishing attribute to my imagination. Because I don't know how you could invent a character like that.

Obviously he is based on reality. He's not based on my own father, but he is based on the fathers of friends of mine. So in my mind it always has been a reality. And even it were not, I have no interest in making documentaries. I've made documentaries and I love doing it but this was not a documentary.

The joy of drama, seems to me to be, that you don't actually have to illustrate what he is. But as Rex said, you can show in drama, in a different world, what might be. So fantasy/reality, I don't know. Is 'The Lion King' any less real, because the emotional experience is any less real because the animal is so blatantly a cartoon, it doesn't actually exist.

But Harry does exist and Geoff does exist and I wanted to create a complete world for them so that the audience going into that world never felt there was anything strange about it. The world itself made sense. And the Opera House and the Harbour and the ferry all help with that I think.

Is the reality of 'The Sum of Us' then, ideals that you perhaps wish you had as you were growing up?

No, people have assumed this. I don't. First of all I don't think it's ideal, because what happened in America was that we had the first ecstatic reviews in the New York Times and everything. And then people started to look at the play more intensely in articles rather than critics reviews. And there was a lot of debate about Harry's motives, a lot of debate about whether he was in fact quite as tolerant and accepting as he seems to be. He leaps on the thing, "Have you done it with girls?", "You never told me", "Wouldn't you like to try it again?" Which suggests that he hasn't totally accepted his sons sexuality at all. I think the decision he has made is that - I want his love no matter what. Its not that I want him to be like this but I want him to love me. He is my son.

And one of the most marvellous moments in the film for me is when Russell takes the opposite view and in all this chaos of looking after Dad and everything he says, "Well, he's my Dad, how can I not." And that is when the film for me becomes its most real because the phrase is so simple and its so simply done by the actor and it has a world of meaning behind it.

So is 'The Sum of Us' essentially a love story, fundamentally devoid of gender and sexual preference at base line?

Yes, that's exactly what it is. I think love is love and it is about unconditional love. More importantly, when I wrote the play and people said, "David what's it about?" Well, I have no idea what it's about and I wrote the damn thing. But when I saw the movie, because I wasn't here for it, when I saw what other people had done to it, I decided what it is about is to tell someone you love them before it's too late. Embrace love.

What about the casting of the film. I mean Jack Thompson, John Polson, Russell Crowe. An extraordinary cast.

And Deborah, don't forget Deborah, because her last scene, I just think she's utterly marvellous. Again I've said a lot of times that seeing the film with an audience, the audience is just way, way, way ahead of me. In that last scene of Deborah's, they actually start laughing before she says the line.

Its a dream cast. The first Australians I've seen do it. I've seen many, many Americans do it. They all attempt an Australian accent with greater or less success. But the Australian actors bring to it a world of Australian-ness that it was written for but I have never seen before. So for me it is a dream cast.

I think Jack fits into the role like a comfortable old slipper. I think Russell is marvellous. I think John is terrific. I love particularly his last shot when Geoff asks him the question and he doesn't say yes and he doesn't say no and he has this wonderfully ambivalent look on his face. I just go aaaah!

It struck me with Jack Thompson, in particular, who I would call an Australian icon, a cinema acting icon, that with material like 'The Sum of Us' he is actually being allowed to reposition himself, to rebuild Jack Thompson. Because here is a story that has fundamentally never been told by an Australian film maker.

I think that's absolutely true. You talk about Sydney icons, the Harbour Bridge, the Harbour, the ferry, the Opera House. Jack is up there with the Sydney Opera House as an Australian icon and I think that because of his position in the society he brings a weight of presence to the film that makes it even more accessible to an audience because they know Jack. So you're in the cinema and your already half way there.

The function of the character is to take the audience by the hand and say come with me. Come to a world you don't know about and you'll be perfectly safe, I promise you. And Jack of course does that because we all absolutely trust Jack. He's such an open and generous man.

Accessibility to an audience, the idea of direct address is something that used to be an alienating thing but you've turned it around and actually made it something which is very inviting to an audience. And also I think comedy, lightening the load, by giving people the opportunity to laugh. When you are writing a story like 'The Sum of Us' are you consciously thinking about, I mean obviously you're a playwright, you want people to see the play, but are you making conscious decisions about how you are really going to draw them in?

Absolutely. I mean a line like "Up your bum," is not accidental, it comes from somewhere. A lot of the gags build in threes - "Whisky makes you frisky, brandy makes you randy, pity we haven't got any rum." What's interesting again is that the audience is way ahead of me because they laughed on the first one in Brisbane, they laughed so loud they didn't hear the second one and the only word they heard on the third one was rum and they were off again. So they are actually way ahead of me.

But there is I hope a deal of craft in the piece because I was trying to test myself as a playwright. And the year that we won the Best Off Broadway Play, Neil Simon won the Best On Broadway Play, and so I was up there with Neil Simon and boy, that's a blast I can tell you, because that's the master craftsman. But as much as anything it wasn't written with a social agenda. It was written as a test of my craft, so the fact that it's getting the laughs and getting the tears is a wonderful feeling.

It's like the Graham and Mary story, what happens to them, the climax of their relationship, is not there for social agenda. That it has a social purpose is another matter. It wasn't put in for that reason but to set a whole emotional territory. And finally I now realised to set up the theme of the film, how do you say thank you for forty years of love? What words can you possibly find? And somebody got stuck into me the other night in Brisbane and said well you copped out, you should have written that scene. I wanted to know what they said. But I can't imagine that scene, can you? I think its much better if you try and imagine that scene – put your words into it not mine.

You wrote 'The Sum Of Us' to test your craft? But how personal is it to you, the whole process of writing the play, seeing it staged, winning awards, seeing the film. What sort of wave of emotion did that bring to you, as the creator of the piece?

It is the most complex process of emotions you could possibly imagine. First of all there is tremendous pride. There is tremendous sense of warmth, when you hear six hundred people belly laughing and foot stomping, and calling out to the screen. I mean there was this show when Greg decides to leave – someone yelled out "I'd stay."

Then there are other processes that attend you to it. I'll remove it from Australia to give you some idea. The first production of the play in Los Angeles, a very small theatre so we were accessible to the audience – the producer, the director and myself. And this young man, a presentable young man in that sort of American clean cut way came to see the play three times and came up to us and said, "My parents can't handle my sexuality. I'm going to fly them into Chicago to see the play and to try and explain to them, may I introduce them to you afterwards?" And we said sure, if they want to.

Well, they came – the sort of sweet, dumpy mid-western couple, not knowing what they were in for, and afterward when we were standing outside the mother came up, she was crying and she embraced Dorothy Lydon, the producer and went away and talked with her. And his father came up to me and shook my hand and said, "All I know how to say is thank-you, and now I'd like to go and talk to my son." And he put his arm around his son's shoulder and went away. And for the first time, I think probably in his life, he had a long and serious and honest conversation with his son.

Now, when that happens it's very moving. It tends to happen rather a lot. You sort of become a father confessor to people who use the play as a vehicle for coming out. Or even for parents who come without their children's knowledge to find out about the world and maybe find ways to raise the matter with their children. And what gushes out of them is extraordinary gratitude and it's very moving.

It's a weight on your shoulders, because you want to back off and say, "Hey, all I wrote was a comedy." But people tell you you wrote something more and it's a very wonderful emotion. I can't imagine experiencing anything quite like it again in my life.

I think for me one of the things that really makes 'The Sum of Us' work, and I'm talking for a broad general audience, who may need some sort of reassurance about their children, is that the way the comedy is written? You allow an audience to laugh at, and with, in a parallel track all the way through the film. How do you do that? How do you write that sort of comedy?

Before I came to Australia everybody said to me, "David don't go to Australia, they don't like Poms and they hate poofters." And when I came here I found out that the more honest I was about myself, the more responsive people were to that. If I was trying to hide something, well people thought he's not been honest with me so why should I be honest with him. And that was the division. And with the play I decide to take the same approach. I will be completely honest.

There are elements of the gay world I don't like. As Geoff says I don't want to live in a world that begins and ends with being gay. Or conversely, just because someone is gay doesn't mean that I should like them.

In my present home town in America, we have a lesbian Mayor. And people say to me when are you going to vote for her, to which my response is, "Well what are her politics? Is she a fiscal conservative or is she a fiscal liberal? I am not going to vote for her just because she is lesbian." And I think there are silly elements to the gay society just as I think there are silly elements in the straight society. And so I try to present the world as I saw it as honestly as I knew how. And because I wasn't writing the play to have it produced, because I didn't expect to make money from it, I could be, I think, that honest.

Now, I get taken to task by some people, a few gay people have objected to the fact that Geoff says I've done it with girls. Meaning he is not completely homosexual. Well, I've done it with girls and its very nice, thank-you very much, it's just that I prefer doing it with blokes.

I think, in Tasmania for example, I would love the film there to achieve something that I don't think they've quite cottoned on to. It seems that so many people are so ill informed. What I would love for the film to do is to say, "Look they don't all have two horns and they are not all monsters", and more importantly I'd like to remove the debate if at all possible, after all it's only a comedy, from the equation of homosexuality = sex maniac.

I am not, for example, rushing around all day in a state of permanent sexual arousal wanting to grab anything I can see. Most of my life with my lover is just trying to work our how to get on with the business of living. And at my age, you know, sex is not quite as important to me as it was. That doesn't make me any less sexual. It is not the homosexual act that makes you a homosexual, it's something quite else. But I don't think, again it's a lack of art, cinema, whatever, I don't think they've quite cottoned on to that in Tasmania yet.

It strikes me that there is a wonderful irony in 'The Sum of Us' in that it is an Australian story, and I can't imagine it being any other story. But coming out of a culture that's known for its macho larrikin maleness. How do you respond to that? Could this story have been told anywhere else?

You'll get me banned from this country I tell you. This whole macho Australian thing, it used to be in London. Which is when I first heard about Australia. The queens there would go down to the boats and meet them coming off the boats, because they were as fresh as daisies and they all wanted to do it. That was the joke about Australians. Of course it's not true, but I don't think the society was as homophobic as we pretend it was.

Gay liberation didn't start with Stonewall, it started a long time before that. As I say, I first came here in 1967 when Playboy was still banned. But what I think happened was that the society recognised, that this Ocker society recognised, it could not go on as a white supremist, racist, sexist society. They had to accept that the possibility that two Wongs could make a White, and I think the society in effect elected to commit suicide. Elected the change. And embraced it extraordinarily well.

If you look at what is happening in Germany and Italy now, they are only now facing the decision that Australia made a long time ago. They've turned to fascism. I don't think there has ever been a case in Australia of people burning six year old children just because they had a different colour skin. There has been pain in the transition here but not as much pain as there is now in other places. And I think that is a great compliment to the society.

Here you'll find the Australian attitude is, "Bugger it let's go to the beach." And of course that's the difference between white Australian society and black Australian society. The black Australian attitude is, "we're already at the beach who needs to go anywhere." It's a white concept that?

I have a very rosy view of Australia because I have found such kindness here and I made my home here. I still really regard it as my home. And I had occasion to be on the set of, 'Robinson Crusoe' in Papua New Guinea, two week ago, just as a rush job. I walked on the set and half a dozen of the film crew, who worked with me when I was a director in Melbourne, well they had to close down for ten minutes, while we hugged, embraced and shed a few tears. You know, it was like coming home. And Australia is that for me, Australia is coming home.

And when the play was on in New York we had the first rush of great notices and then someone wrote the most beautiful thing when they said it is wonderful to go into the theatre and imagine home again as the place where you are most loved. And that's how I feel about Australia, I feel most loved here.

You are a well travelled bod?

Yes.

Could 'The Sum of Us' come out any other culture?

Yes. I've always begged them to let me translate it into American or into English North Country, because it must be able to, otherwise it doesn't have universal appeal and blatantly it does have universal appeal. I mean the fact that New Yorker's regard it as the play's natural home, even though it's done with appalling Australian accents. They don't care about the accents, they care about the message. The play is communicating - we are family. I am my brother's keeper.

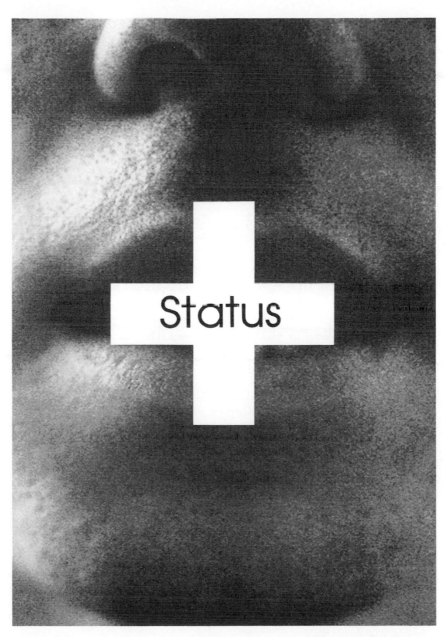

Status

STATUS

A documentary film treatment

Stephen Cummins

DIRECTORS STATEMENT

THE SOCIAL STIGMA ATTACHED TO AIDS makes the diagnosis of HIV status an emotional labyrinth. One of the major factors of this phenomenon is disclosure. I have chosen a small number of stories which from my research were both typical and interesting. As someone who is HIV positive these experiences mirror or contrast with my own. The voice of the narrator is my own voice. The dance and drama sequences function as moments when the audience can experience the material emotionally as well as provide some black humour.

Stephen Cummins was one of Australia's most promising young film makers. The following script 'Status' is a shortened version of a film treatment completed in early June, 1994, following an initial development grant from the Australian Film Commission. Soon afterwards Stephen rapidly became ill with Lymphoma and died on August 23, 1994, surrounded by family and friends.

"I was initially to be composer on 'Status,' and when Stephen became ill, to be co-director. I have tried to stay true to his intentions in the excerpting of the script. Although Stephen, who was my best friend, died before the film reached production funding level, those of us who were working with him wish to eventually bring out these ideas in various projects, of which this publication is the first."

"His inital Super-8 work established concerns that were to remain with him through his career: multi-layered examinations of sexuality, the body, and identity. Stephen went on to win several international awards in the late 80's for his short films 'Elevation' and 'LeCorps Image.'

He was probably best known for the 1991 short film 'Resonance,' an experimental piece about anti-gay violence that we made together with the dancers Mathew Bergan and Chad Courtney. After winning Best Short Film at the 1991 Sydney Film Festival, 'Resonance' went on to win several international awards and has been shown at more international film festivals than any Australian short film this decade. He also directed 'Life's Burning Desire,' an SBS Masterpiece documentary on the dancer Paul Mercurio, and 'Body Corporate,' a dance video for the SBS program 'Carpet Burns.'" - Simon Hunt

Status will be shot in colour on 16mm, mostly in a studio. To emphasise the performance element of disclosing one's HIV Status, I am interested in shooting the interviews and the drama and dance elements of the film all in the studio, with the same lighting and similar sets.

INTERVIEWEES

Arie   An HIV positive gay man who was diagnosed in his early 20s.

Amelia Strong independent heterosexual women in her mid 30s.

Stuart HIV negative dancer and activist in his early 30s. His lover, dancer Kelvin Coe, died two years ago of AIDS.

Alan   Co-Convenor of PLWHA (People Living With HIV and AIDS).

Bruce An HIV-Positive man in his 30s, who died during the writing of the script. We hear his voice from recordings.

Narrator The film maker's voice. An HIV-Positive artist in his early 30's.

SCRIPT

The camera pans up a bed and over the bodies of two men kissing. Their bodies intertwine in an almost dance-like movement. Suddenly one stops, and whispers inaudibly. There is a silence and both bodies are very still. The image changes to negative and then back to positive and repeats a number of times.

A large "plus" symbol appears with the word **"Status"** on it. The soundtrack consists of barely audible whispers which build to become a loud shout.

DIAGNOSIS

TEXT ON SCREEN (slowly emerges out of TV Static) -

   "What's your sign +/-?" "Do you know?"

DRAMA SEQUENCE - In an oversized clinical surgery

We see two doctors outside the door of the surgery fighting over who doesn't get to break the news to the patient. Inside we see a female patient in a doctor's surgery.

Doctor (Woman) I'm afraid the results have come back positive. This doesn't mean you have AIDS but it does mean you have been exposed to the virus.

The patient appears preoccupied with an object on the desk and doesn't respond to the news. We hear the director's voice.

We'll try that again, you look half dead. Try to focus this time, put more into it. This is meant to be dramatic.

Actor playing the patient looks bored.

Arie   "When I found out from the doctor, I felt I'd been shot with a speargun so I was actually in shock for about an hour. I thought I had it tattooed all over my body."

Narrator   When I walked into this room I was a normal, fun-loving, healthy kind of guy. Now, when I leave, according to the science of virology, I have some terrible virus. But I don't feel any different, except confused about the conflicting claims science now lays on my body.

IMAGE- The camera pans a naked male body. Slowly words become projected onto the body - ie virology, immunology, CD4 cells, disclosure - until it is covered.

IMAGE- Overhead shot of Arie lying on a bed. The camera begins to slowly spin around as we hear the following. We hear the sound of a heartbeat getting faster. The scene is shot to look a little like a horror film.

Arie   "I felt poisoned, like I was being taken over - I felt like it was flowing around my body like little fish. It had come from the outside in through the skin. And the way they talk about the body fighting the virus, the language they use in medicine, I was having visual responses to that - there was this kind of mock fight going on inside my body."

The image begins to strobe from positive to negative during these comments.

IMAGE - We see Arie sit upright on the bed. He walks to the bathroom like awakening from a dream. He examines his face in the mirror during the following:

"For a little while there I started to feel I was fitting into a stereotype of what, I thought, I would soon look like. A kind of emaciated, disturbed look in the eyes, leatheriness of the skin - all these weird sort of images. They were basically images I had seen of people on their death-beds."

Arie addresses the camera.

"That didn't last very long because that was obviously a stupid thing to think. Finding out one way or the other has probably dumped a whole lot of stress and I think I even look a little younger, I don't have that underlying stress or question mark in each eye which I think I might have had previous to that and which I think I've noticed in photographs too. I've noticed a difference in my face reflective of a sense of underlying calmness."

A small question mark symbol changes into a "plus" graphic appearing on his face, then grows larger to fill the whole screen obscuring his face.

QUIZ SHOW

We see an elaborate Quiz Show set. We see the three contestants (who are interviewees) wearing numbers 1, 2, 3 on their T shirts. They are seated behind a counter. At the front of the counter are their numbers and a stylised thermometer for each of them. The thermometer is a measure of each contestant's T cells. The host runs on wearing a suit and has a doctor's stethoscope around his neck. As the show opens each of the contestants is having blood drawn by doctors with huge hypodermic syringes.

Compere   Tonight we have three lucky contestants (names each of them). And now for the first test, T cell scores. You all know the rules? (All contestants shake their heads, however the compere ignores them)

The latest T cell counts have just come in from pathology. (The numbers appear on the scoreboard) Contestant No 1 with 100, No 2 with 350 and No 3 with only 25. It's not looking good No 3, but on with the HIV Game Show. Even you have a chance to win back those elusive T cells.

(BLACK SCREEN)

Narrator   The first person I wanted to tell was my lover so I rushed home. He wasn't home so I went to an art opening instead and didn't tell anyone. The art was about AIDS!

INITIAL DISCLOSURES
TEXT ON SCREEN -

"Let the performance begin!"

IMAGE - A Close-Up (CU) of a mouth speaking, as the following Voice-Over (V/O) continues. The image gradually becomes slow-motion until its movements are almost undetectable.

Narrator   I felt like a character in a movie. As I told each of my friends, it began to feel more like a performance. I spent my time comforting others. It seemed strange because I was the one with a potential life-threatening illness, but I felt numb and spent the day with my dearest friends sobbing on my shoulders.

DANCE SEQUENCE - We see a man being hugged by another, they part and another dancer moves in to hug the man. The action is repeated with a number of dancers being "told the news". We hear an off screen voice: "next!"

IMAGE - We see Amelia dialling a phone number. The tone is engaged. She tries another number.

Amelia   (Speaks about telling her sister who fainted on the phone)

"I talked about having AIDS at that point in time and I just heard her go "uh" and I heard this thud and she fainted. "Angela, Angela, come back, come back." It was not the response I expected."

DRAMA SEQUENCE - In lounge room of suburban house environment

(Close-Up) Son

Mother, I've got to talk to you !

CU Son   (repeat -from another angle)
Mother, I've got to talk to you !

CU Mother

Sure, what's bothering you?

CU Son   (Pause)......

Cut to: CU of Son, camera then reveal he is lying in the bath.

Son   (practising, talking to himself)
It's a year since Jamie died of AIDS.
You remember that we went out for a short time many years ago? You know he died of AIDS? You've never asked me about my HIV status!
............No no no, too accusatory, morbid, ...
Try something more upbeat.
I went for a HIV test, after Jamie's death.

Stuart   "AIDS isolates people. Kelvin was naturally a loner, he didn't know anyone else with HIV/AIDS. He was scared, very very scared."

DRAMA SEQUENCE- Suburban House Environment

Mother   Sure, what's bothering you?

Son   (Pause)......

DRAMA SEQUENCE - We see a montage of close-ups of the same character telling a number of different people, followed by a number of close-ups of their responses.

Last image - a series of three close-ups of faces with people gasping in comic disbelief.

GRAPHIC - A white screen gradually zooms in to form a "plus" with a close-up of different mouths (ie four different people) in each corner. Each of the mouths say in turn "I'm HIV positive" and then they chant in unison.

Narrator   After a number of disclosures the whole process of telling becomes more of a performance, until HIV itself becomes the performance of an identity. It's a never-ending process, there's always someone else to tell, or yet another reason to have to tell someone.

TEXT ON SCREEN-(in inverted comas)

        "Re-enactment"

IMAGE - CU of phone. It rings for a long time, eventually a hand reaches over, lifts it and hangs up again. The phone begins to ring again.

Stuart   "Nobody apart from myself knew that Kelvin had HIV/AIDS and so the first thing that they heard about this was when Bob Cremin from the Herald Sun rang them up and said 'Do you have any comment about Kelvin Coe having AIDS?' These people were upset so not only did we have to deal with these inquiries but had to provide a caring capacity for people who were very upset because they were close to Kelvin."

IMAGE- Bruce at ACTUP demo in slow motion.

V/O Bruce   (Speaks about three stages of coming out: as gay, as HIV+ and as an activist)
"What are they going to do to you? Once you've come out there's nothing more they can hurl at you. So that's a position of strength."

Arie   "Some days I can't be bothered telling people because it will take an hour of my time."

DANCE SEQUENCE - We see one person (A) in the foreground close to filling the frame but not facing the camera, looking at another person (B) in the background of the shot. (A) then approaches the person in the background to speak, but can't and retreats back to the camera but this time facing it filling the screen. He then turns around looking back, sees two people B & C (a couple) he repeats the move and approaches them only to retreat again at the last minute. This movement is repeated with more and more people in the background. The murmur of the background crowd increases-we hear comments like: "What's wrong?," "Cat got your tongue," "Go on spit it out."

QUIZ SHOW

Compere   Welcome back to tonight's HIV Game Show folks. We're coming to you live from St Vincents Hospital. To get the ball rolling what better place to start than.....

TEXT ON SCREEN -

"Disclosure Technique"

(Advertising-style music and introductions by compere)

Compere   Contestant No 1 - confession!

We see No 1 looking uncomfortable, shuffling.

Contestant No 1
           There's something I've been meaning to tell you about.

Compere   Contestant No 2 - activist!

Contestant No 2 rips open his shirt to reveal a T shirt saying "Nobody Knows I'm HIV+"

Compere   Contestant No 3 - anger!

Contestant No 3
           (outburst)
           You think you've got problems! I'm HIV+, I can't find a job, I can't find a lover, my skin's breaking out, my cat just died.....(etc)

Compere V/O   Contestant No 2 - martyr!

208

Contestant No 2

>Don't cry for me, I'm HIV+... *(sung as trashy pop song)*

Compere V/O Contestant No 3 – again casual.

Contestant No 3

>By the way I'm HIV+.

Compere Thank you Contestant No 3, just love that casual approach, very smooth. And over to our panel of experts for the results.

(We see a panel of three experts, a sociologist, a counsellor and a doctor.)

Sociologist Well, Bob, of course our favourite is the confession, so congratulations Contestant No. 1. You have won our signature range of diamond pill containers and decorative wrought iron transfusion stands.

(No. 1 looks pleased while the others murmur "Set up")

SEX AND RELATIONSHIPS
IMAGE – *Close-up of mouth. The voice is stuttering and faltering.*
"I'm ....I ....I want to talk......." "I"

Arie I'm not going to disclose my status unless I feel that I've been in a situation where there's a potential relationship. I practice safe sex and there's no problem for either party.

DRAMA SEQUENCE-

Rough Trade "Haven't got AIDS have ya?"

Other Man (gulp) 'No'

Amelia Talks about her fear of infecting negative partners even though it is a mutual responsibility. That positive people are normal people with the same needs as everyone else and yet are made to feel guilty about wanting to have sex.

Stuart "I'm a single man now and when people put two and two together and realise that I'm Stuart Robertson and my partner was Kelvin Coe, who died of AIDS, they tend to run a mile. They think that I have AIDS. I refuse to meet someone and say 'by the way I'm HIV negative', I think that's totally inappropriate."

Narrator   As I walked home, I thought about the future of my relationship. We had been together five years. I remember he'd said he would never sleep with someone who was positive. We'd argued about it, as we often did, but it was just rhetorical. I had to disagree no matter what. But now it was me. I was positive. Would he make an exception? He might say it doesn't matter. Could I believe him?

IMAGE - Feet walking. After walking a few metres they turn back, repeat.

IMAGE - We see a male torso in the shower washing off what looks like cum. The washing becomes more and more obsessive.

Amelia   (Tells the story about going to Mykonos after her lover died from AIDS. She meets a beautiful Greek hunk and on the second day they go back to his place, where he asks why she isn't married or doesn't have a boyfriend. We also hear the conflicting voices in Amelia's head whispering, "Tell him, don't tell him." She explains that her lover died of AIDS. He then asks about her status and cries when she tells him she is HIV+. They end up getting together any way. One night a condom breaks!)

IMAGE - We see an empty bed and the sound of two people having sex. As Amelia mentions the condom breaking, the bed becomes covered with blood.

"He jumped up! He doused his dick in bleach which I thought was quite radical and I was sitting there saying, 'soap and water would have done it you know!'"

IMAGE - He throws her around, bailing her up against the wall and screams at her. Image continues, as Amelia finishes the story, location sound fades out.

DANCE/DRAMA SEQUENCE - Same Bedroom Again
We see a "duet" between two dancers A and B as a series of jump cuts. They are both wearing long pyjamas (1) A sits on the edge of the bed looking depressed while B is lying on the bed face up. (2) A has moved up the bed, B is now lying face down. (3) Both A and B are lying on the bed looking at each other but not touching. (4) B is now sitting on the edge of the bed. (5) B gets up and leaves the room leaving A on the bed.

INVOLUNTARY DISCLOSURE
IMAGE - Close-up of a phone to someone's ear.

Voice 1   I saw *(bleep)* outside Albion Street yesterday!

Voice 2   Do you think...

Voice 3   Have you heard that *(Bleep)*... is positive?

Sound: Fingers dialling.

Voice 4   Did you know that *(Bleep)* has AIDS?

In an open plan office we see the back of someone leaning back on a chair speaking on the phone. We hear echoing and whispering on the soundtrack. We see him put the phone down. He gets up to go to another desk and tells. The person at the desk then turns to the person beside her and tells. Another person at the desk then walks to the water fountain telling the others. We see someone waiting for a lift. The doors open. The conversation stops and the crowd looks uncomfortable as the camera joins them in the lift.

IMAGE - Two middle aged women in an office. One asks the other:

"Is fisting in category A or B?"

TEXT ON SCREEN-

"How did YOU get IT?"   "Who wants to know?"

Stuart   (walking along a street at night)
"One Sunday I went out to get the paper. Kelvin was asleep in bed. I turned through it and on page nine there was a photograph of Kelvin and the headline 'Ballet star dying of AIDS'."

IMAGE - Close-up of newspaper headlines

"We always used to go out for breakfast on Sunday mornings. But Kelvin didn't want to go and eventually broke down. I decided he was going, so we went. The atmosphere when we walked in!   It wasn't to enjoy breakfast but to prove a point. It was a breakfast restaurant, there were Herald Suns everywhere, with people reading them. I'm glad we did it otherwise we would have allowed ourselves to become victims."

DANCE SEQUENCE - Dancers perform a "Chinese Whispers" type dance. As the positive character walks, the information is passed from person to person behind his back. Some people look scandalised, others embarrassed and others distressed. Towards the end of the chain one of the dancers becomes angry at being told behind the positive character's back and rushes to embrace him. He looks overwhelmed by this emotional response.

DISCRIMINATION

DANCE SEQUENCE - The camera moves through groups of people standing and talking in a bar. One of the dancers whom we recognise from a previous sequence as being 'positive' is being ignored by the others. As the camera (slo mo) gets to each group they turn away. The positive person falls or is pushed. One of the guests kicks him while still balancing a drink in his hand. Another guest also kicks while a third spits. CU of camera being spat on.

Amelia
(Discusses the assumptions made by heterosexual males about women who are HIV+)
"To heterosexual males I think it is very much that attitude nice girls don't get that sort of thing, nice girls don't really talk about sex or enjoy it. They want you to be a whore in the bedroom and Doris Day at the dinner party."

IMAGE - Extract from the 60 Minutes episode in which Amelia took part, with the interviewer in a case of misplaced hysteria parading as concern, stressing "how important" the issue of HIV is among heterosexual women.

Amelia
Talks about the repercussions of her 60 Minutes interview, such as people staring at her in the street, walking on her roof and throwing condoms into her yard.

HIV COMMUNITY

Bruce
"I remember a couple of years ago, I was in The Stud in San Francisco and this guy was standing next to me. I looked at him and I thought, that looks like Robert. He looked at me, he said 'Bruce' – 'Robert' – 'You're still alive.' I said 'So are you.' He said 'Do you have AIDS?' I said 'Yes, do you?' 'Oh yes.' So that's a typical reunion in San Francisco, it's not quite that bad here but it's getting there."

IMAGE - CU of a thumb being pricked, then a second, then the two thumbs are pressed together as "blood brothers."

Alan
"The desire to create a positive safe space is a response to the level of discrimination faced by HIV+ people even within the gay community. It may be the only place where positive people don't have to spend half their time educating and negotiating, instead black humour reigns!"

DANCE SEQUENCE - A number of dancers are lying on the ground. A body is being pulled by a rope across the top of them. Each person reacts physically to the body either a hug / laughter / tears / other gestures.

IMAGE - We see a mid-shot of a good-looking man smiling into the camera. Details of a classified ad appear as text over top of his image. "HIV+ guy seeks same for fun time possible relationship."

Narrator I approached my first support group with some trepidation. I guess I always felt there was much more to my personality than just being gay and similarly being HIV+. But then I thought maybe I'll get to meet some really cute man there who is also positive. But unfortunately my next boyfriend wasn't there. Maybe next time.

(after V/O finishes) We see a close-up as he learns forward and whispers secretively:

"I'm actually negative you know."

DRAMA SEQUENCE - We see a couple walking down a corridor. One enters the door saying "positive support group", the other "negative support group." We follow the second. We see a group of people sitting in a circle.

Facilitator When did you first feel negative?

Narrator At the first national AIDS conference, Jim Dykes stood up and asked all the positive people in the audience to stand up. He was hissed down. Now a number of years later at a recent conference of NAPWA (National Association of People Living With AIDS) there was a demand for all those that weren't positive to leave the room. Although this was seen as very controversial there is now growing pressure from activists to disclose, to the community, as a political decision.

IMAGE - We see an image of a person's back, camera tracks to see the backs of a number of people sitting on seats. The first stands up, the others follow. They begin to stand and sit down, firstly in sequence and then quickly and at random.

Sound - we hear a loud cacophony of shouting voices.

IMAGE - The word OUT is barely visible and very small, and then very slowly fades up and grows larger at the same time until it fills the screen.

QUIZ SHOW

Compere Welcome to the next part of the show. Good to see you all still here. Things are getting tense here with Contestant No 1 with 200 T cells, No 2 with 180 T cells and No 3 with 240. I notice No 2 has had a change of outfit. Nice frock No 2 but with a T cell count like yours you need all the glamour you can get. But not to be outdone and just to remind you of our grand prizes here's 'Nurse' Julie.

'Nurse' Julie As always we have some fabulous prizes, donated by our sponsors, Coughman La Roach and Borrowes Hellecome. You have an opportunity to take part in a brand new experimental drug trial QT2748RZ, which may be a cure for AIDS. Or we have the bitter lemon enema which has proved very successful in the test-tube, although it takes a little practice to get your method right.

Compere The next part of the game is Social Security and Housing Skills, and here we are at the Department of Social Security.

Each of you will be given 20 different forms to fill out and you have three minutes, starting from now.

We'll be back in a minute with the results after the break.

IMAGE - 50's style advertisement, of a number of heads smiling and popping a pill, like clowns at a sideshow.

QUIZ SHOW

A dispute has occurred. The compere is standing in front of Contestant No 2.

Medical Expert

He should be disqualified for taking the wrong drug! We've just decided that DDC is this week's drug.

Compere I'm sorry Contestant No 2 but in the bylaws it says we can change the rules any time we want. You are disqualified for taking AZT on set.

Stuart "The next day I rang Bob Cremin up at the Herald Sun. I told him I'd read the article and that if he was interested I had a lot more interesting information about other people in the dance world who had AIDS. He was drooling at the mouth. We arranged to meet at a coffee shop.

He said 'What have you got for me?' and 'Who exactly are you?' 'Actually Mr Cremin, I'm Kelvin Coe's lover' and threw the paint over him."

We see red paint thrown at the camera. Stuart continues, obscured by the red paint.

"It went a long way. All over him. I was angry and my voice was shaking. I told him he had the morals of the gutter and what he had done had caused a person with AIDS a lot of worry and he deserved to get a lot more than this and he'd got off lightly. I was crying by now. They sat there then said "let's go" and dripped off. The manager came out to see what was going on. I explained. He said, "that's OK don't worry about the mess. Do you want a drink?""

A waiter begins to wipe the paint off the camera restoring our view.

(Stuart speaks about the process of blackmail used by Bob Cremin to out Stuart Challender and the lack of protection under the law. He then speaks about the ACT/UP team and the media campaign to explain the action, and the sympathetic response of most of the press. The Herald Sun began to try and spread rumours about Stuart holding up Bob Cremin with blood infected syringes. He also talks about how the AJA dismissed the outing of Kelvin Coe as trivial.)

Bruce   Explains how even within the HIV community there may be discrimination against people who are activists since other positive people don't want to be associated with them.

DANCE SEQUENCE (same sequence as the above body passing)

We see a number of people (standing this time) passing a person between them, suddenly they drop the person and walk away.

CHANGES IN SOCIETY

We see an image of a Sydney cityscape at dusk. We hear various phones ringing in different rooms but no-one answers. Text appears over image.

TEXT ON SCREEN -

"Tolerance is a more refined form of condemnation - *Pasolini*"

QUIZ SHOW

Compere   Now for the part of the show you have all been dying for. Can you find a cure for AIDS? We're here as guests of one of the largest pharmaceutical companies in Australia.

Contestant No 3 wins "Questionnaire Skills", but a disappointing T cell count of only 180. Contestant No 1 won "Disclosing Moments", "Pharmacy Sweeps" (cutaway to see the three contestants running through a pharmacy with shopping trolleys) and the "Outing Competition" (we see a photo of Liberace with a question mark over it) and wins with a overall T cell count of 450.

Congratulations No 1! You get to pick a box. We have a fabulous range of treatments available but beware **the placebo**."

Contestant No 1
I'll have the pretty pink capsule!

Compere   With the purple stripe or without?

Contestant No 1
With the purple stripe of course!
(drum roll)

Compere   I'm afraid it's the placebo, you're out of the game No 1.

Two ambulance officers come in and take him away on a stretcher as he struggles against them.

Compere   Well, that's it for the show tonight. I'm sure all you people at home can't wait for us to trial the next round of drugs but I'm afraid you have to wait another year for our next show, which will be brought to you from the International AIDS Conference where we'll be partying with all our scientific friends.

DANCE SEQUENCE - We see A's head in close up. It is partly obscured by very fast movements that at first look violent. These slow down to reveal fast hand movements which slowly become sensual. Still in close up we see A's head being balanced as if it were a ball. A game of movement and support begins. The two dancers both at various times in the dance cradling the other in their arms. It is a dance of love and support. Fade to black.

Bruce   *Black screen during V/O*
"I think there is a definite change but it's not the kind of

change that AIDS agencies like to trumpet because of all their campaigns. It has to do with several simple things, one of which is simple familiarity and the loss of the sensationalism. People have got tired and moved on to other topics that they are more interested in, Somalia and Bosnia and Romanian children and stuff like that.

I think a lot of gay men just wish it would go away. These AIDS people are kind of spoiling our good time, why don't they just dry up and die and blow away?"

Amelia   "When it comes down to gut reaction, and someone is put face to face with it, I think people are still absolutely petrified of this. It's basically unacceptable, you know, for a lot of people it's just too scary. You can talk about it and talk about it and talk about it but kiss me, hold me, fuck me, I'm HIV positive!"

Silence as Amelia leaves the room.

END
Copyright Suitcase Films, 1994.

FF: A FILM AND A FUNERAL

Michael Hurley

I MOVED MY THUMBS TO THE NAPE OF HIS NECK
and felt the lumps in the nodes of his lymphs.
He went still and tense.
"You're like my doctor," he said.
I ran my knee up his thigh.
"Does he do that?"
"No," he said. "I would hit him."

"I know who you are," he said.
"I know," I said. "We've been here before."
"You want more," he told me.
"Please," I said.

Michael Hurley recently received a 'Writers in the Community' grant from the Australia Council to work with the AIDS Council of NSW.

'FF: A Film and a Funeral' was a plenary presentation at the 'AIDS. HIV and Society,' annual conference of the National Centre for HIV Social Research, Macquarie University, July 1994. It is dedicated to Robert Martin, and appears here in a shorter form.

Michael is currently completing 'A Companion for Gay & Lesbian Writing in Australia.' His fiction has appeared in 'Two Timing. Sex, Writing and Writing of Sex,' co-written with Jan Hutchinson in 1991 and in the anthologies, 'Love Cries,' 1995; and 'My Look's Caress,' 1990.

He lives with Warwick, in bushy splendor, near the Marrickville Seven Eleven. He came 'out' in 1972 after growing up in army camps. It took him a long time to start liking uniforms.

I moved my thumbs into his mouth.
He moved his mouth to mine.
He pushed fingers into me.
I was held, fixed.
He moved his fingers and I came.
His spit dribbled down my thumbs.

Days later, I saw him at the clinic and we smiled.[1]

I keep thinking about the film 'Four Weddings and a Funeral'. I think about how it contains one of the most profound representations of one gay man grieving the loss of another that I have ever seen. And then I think about how that representation of a gay man's grief is used to signify the importance of love, a love in which the specifics of gayness disappear.

I think about how the relationship between these two men is empty of any hint of sexual activity between them, of how they barely touch at all, of how any notion of a wider gay community is absent from the film. There are no representations of HIV, safe sex or AIDS, though there are many instances of heterosexual sex.

It's a lot to think about, in a film that otherwise I found pleasant enough but nothing special.

At the same time as I think about this film I think about my friend Robert, who died last week and whose funeral I helped organise and spoke at last Friday, and of his partner, one of my closest friends. Robert is the eighth person I know to have died since October.

I'm not claiming any special status, here, many of you will be in the similar situations. The practical problem, for me as a writer, is how to tell the stories I want to tell without being abject or maudlin. If I were a drinker, these pages would reek of gin.

For an awful occasion, Robert's funeral was close to as good as they get. We draped the rainbow flag over his coffin, we colour co-ordinated, we played Queen and Elton John and Diana Ross, we spoke of his life and friends, of his partner, of his family, of his workplaces, of HIV and AIDS and we gathered in his name afterwards. We kept grieving his loss and were glad his long struggle with pain had ended.

So I want to talk about this film 'Four Weddings and a Funeral', about Robert's funeral, about loss and melancholia, about gayness and HIV, and, more allusively, about story telling, about living in, with and through the epidemic.

Again, this poses challenges for writers of all kinds. I find that if I tell a grand narrative of the epidemic, especially in all its international dimensions, then it's overwhelming. Cecil B. De Mille is a limited model, as is *Gone With the Wind*. AIDS does not have the cultural purchase of *The Bible*, and cannot be reduced to romantic nostalgia for a lost way of life. So I find smaller narratives more useful and more cheerful.

However, the smallness of a narrative does not automatically make its meaning clear. And it's this question of meanings that is my prime concern. I care about the stories that are told to me and that I tell because thay are part of negotiating living in the epidemic. What follows then is an exploration of some of the stories that are being told to us in this film and a consideration of the stories that I in turn tell myself. What you have to do is work out what these kinds of stories mean for you. It's not a matter of us agreeing on the stories and how they might be told but of recognising the importance of them to the quality of our lives.

The centrepiece for 'Four Weddings and a Funeral' is the funeral. It's the funeral of a gay man who dies from excessive living, probably of a heart attack. The man was a hedonist, in the sense of someone who lives life to the full through sensual pleasure. At the funeral, the dead man's lover speaks his grief and mourns his loss by reading W.H. Auden's poem 'Funeral Blues.' The performance of the eulogy and the reading of the poem allow two of the heterosexual male characters to recognise that the relationship between the two gay men is the fullest embodiment of love and commitment that they have ever known.

Unlike the various heterosexual weddings which formally announce and institutionalise love and commitment – and on which the film comments in a variety of ironic ways – the relationship between the gay men is only formally acknowledged with the funeral. The film uses the funeral to explore and demarcate the difference between officially sanctioned relationships and, if you like, real relationships.

Love between men briefly appears centre screen as symbolic of the real. This recognition that what matters is the relationship and not its status, as a social institution, then allows the lead heterosexual male to jilt his bride-to-be at the altar and to commit to his true love in a marriage of the heart. Herein, says the film, lies the real possibility of living life to the full.

Whatever we think of this collapsing of friendship, sex, love and commitment into notions of permanent relationships, this is the territory the film is set up to explore.

Having the gay men signify love by giving them a wedding in Westminster Abbey would have been both too camp and unpopular for this kind of film. What you *can* give gay men in a film such as this is a funeral.

Now, if you haven't already guessed, I'm fairly ambivalent about all this. Firstly, the funeral scene, as I keep saying, is immensely powerful. One man speaks of his love for another, from 'Funeral Blues':

> *He was my North, my South, my East and West,*
> *My working week and my Sunday rest,*
> *My noon, my midnight, my talk, my song;*
> *I thought that love would last forever: I was wrong.*[2]

The man being mourned was portly, maybe in his late forties, given to colourful waistcoats, good food, the pleasures of drink and dancing, cigars; he had an eye for the tasteless and mocked pretension; he loved life and his partner. He is, in this sense, represented as a classic pleasure lover who pays the price of high living. He is also a working class man who makes good by adopting particular epicurean habits which make him socially acceptable to the bohemian edges of upper class English society as represented in the film.

His partner is, at first sight, quite different: slighter in build and a little younger, more socially restrained, sober if not sombre in dress and highly eroticised by his delightful Scottish accent. You'd lie down just to hear him speak. He lives, and gets to deliver *the funeral oration*. On the surface, at least, he's not a hedonist but *why not?* He has the same friends, attends the same parties and is very much part of the social circle. He also appears to be living life to the full. We see this in the pain at the loss of his partner:

> *Let aeroplanes circle moaning overhead,*
> *Scribbling on the sky the message He is Dead.*

And in the final verse:

> *The stars are not wanted now; put out every one;*
> *Pack up the moon and dismantle the sun;*
> *Pour away the ocean and sweep up the wood;*
> *For nothing now can ever come to any good.*

It's an extraordinary performance of homosexual love, albeit in grief, and this must be given full acknowledgment – for its rarity in mainstream cinema and for it, superficially at least, remaining outside the arena of the epidemic and AIDS films.

And it is important that it chooses to signify that the epidemic is not the sole cause of gay death, nor the sole constituent of gay life, however much it sometimes seems to be.

I want to return to those images of two gay men living life to the full. They are themselves constrained in the film. This constraint is productive, although I would argue in a negative way. Firstly, while the relationship between these two men is made exemplary of love and commitment, there is no hint of sex and little if any of touching between them. Why not? The reason, I would argue, is a calculation about the acceptability of representing gay sex to a general audience in the Age of AIDS. It's a calculation about risk. It is a calculation that says, not so much gayness = contagion = AIDS, but that gay sex *will* signify AIDS. The possibility, the fear, that gay sex would be read as HIV infectious sex by an audience has the effect of removing all notions of sex between the film's gay lovers. The film's ethic of representation tends to sanitise their sexuality in order to make them generally acceptable as models of love and, thus, to establish the central metaphoric structure of the movie.

This sanitisation allows for heterosexuals something which has been consistently refused for gays in the cultural panic surrounding sex and HIV. It allows the question of viral transmission to be silently separated from the question of sex. In this sense, the virus is present in its absence for both heterosexuals and gays. I don't want to decry this presence in absence. Rather, I want to look at its implications at the level of what the film actually attempts and achieves.

After all, it does reverse more conventional, predictable representations of gay love by making it a metaphor for *real* love. Its achievement at this level can be seen in the film's success at the box office and in the subsequent public demand for the Auden poem, necessitating its rushed and relatively mass reprinting by Faber & Faber.

So, I am arguing that the film positively enacts a version of gay grief/love, which is then shifted and reincorporated into a narrative of heterosexual melancholia in which masculinity is the lost object.

In terms of the film's frame of reference and its popularity with gay and gay friendly audiences, it doesn't appear to matter that the gay sex is never validated, nor that masculinity should not be perceived as something *heterosexual*, to be lost. If I were any more despairing, I might suggest that the normalisation of gay love and the sheer power of the funeral scene are found to be sufficient crumbs at the banquet of life.

What I would rather suggest, however, is that the film allows us as people living in and with the epidemic to reinscribe *gayness* into the heart of the epidemic - on our own terms. This film also contains a rare instance within mainstream culture of asserting what the gay communities have known for some time: that the communal speaking of grief is central to living in the epidemic and that celebrations of gayness are a life affirming rejoinder to a world which prefers the grief to remain unspeakable.

So, in the wider context of the AIDS epidemic, I want to argue that this evacuation of gay content from the film matters very much, that the stories we narrate about gayness, masculinity, HIV, shame and melancholia are central to how we live in and through this epidemic.

On Saturday, the day after my friend Robert's funeral, I had to begin writing this paper. As it happens, Saturday was also the third anniversary of another friend's death from AIDS. I forgot until the next day. Writing this paper was the last thing I felt able to do. Part of me would rather have said, "No, it's too hard," and gone to bed, there to ask my partner to fuck me into oblivion.

This desire to be fucked into oblivion, into forgetfulness, might be characterised as symptomatic of both a specific grief over Robert's death and of a more general AIDS melancholia and a desire to escape from it. It could also be seen as an acting out of grief. I cannot pretend that the epidemic is not affecting me. Nor do I want to.

The poem 'Funeral Blues' suggests that grief never ends - *For nothing now can come to any good.* That last line captures the intensity of the felt experience and speaks it as an everlasting finality. I like it for its force, although I fear the attractiveness of its despair. In Freudian terms, it suggests both aspects of melancholia - a sustained identification with the object of loss, and the possibility of that loss being continuously acted out. That is, and somewhat paradoxically, melancholia involves an unresolved grief which reproduces itself, not necessarily because the loss can't be acknowledged but because it can't be let go of. Melancholia involves a fantasy in which the lost object is an ever-present phantasm. A phantasm whose presence respeaks and intensifies the original loss. And the pain this reiteration causes can become a self-directed rage of suicidal proportions.

I said I had known eight people who had died since last October. One was an HIV negative man who suicided. He was twenty-three. I'm told he left a note saying life had neither purpose nor meaning. He was closely engaged with the epidemic.

While 'Funeral Blues' suggest the possibility of melancholia and despair, 'Four Weddings and a Funeral' refuses it. The speaker of the poem, the aggrieved lover, is shown nearly a year later, going out with another man. The character's grief, in that sense at least, is resolved.

The sanitisation of gayness in the film alerts us to the difference between how gayness appears in the film and how it signifies in the wider culture. We have seen that the film chooses to bar sex from the signifiers of gayness because of a fear the audience might mobilise discourses which collapse gay sex into HIV infectiousness.

There is a dematerialisation of the body, a removal of the flesh, through a tidying up process in which dicks never meet arseholes in a flood of sweat and semen. Condoms, in this scenario, would simply signify the messiness of undifferentiated body fluids.

For this fear, it doesn't matter whether the sex is safe. The HIV status of its participants doesn't even make it over the horizon of consideration. There is another aspect, however, to taking gay bodies *out* of the epidemic. We could for our purposes see it as a strategic way of making gayness signify ways of living life to the full, ways that are not pathologised by notions of either melancholy or disease. This is, of course, the tricky bit, the bit that has preoccupied us politically for at least the last twenty-five years. The bit that has been even more difficult since the epidemic began. I'm referring to how we have never really achieved public narratives that articulate either the relationships between HIV and the gay community, or the close relationships between the PLWHA and gay communities without collapsing one into the other.

Maybe speaking my desire for such narratives is misplaced, is in itself a sentimental gesture. I would argue, in a way loosely parallel to the film, that this imaginary in which queer life and living with the epidemic are narrated separately and together is a crucial element if we are not to lock ourselves into an allegory of life in the epidemic as a life ultimately doomed to emptiness. The silence over gay sex in 'Four Weddings and A Funeral' does precisely that.

I used queer deliberately here, because this project of speaking for ourselves has to allow for the chaos of multiplicity. There is for these purposes no single gay body, no single imaginary that can easily encompass us all. For these purposes, however, Mardi Gras and the contestation of who it is for is a site of the imaginary. Of whom we might be and what we might have to say.

At the time I was preparing for Robert's funeral, I was meant to be attending a family reunion in Perth. I spoke to one of my sisters, biological not tribal. I like this sister, she was the first member of the family I came out to and has always been generally supportive. I told her I would not be at the reunion. (She knew Robert had a partner) She asked why Robert's parents were not organising the funeral. I asked her, if she died, would our parents organise her funeral. The answer was obvious. No, her husband or children would. What staggered me was the unintentional ease with which she ignored Robert's death, Robert's partner and my own twenty-five-years friendship with Robert.

It would be easy to be bitter about this incident. It meant, however, that I had some understanding of the bitterness when someone at the funeral remarked that *you would think they'd have discovered a cure by now*, and someone responded by saying he sometimes suspected a cure had been found only it wasn't profitable enough to release.

I want to use these anecdotes to illustrate two points about how we narrativise stories about the epidemic. My first point is that you get out of narratives, which you tell yourself, precisely what you put into them. For instance, what I didn't tell you, back there, was that I have another sister who encouraged me to ignore the family reunion and to be with the people with whom I really live my life. Since saying that, she has telephoned back several times. If I incorporate both sisters into my narrative then the world is not so bleak. Nor is it so simple.

My second and final point is even more straight forward. I don't want to either deny or pathologise the bitterness that AIDS creates. Nor do I want to elevate that bitterness to being the story of our times. Robert once told me a very macabre joke: *How do you know your garden has AIDS? All the pansies are dead.* We laughed together. Then he went out and lived the fullest life he could for as long as he could.

If I stop at this point then there's a good chance that I will feel overwhelmed by feelings of loss at Robert's death and by the relentlessness of the epidemic. While I want to acknowledge these feelings I don't want to be permanently disabled by them. Like Robert, and like the lover who survives in 'Four Weddings', I want the fullness of life. I have to find and tell other stories that give meaning and purpose to living. Storytelling is part of keeping on finding and making new perspectives on harsh realities. Keeping on requires delight in daily living. We can find and make that delight in the stories we tell to ourselves and to each other.

It is the Sunday before the Tuesday. I have a date.

Moving bodies and behaviours, places, people, around pages.

He is in a strange city, in a new place. He is in the dark. It's humid in there. Maybe twenty men in a space three metres by three metres. His torso is almost bare, Sweat courses his spine. He is encircled, embraced, groped, separated out, kissed by someone he can only touch. He is in the dark. Is it you? He touches the body. Feels its shape. No, maybe it's that other, yes, there, suck me there, and yes squeeze. His T shirt goes over his head, he straddles to keep his pants from the ground. He groans, he fingers and mouths and breathes and runs with sweat and the voice of the body, the getting to be known body, the knowing body, the voice of that body, speaks: "Do you love me?" Silent at first, incredulous, shocked, he begins to laugh; he breaks into hysterical laughter. Romance often takes him this way. In the dark. With twenty strange men. He senses prohibition. (In this place only certain sounds are desired: zip sounds, moist sounds, grunts,

moans. Speech and laughter are intrusive. Unerotic. Like this parenthesis.) The held body stiffens into affront as he laughs into breathlessness. He clutches it, denying rejection, presuming a joke, encouraging complicity. You're clever. Look what you've done. The wit. The speaker too begins to laugh. They cannot see. They are too weak to stand. They fall into the darkness. They laugh together.

I am in a strange city in a new place.
I am living in the dark.[3]

1,3   Michael Hurley and Jan Hutchinson, 'Two Timing. Sex, Writing and the Writing of Sex,' Local Consumption Publications, Sydney, 1991, pp. 21,22,25.

2   'Funeral Blues', 'Tell Me the Truth About Love.' Ten poems by W.H. Auden, Faber and Faber, London, 1994.

N.B. 'Four Weddings and a Funeral' released on video December, 1994.

LAST CHANCE FOR VESUVIUS

Ben Widdicombe

R OBERT AND I ARE AT SEPARATE
tables. He has spilt something from a tall glass and a waiter is lifting his plate to lay
a napkin underneath.

I can see the waiter holding the plate high above peoples' heads, saying "No sir,
no trouble at all." Next to him a woman changes place with her husband.

"...and a toaster and a blender and a thing to juice oranges. And an espresso
machine, well, I think it's an espresso machine. Maybe it's a cappuccino maker."

Nasi squeezes my wrist as she speaks. In the last forty minutes she has acquired
two dinner - sets, a kitchen full of appliances and a husband.

"It's both," I say. "From Robert and me."

My place-card is in the shape of two bells, tied together with pink and blue
ribbon. It says 'Best Man'.

"Oh, David. You always know just the right thing." She squeezes even more
tightly and smiles.

Around us the room is dotted with sprays of white roses on white damask table-
cloths, with page-boys and bridesmaids in pale, pale beige. Nasi is dressed in the

*Ben Widdicombe lives in London, but just now he's wondering why. You have to be a millionaire to own a
dishwasher and the hot and cold water always comes out of different taps.*
*He attended secondary schools in Queensland and Kent, before graduating from the University of California in
1991. He works in the arts and contributes to newspapers and magazines around the world.*
In Australia his fiction has been published by Black Wattle Press and Outrage magazine.

purest white, and her skin pours from the dress like coffee out of porcelain.

She is beautiful.

" Can you believe he still hasn't told me where the honeymoon is? I said it had better be somewhere warm or I'll divorce him, but he says he wants it to be a surprise."

In front of us are three hundred people. There is a bench for presents along the back wall and a photographer with a moustache who has spilt Coronation Chicken on his suit.

I hear Robert's voice rise above the crowd for a moment and say "darling," but he is not talking to me. He is telling a story, and between the heads of the other guests I can see pearls of spittle flying out of his mouth, the way they do when he's drunk. The photographer takes his picture.

"I've got to get back to my chair," says Nasi, "here comes the pudding. You're not going to say anything too embarrassing, are you?"

"I..."

"Has anyone seen my wife?" Dai calls from three places along.

Nasi laughs and says, "David was just chatting me up."

"You have to watch him you know," he says, and then to me, "she's spoken for now."

I unhook part of Nasi's dress from the chair as she rustles back over to her husband. She arranges herself at her place and, once settled, her father takes the napkin out of his lap. He is a stout man and takes a moment to rise.

I take a sip of water and wait for his knife to strike the glass.

"God, my grandmother actually remembers the Raj," said Dai in the vestry when I was helping him with his cuff-links. "And Nasi's grandfather offered her five hundred pounds to marry some man he found for her in Croyden. I can't believe these people are going to be in the same room. Did I give you the ring already or do I still have it?"

"I have it. Hold still."

"Christ. You don't know how lucky you are, never having to go through this."

"Mmm," I said, closing the cuff around his wrist.

"Not too tight," he said.

"Sorry."

Some one has turned on a spotlight. The three hundred people have settled down to their coffee and summer-fruit trifle, but to my startled eyes they could be three thousand.

The photographer has set up his camera.

"I suppose," I say, peering into the bright mist of faces, "that it's customary for, um, the best man, to say a few words," I am turning my place card over and over in my hand, wishing I had notes to hold instead, "and I'm sure you'd, um, like those words to be as few as possible."

There is a little laughter and shapes shift slightly in the gloom.

"But I would like to, perhaps, tell a story about the groom before the other speakers have a chance to get up and tell you what wonderful people the couple both are. To mix a little truth with wine, so to speak and ...I thought I might tell you the story of how Dai broke his nose."

There is silence for a moment and Robert makes a sound like a snore. I swallow. I remember.

On graduation day, Dai's parents came down from Cheshire, they came in a burgundy Ford.

'What's that?" he said, after he had shaken hands with his father and hugged his mother so that it bent the brim of her hat. "It's a new car," said his father, sullen in the way fathers are.

Dai curled his lip. "You're joking. Dad, what have you done with the Jag?"

And when his father pressed the keys in his hand he understood.

I was tying my tie at the time, four stories up from the gravel in our little attic room. The window was on Dai's side, and to step up and look out of it was always a little illicit. I had to touch my forehead to the top of the glass to see.

Then Dai motioned to someone standing in the door of the boarding-house and Alison stepped out from the building. She seemed nervous; his mother smiled.

"It was after our last year of school, you see, and Dai ... Dai and I had agreed to go around the continent together."

I am scraping beneath my fingernails with the place-card and as soon as I realise I'm doing it I put it down quickly.

"And so we bought the tickets, you know, two of those all inclusive month-long things that used to let you go anywhere, and we made up a list of things to take. Oh, and Dai insisted on buying a propane stove which he carried around for the whole time and didn't use once."

I am distracted for a moment by the memory of he and Alison on the driveway. He kept that Ford right through University, until he crashed it one night on the drive up to Cheshire. He could have killed himself.

"At least, I didn't see him use it." My hand finds a water glass. I drink.

"Excuse me. I can, ahem, remember, though ... in those days the tickets came with a big map of all the routes they covered, which you could fold out, and I remember spreading it over the floor of the room at the top of the boarding-house which we shared and plotting our course across Europe. I kept a list of the cities we wanted to visit, and dates we had to be there by.

"But there was a girl around at the time, you see, called Alison. She was in the year below us and I guess Dai had always fancied her and never done anything about it, but then one night, about three weeks before we were due to leave, she cornered him after dinner and said how sad she was that he was going. And then it was on."

People laugh, now, and begin to recognise the elements of a Best Man's speech. The bride and groom both look pleased to be uncomfortable.

"So that was fine, I mean, it was only going to be for three weeks right? I wasn't too worried. But then one day about a week before we were going to start our trip Dai comes up to me and tells me he'd invited Alison to come with us."

The men in the audience go "oooh", as if they were at a pantomime. Robert has begun talking with the woman sitting next to him.

"And I ... well, you know, I was a little disappointed because I was looking forward to having the trip, you know, just the two of us. But Dai says it's alright because it won't make any difference and it'll still be our trip just the same. And since he seems like he's already made up his mind I say yes. Big mistake."

There is more jovial laughter, now, and people use the pause to pick up their drinks. I can tell from the sound of glass that most have moved back to wine.

"When we got to France, it was all rose gardens and bistros and walks by the river. No Louvre. Alison didn't like art. No opera. Alison didn't like opera. And that was alright, because I'd made a mental decision that I wasn't going to be a bum, fussy, right off. I mean I could afford to give them a little space. After all, I'd just done a lot better in our A-levels than Dai and I thought I could afford to be generous."

Dai laughs. Nasi sighs. Dai and Nasi's parents laugh. I remember.

I remember a pensione in Ercalano with lemon trees. It had a view of the sea if you stood on the roof and a view of the town from our room.

We had brought little glass vials, stolen from the college laboratory, which we had labelled together at school. The labels had name like 'Water from the Seine' and 'Marble from the Acropolis', and were meant to be things we could keep to remind us of our trip.

The empties were wrapped up in tissue-paper. I went through my pack and found 'Dust from Vesuvius'.

"*We won't be closer,*" *I said,* "*we should get it now.*"

I remember Alison was sitting on the windowsill, rubbing something unnecessary into her legs. She had eyes that were always half closed, no matter what time of day it was.

"*I'm sleepy,*" *she said,* "*you go.*"

Dai was sitting on the only chair in the room, rocking backwards and forwards with his feet on the edge of the bed. Alison was looking at him with her intentful, lazy stare.

"*We won't have time before the train tomorrow,*" *I said, purposefully making it difficult for him,* "*it's our last chance.*"

I thought - you owe this to me.

"*I'll come right down,*" *he said, looking at Alison and then quickly back at me.* "*In a second.*"

And his eyes said he meant it, so I went on ahead.

Forty minutes later I let myself back in through the door. I had cut the heel of my hand, scraping dirt into the jar, and it was still only half full.

Alison was asleep, and Dai lay weakly against her. The light from the window had fallen away from the bed and the air was sick with the smell of them.

When Dai heard me come in he stood quickly, reflexively. He grabbed the thin cotton sheet to cover his nakedness, and as Alison stirred I hit him.

'Dust of Vesuvius' shattered across the floor and I left the room, the pensione, Italy.

Three weeks later he posted me 'Marble from the Acropolis' and we had lunch.

"And I suppose everything must have been alright because here we both are tonight."

There is laughter and applause and clinking of glasses when I sit back down. Dai is shaking a finger and smiling from ear to ear. Nasi is clapping.

After the rest of the speeches we move to the back of the room where the wedding cake has a table of its own. There are three large layers, with little plastic columns in between. On the upper-most layer a model bride and groom stand beneath a flowered trellis.

Nasi is saying "Is this low-fat, darling? I hope this is low-fat." And people laugh.

Robert puts his mouth to my ear and says, "This is so incredibly boring. The next time one of your friends gets married, leave me out of it."

Dai and Nasi touch their hands to the knife and as it sinks through the cake a flash bounces off their white, white smiles.

FREEFALLING

Peter Dickinson

T ODAY MY BOYFRIEND AND I ARE
moving in together. The next logical step, you might say. For the past year or so I've
been spending at least four nights out of every week at Stephen's place. Got my own
tooth brush, a chipped and stained mug in the cupboard that seems almost to have
moulded to the curve of my palm, the press of my lips, a corner in the bedroom for
some of my school stuff. Most of my clothes are already hanging up in his closet.
It's just a matter of bringing the rest over, along with a few books, and some minor
personal effects. Like my collection of angel ephemera. And Myrtle, the little
plastic turtle my friend Lila gave me.

Lila lived across the hall from me in residence at Uof T. She had real turtles then.
Until she was forced to get rid of them after someone complained about the smell.
Lila always maintained it was Persimmon, the pseudo-anarchist from Etobicoke with
the fake British accent, who ratted her out to the Dean. Soon after she'd deposited the

*Peter Dickinson lives in Vancouver, Canada, with his partner, Richard, amid an odd assortment of perennial plants
and a growing collection of crystal phalli. He is a Ph.D. student in the Department of English at the University
of British Columbia, but would really rather be a dancer. To this end, he is currently enrolled in an adult beginners'
ballet class and has dreams of working with 'Mischa' one day.*

*He has published critical articles in a wide variety of scholarly journals across Canada and his short stories have
appeared in the 'Sodomite Invasion Review' and 'Queeries: An anthology of Gay Male Prose' (Vancouver:
Arsenal Pulp, 1993).*

*"My partner and I would love to come to Sydney for Mardi Gras. We've heard that Sydney is the 'queerest' city
in the world these days."*

last of her slimy hard-backed friends with an obliging, if not overly eccentric, aunt who ran a boarding house in the Annex, Lila purchased an army of plastic turtles — 200 at 10 cents a piece at Honest Ed's — which she proceeded to leave discreetly all over our floor: in the common room, on toilet seats, in Persimmon's bed.

Lila and I both moved out of residence after second year. She'd fallen in love with some Frenchman she met on a plane and was chasing after him to Paris. I'd simply grown tired of having the word *faggot* scrawled across my dorm room door. Myrtle, the sole survivor of Lila's reptilian army, was bequeathed to me as part of a tearful exchange in a bar on Queen Street. Take care of her, Lila said, removing a tiny match box from her purse and placing it on the table. Then she kissed me, turned, walked briskly toward the exit, and slipped quietly into the dusky Toronto night.

Most of the time I keep Myrtle hidden in the same tattered match box, at the back of a bureau drawer, underneath some sweaters. I only take her out on special occasions. Or when I'm feeling sad. But I'd never leave her behind; I'd never forget Myrtle. I don't own much furniture, at least nothing of any value, or weight.

Stephen and I met two years ago in a graduate seminar on 'The Social Construction of Memory' at the University of British Columbia. He sat down across from me and smiled and I forgot all about my previous lovers. Their faces just disappeared from my mind. Phhht! Whoosh! Gone, without a trace. Which, for a time, is exactly the way I wanted it. Then, slowly, he helped me to remember. The way he rubs the back of my neck when we watch television, elbow resting on my shoulder, thumb and fingers working in opposite directions, pinching squeezing stroking, that reminds me of Malcolm. And whenever he cooks Italian I always think of Ken because they both like their pasta aldente. Never too soft, Stephen explains, tonguing a half-cooked noodle lasciviously and eyeing my crotch. His laugh is similar to Paul's — high-pitched and sing-songy, almost a giggle. Not that I think of him as a mere composite of all the men I've ever dated or slept with. He has his own idiosyncrasies, most of which I'm rather fond of.

But, you see, I can't leave it at that. It's not enough. Because what I love most about Stephen is precisely that which I cannot describe in words, that connection between two people that occurs only in lovemaking, captured in that end-time of desire when he throws his head back and clenches his teeth and comes inside me, and I see reflected there in his eyes, in the pupils, refracted by the light, a look that says you move me, you're moving me, don't let go, hold on.

Because that's what it's all about, I've decided. When you fall for someone new. It's an act of gravity: three parts inertia, one part leap of faith. And for a second there you're suspended. Like Wile E. Coyote after he's chased the Roadrunner over the edge of yet another cliff. But then — Beep, Beep! — gravity kicks in again. And all you can do is hope to hell that someone is there to catch you before you hit the ground.

Stephen has booked the afternoon off work to help me move. The plan is that I'll spend the morning packing up my apartment (since I'm between jobs at the moment), and then Stephen will swing by with a rental car around 2:00 p.m.

I'm sorting through the last of my clothes, trying to decide which items are necessary components of my wardrobe and which I can safely donate to Goodwill, when the blaring of Erasure's cover of ABBA's *Take a Chance on Me* outside my building indicates that Stephen has arrived. I have a hard-on the size of a rocket ship, he announces as soon as he's through the door. (Driving always makes Stephen horny. Something about working the gear shift, I think.) "Did you know I have six pairs of these?"I say, holding aloft faded and ripped Levis for his inspection. "Why would I ever need six pairs?" I continue, somewhat rhetorically, all the while coyly pretending to avert my gaze from Stephen's gyrating hips. "Some of them must be at least eight years old," I'm just plain prattling now, retreating across the room in the wake of Stephen's advancing hips, tripping over piles of clothes and books and computer equipment —"I mean, who knows if they even fit anymore?"

"Try them on and see,"Stephen suggests, pinning me up against the radiator in the corner and licking the inside of my ear, soft and cool, like a wet Q-tip. "Shouldn't we start loading the car?"I protest half-heartedly, feeling the rise and swell of my own cock. The thought of making it in an empty apartment — on the floor, against a wall, perched on a counter-top — does excite me, I have to admit. I'm already anticipating the scars we'll receive, how to avoid possible splinters, the pattern the bathroom tiles will make on our elbows and knees."Plenty of time,"he says, tossing me what's obviously the tightest and most revealing pair,"I want to see you strip first."

An object at rest tends to stay at rest. An object in motion tends to stay in motion.

Newton's first laws of gravity. Or so I was taught by Mr. Steenhof in Grade 11 Physics, a class I almost failed. It was those goddamn navigational diagrams. No matter how hard I tried, I couldn't seem to get my car or bus or train or ship going in the same direction as everyone else's. And even when I did manage to set them off on the right axis or angle or trajectory, they inevitably arrived half an hour behind schedule. A panic-induced cram session the night before the final exam, along with some neatly cribbed formulae on the back of my trusty Texas Instruments calculator, saw me passing by the skin of my teeth.

That was in 1983, when the only consolation offered by Mr. Steenhof's class was having the divine Brent Hathaway as lab partner. Back then Brent was what

Stephen and I would now call a definite L.O.I. That's short for 'lad of interest.' He had it all: great jugs, lovely handles, gorgeous spout. The whole kitchen sink, as Stephen would say. He was also class president, captain of the hockey team, and, oh yes, resolutely straight. Studying with him after school, in his bedroom, while his parents were still at work, I did my best to alter certain laws of physical attraction. But the most I could coax out of him was the occasional sixty-nine. Now, a decade and a bit later, I find myself thinking about Brent more and more, especially while waiting at airports, or, like now, when stuck in traffic.

"No one is *resolutely straight*,"Stephen says to me as we inch along Broadway. Leave it to a couple of dizzy fags like us to choose the Thursday afternoon before a long week-end to transport one medium-sized car load of stuff eleven blocks. "A shopping cart would have been faster," I mumble under my breath.

Stephen points to Brent's willingness to suck and be sucked off as proof of his assertion. Then he launches into a five minute harangue against the evils of *compulsory heterosexuality* and life in the closet, during which time I study the big welt forming on the inside of his left arm. Over the past half hour it's slowly turned from white to red to a most wondrous shade of mauve, so that it now matches the colour of the oval border outlining the logo on the *Stonewall 25* T-shirt Stephen is wearing

One of the hazards of sex with me. I used to think I was a clumsy lover until Stephen convinced me I was just passionate. He said we would always be able to judge the ardour of our relationship by the number of bruises on our bodies. So far so good, I think, examining the tiny cuts and abrasions dotting my own exposed shin. Although after today our friends are definitely going to start suspecting certain proclivities toward S/M.

My parents moved around a lot when I was a kid. Fredericton, New York, Sherbrooke, Montréal, Mississauga, Montréal: we were the only Anglos I knew of who headed back into the fray of Québec separatist politics after making it to the apparent safe haven of life in the Toronto suburbs. I think I must have picked up something of their peripatetic bug. It's not that I've lived in tons of different cities since moving out of my parents' place — just Toronto for four years, and now here, in Vancouver. But I do tend to change apartments quite frequently. For a while there it was every six months, until my friend Caitlin screamed that she had no space left in her address book under the *D*s. I stayed put for a whole year after that, just so I could get a Christmas card from her without one of those little yellow stickers pasted on it from the post office. I'm quite adept at packing now. I can be out of a place in a matter of hours. I don't even bother with boxes anymore. I just shove everything into plastic bags.

"I've married a bag lady," Stephen exclaims as he hoists the last of my stuff out of the trunk: a large Gap bag containing some books, and a couple of generic-plain-white-convenience-store-models into which I've dumped sundry toiletries. "Bag person," he amends, noticing my menacing glare.

Stephen is far more rooted, I think. He's lived in the same place for the past eight years. Hasn't so much as rearranged a stick of furniture in the time I've known him. For a while this terrified me, but now I find it reassuring. To know where everything is. To be able to walk around in the dark and not stumble. To be able to reach out and grab onto something solid and permanent: a chair-back, the corner of a desk, the body lying next to you.

It's not a big space, Stephen's apartment. Mine too now, I guess. But it's irregularly shaped, so there are lots of little nooks and crannies. Just waiting to be filled with my stuff, he says to me, grinning foolishly. I appreciate his eagerness. Part of me is worried about upsetting the delicate balance he's created in the years he's spent here without me. With someone else for at least two of them. How will his already over-stuffed shelves accommodate the weight of my books, their dust? Do we each get a separate drawer in the bureau and a portion of the closet, or do we actually give a fuck if our clothes get mixed up, whose socks we're wearing? How will the molecules in the air adjust to the arrival of foreign objects, new things, me?

I confess my anxieties to Stephen but he just laughs and gives me a hug. He's already started sorting through the heap of junk in the middle of the living room floor. He's decided to hang my Japanese wind chime — another gift from Lila — in front of the sliding doors to the balcony, so that it will clink and jangle whenever there's a breeze. Barring that, he says, we can always use it as a dinner bell. I pass him the hammer and a nail. Then I hold the chair on which he's standing. So he won't fall.

I have this crazy dyke friend, Viv. We used to be room-mates. She once tried to convince me and my then boyfriend, Jeffrey, to go bungee jumping with her. She'd heard it was the greatest high. Just attach a springy rope to your feet and jump off the nearest bridge or building or construction crane. Nothing to it, she said. Completely safe, she said. No way, we said.

A month later, Jeffrey left me for some blonde bimbo with his own MG and I was seriously contemplating jumping off any tall structure, with or without a cord. Viv gave me a superball instead. No matter how high you bounce it, she said, it will always come back. Within five minutes it was lodged in the styrofoam ceiling of my basement suite.

Viv called the other day and invited Stephen and me out dancing with her and her girlfriend, Louise. They had just decided to move in together, as well. "Lezzie smoker finally finds same," she screamed into the phone. Then, a little quieter: it would be like a group house-warming. "A house-warming without the house," I said, mulling over the idea. "But with House music," she said, trying to sound encouraging. The closest queers get to marriage, I said.

It was a fun evening, although the dancing part kind of sucked. The music was terrible — not even house, some sort of techno-flamenco fusion, I think — and the club was overrun with straights. The four of us took over a pool table and proceeded to get pissed. At one point Viv leaned over as I was lining up a shot, trying desperately to get the three balls I was aiming at to focus into one, and asked me how you spotted a straight woman on the dance floor. I shrugged my shoulders. White pumps, she said. A dead give away. Then she asked me if I knew which men were straight. Sure, I said, missing the cue ball for the fourth time in a row, the ones whose pants hang low at the back.

I'm hanging up my six pairs of faded and ripped Levis in the bedroom when Stephen bursts in and informs me breathlessly that tomorrow is the twenty-fifth anniversary of the American moon landing. He heard it on the news just now. They're planning all kinds of celebrations at the NASA headquarters in Cape Canaveral, he says. Imagine, human beings landing on the moon less than a month after the Stonewall Riot in New York. You'd think the two events were connected somehow. Not that you'd ever guess it from the amount of mainstream media coverage afforded commemoration of the latter. Astronauts versus drag queens. I mean, who would you choose?

In 1969 I was one year old. Stephen was ten. But he doesn't remember where he was or what he was doing when Apollo 11 landed. He likes to think he felt something when that rag-tag bunch of queers gathered at the Stonewall Inn to mourn the death of Judy Garland hurled pennies at the cops.

The moon isn't such a hot spot anymore in terms of space travel. Mars, maybe. Jupiter and Saturn, certainly. But not the moon. I mention this to Stephen, who's gone back to alphabetising the CDs, interspersing my meagre few among his massive collection. He agrees, but thinks it's just a phase. Pretty soon people will be travelling to the moon again, he assures me, adding that when they do, we'll be first in line. And then he proceeds to tell me how when he was nineteen he won this contest sponsored by Air Canada. First prize: two free tickets aboard the airline's inaugural commercial flight to the moon. "Do you still have them?" I ask. "Of course," he says, selecting a disk to play from the pile on the sofa.

Queers in space. Sounds like a B-movie from the fifties. Stranger things have happened, I suppose. I mean, look at the Muppets.

I look across the room at Stephen. He's cranked the volume on REM and he's already dancing toward me, limbs flailing in that frenetic sort of way he has. "We could always hijack the plane," I yell. "Pick up all our friends before we leave the stratosphere," he shoots back, almost on top of me now. Start our own colony, I think, just as his mouth covers mine and I reach inside his pants.

If you believe they put a man on the moon. . . .

Ever have one of those dreams where you're falling? All day today it hasn't felt like that.

THREE FABLES

Suniti Namjoshi

The Example

AND THE SPARROWS' CHILDREN NEED
a tutor, so they hired a wren. The wren did her job conscientiously and diligently, but the sparrow parents criticised her colour, her modest exterior, and made fun of her sometimes because she wasn't married. And the sparrows' children were like any other children, wily and wilful, simple and gentle, and sometimes very kind and sometimes mean. Then, one day, there was a tremendous scandal. The birds has discovered that the wren's sexuality was not what it should be. They feared for their children. What if the wren should corrupt them morally? They summoned the wren and demanded an explanation.

And the wren said, "What is private is private, and what is public is public."

"Oh no," said the parents. "We understand, you know, that you are not only a lesbian, but also a feminist, and feminists maintain that the public and private are not distinct."

"But I don't teach sex," said the wren, "I teach reading and writing and simple arithmetic."

"Ah, but what you are, after all, is something that our very own children

---

Suniti Namjoshi was born in India. She has worked as an officer in the Indian Administrative Service and in academic posts in India and Canada. Since 1972 she has taught in the Department of English at the University of Toronto and now lives and writes in Devon, England.

She has published numerous poems, fables, articles and reviews in anthologies, collections and journals in India, Canada, the US, Australia and Britain.

Her publications include five books of poetry in India and three in Canada.

might turn out to be. And what you are is dreadful and horrid."

"I am not dreadful and I am not horrid," said the wren indignantly.

"That makes it worse. You set an example," said the parents sternly.

"So do you," said the wren.

"Well, you're fired," was the parents' verdict.

And so the sparrows' children grew up anyhow and some were horrid, and some resisted it.

THE WICKED WITCH

A rather handsome young dyke strode through the forest and knocked at the door of a small house, which belonged to a witch. The witch answered the door, and the dyke said, "I'm sorry to bother you, but I've come on a quest. I have a question and had hoped you could help me."

The witch considered for a moment, then asked her in. She made some tea. "What is your question?" asked the witch.

"What is the Real Thing?"

"What?"

"That is my question," answered the dyke, "I fell in love with a beautiful woman, and though she professed some affection for me, she assured me nonetheless that what I felt for her was not the Real Thing."

"And did you ask her her meaning?"

"Yes" said the dyke, "She said that the love between a man and a woman is the Real Thing."

"I see," said the witch, "Well here are your choices. Turn into a man, go to this woman, and say to her this time, "Look I'm a man, and therefore capable of the Real Thing."

"No," said the dyke, "I'm not a man. How can an unreal person feel a real thing?"

"Well then," said the witch, "Get 500 people to go to this woman and say to her loudly that, in their opinion, what you feel for her is the Real Thing."

"No," said the dyke, "I feel what I feel, what difference does it make what other people say they think I feel?"

"It helps," shrugged the witch, "It's known as the Principle of Corroborative Reality. However, here's your third choice. Forget other people and find out for yourself what you really feel."

"I see," said the dyke, "And when and where and how shall I begin?"

"Now?" said the witch and poured tea.

A MORAL TALE

The Beast wasn't a nobleman. The Beast was a woman. That's why its love for Beauty was so monstrous. As a child the Beast had had parents who were both kindly and liberal. "It's not that we disapprove of homosexuals as such, but people disapprove and that's why it grieves us when you think you are one. We want you to be happy, and homosexuals are not happy, and that is the truth."

"Why are they unhappy?"

"Because people disapprove..." The Beast considered these arguments circular, but she discovered, also, that she was unhappy. Boys didn't interest her. She fell in love with a girl. The girl disapproved, and she found that she was now the object of ridicule. She became more and more solitary and turned to books. But the books made it clear that men loved women, and men rode off and had all sorts of adventures and women stayed at home.

"I know what it is," she said one day, "I know what's wrong: I am not human. The only story that fits me at all is the one about the Beast. But the Beast doesn't change from a Beast to a human because of its love. It's just the reverse. And the beast isn't fierce. It's extremely gentle. It loves Beauty, but it lives alone and dies alone."

And that's what she did. Her parent mourned her, and the neighbours were sorry, particularly for her parents, but no one was at fault: she had been warned and she hadn't listened.

DROWNING

Sara L. Knox

KATH KNOWS THAT TOO FAR IS A place from which she will never return; a place she will not even be able to describe to others in a warning phone call. I, on the other hand, know that going too far can be a wrong word; an enquiring look not returned, or a sudden silence at the dinner table. Kath does not see this at all – too far is a place: somewhere she once glimpsed.

By rights, I should never have known Kathleen Constance Kent, but coincidence is habit-forming. She became one of my stories, just as her father before her was converted to a good story by my father, whose penchant for anecdote led him to the bottle. Ray Knox and Bob Kent went to the same Catholic boys school (until my father – the heathen – was expelled); later they would work together at the DSIR. Once, after they'd been out drinking, her father would crash the car they'd borrowed from work. My father pulled himself free, cursing Bob for a blind man. But, being young men who couldnt imagine age, let alone death, they laughed and all was

---

Sara Knox has a long, if irregular, publishing history. Most of the poetry, short fiction and essays she has written have been published in New Zealand where she lived until recently. She is currently completing a PhD on murder narratives in modern American culture at La Trobe University, Melbourne.

Sara won the 1994 Brother/Sister newspaper writing competition with 'Drowning'.

Among the many identities to which she is loyal can be counted: being queer, being a leathergirl, being a youngest child, being as clever and charming as is humanly possible, being a slut, being studious, being lazy, and being blonde. In other words, Sara believes in the diversity of self, as well as the diversity of the communities to which she 'belongs'. Sara has trouble being grown-up and continues going out to clubs far too much for her health. She is possibly the oldest techno-head in existence. Her ambition is to be a TV evangelist in the States.

forgiven. Ray danced in the road while the other survivors searched for unbroken bottles of beer in the overturned car.

The next Friday Bob got uncharacteristically drunk and boasted to my father that he'd once killed a man: he'd drowned an Egyptian in a barrel of oil, one night when he and his boisterous soldier friends decided they didn't like the selling price of some native trinket. Bob seemed proud of this little adventure. My father, appalled, turned his face away, the other man's spittle painting his cheek in spite. Years later, my father told me that he could never understand the joy that showed on Bob's face as he confessed, nor could he fathom the undeniable beauty of the woman that married the bastard. (My father and I agree on many things, not least of which is the loveliness of certain women).

I carried the freight of these stories into my relationship with Bob's youngest daughter, Kath. She, too, went to a good Catholic school. She wore white gloves and a uniform pressed freshly every day. She always walked home flanked by other girls. This mobile armour protected her from our depradations – we who attended what St. Marys students called a slut school. We would loiter at the intersection of Hill and Molesworth streets to light one another's cigarettes; then call the St. Marys girls over for a smoke. If they acknowledged us, we'd yell – as if in second-thought. "Oh no, better not, you'll stain your gloves!" They'd look at us shyly, almost longingly, then hurry on, propelled by the myths of sin the Sisters told. The wind would grab the churchy sound of their school bells and bring it to us as a reproach. Our defiant answer was to smoke furiously, struggling to take more of the cigarette than the wind could. I'd see the Catholic girls turn the corner, hair uplifted and the hems of their skirts beating faint red marks against the backs of their legs.

I didn't remember Kath exactly, although I know she was there. She said she remembered me.

My father guessed who she was from her resemblance to her mother. The day she first met my parents, Dad drove me to the shops so we could talk.

"She's beautiful!" he announced, gravely.

"I know." I replied.

"Like her mother..."

"I know."

What else could one say?

Her hair would fan the pillow about my face when we fucked. For that reason alone I liked her on top. She was completely without candour; could say and do anything: she read my diaries, lied charmingly and stole from me. I loved her without respite. She would sail into the black waters of a bad mood and stay there, becalmed, for days. I would watch her from afar, wishing the wind would blow her back toward me. Sometimes I wished she spoke another language so I could legitimately fail to understand her. Of all of it, her face was like a light. Her beauty held me; it alone was intelligible.

One summer we went to Waiheke Island. Our holidays were a welcome extension to lives already misspent on leisure. We walked the red soil roads that ribboned the hills and avoided the thick greenery of the bush. The sea looked up at us and we down at it, doubtful. We'd had enough of the voyage out - indeed, I had nearly vomited. But the sea began to look forgiving enough as the days wore on. Eventually she suggested we swim.

I saw the idea come to her as we lay sunbathing on the deck of the beach-house. Her brown eyes opened, oblivious to a light that made me squint, even behind dark glasses. She stared up into the blue sky, holding the heat of the sun; storing it away against the cold recesses of her soul.

"Shall we?" She asked, her tone itself an anachronism.

We walked down the track to the beach, which was vast and empty, crossed only by the rider of a trail bike. We averted our faces from the noise of its engine, waiting till it receded behind the plaintiff cry of the oystercatchers that were diving for fish in the bay. I stood by her and shaded my eyes, pretending to watch the birds. She walked from under the flat of my hand, down to the water.

I trailed into the water behind her, not quite sure that I wanted to. Sometimes, particularly when you are stoned, water wraps around you in a way that is anything but soothing - it is claustrophobic. As the sea gobbled up my toes, my feet, then my legs, I remembered every story of drowning, of sharks, of jagged rocks, of cramps. But it was warm, it was summer, and, of course, people do swim.

She swam straight out from the beach, her freestyle messy but efficient. I followed her, sidestroke, determined not to lose my bearings in a wake of water. She swam fast and far, pulling away from me. I trod water for a moment, turning on the spot like a sluggish Peter Pan. The water was deep, for ours was a rocky beach with a steep slide off into the channel of the bay. I did not like not knowing what distance I hung from the ground, regardless of the fact I could not fall to it. I called to Kath again, and, this time, not even the birds cried back. She was further away than she'd been before. I began to swim again, overarm, hating every minute of the thrash and fall of the water. I tried breast-stroke and found that better, more sedate. Then I heard myself thinking out loud, in a breathy voice, that I should turn back to shore. To shut myself up I swam freestyle for a while longer, but navigated poorly. Kath was now not just further ahead but out - south of me - squarely between the arms of the bay. I righted my course and swam onward, not yet tired. I finally caught her just at the point where the bay opened out into the gulf. She was floating on her back, arms outstretched. She seemed surprised when I called out to her, as if she'd come all this way to lose me. Feet descending to tread water, she faced me.

"Aren't we too far out?" I sounded angry, rather than nervous.

"Well, you didnt have to come this far... "

She flicked water out of her eyes, wet dark hair framing her high forehead. I wanted to lecture her about the sea. My father had been a merchant seaman, had seen people drown, had seen them savaged by sharks - he had a healthy respect for the sea. But I didn't want to appear spooked.

So, I suggested we float.

We slid onto the surface of the water, inscribing slow arcs in the sea with our arms and legs. The oystercatchers were keening, and we listened to their trouble without comment. Kath's hair reached through the water to tickle my shoulder. If she had not lured me out there, I could have forgotten her until then.

"Let's start back."

And that was when I felt the tug of the outgoing tide. She had started our run out to the sea, and now the tide was determined to complete it. The sea was syrupy, resisting my attempts to swim shoreward. By my side, at a distance of a metre or so, Kath was trying to tunnel into the stone lip of the sea. She panted. I breathed in a mouthful of water when I turned my head to watch her. We were not getting anywhere. The shore stayed put, deceptively close. Fear conducted easily into my body from the fingers gripping my upper arm.

"Were not going to make it."

I shook her off, indignant, and told her to shut up. We swam and found ourselves where we'd always been. Waiting to drown. She took hold of me again and, this time, I bit her. She flailed away and back, hitting me in the face with the palm of her hand.

"Your father's a murderer! A fucking murderer!" I yelled at the face, lively with fury, veiled by foamy water. And then, being my father's daughter, I gave myself up to the sea - swimming with the tide, rather than against it. I swam along the edge of its pull in the hope that I'd hit the northernmost tip of the point. Eventually I had to swim on a tangent to the tide, fighting the languor in my thighs and shoulders. In one moment of terrifying precognition, I saw myself swept out into the gulf just twenty feet from the rocky spit of the bay. And then I was wading up onto the shore, my body so heavy I felt I'd sink down through shell-encrusted cracks of the rocks. I walked to the uppermost edge of the beach and sat down. Behind me the bush conversed quietly with two Wax eyes. I watched Kath's head, the sunlight flashing occasionally on the plane of a cheek as she swam against the tide for the shore she'd started from. I wondered at that stubbornness. She must, after all, have understood what I meant to do when I started to swim out of the bay.

When I was certain that she could not possibly reach the shore, I ran along the track heading the beach. At the first occupied beach house I managed to panic the middle-aged man who had, till then, been spending a productive afternoon noisily trimming his Manuka windbreak with a chainsaw. He nearly ran out of his jandals in his urgency to launch the motorised dinghy that perched, largely unused, on the rust-stained slipway. I pointed out to him the dark spot on the water that was Kath's head and, shivering, said I could not come out with him. He draped a paint-flecked woollen jersey over my shoulders and went to rescue the drowning girl whose name, for some reason, I'd told him. I could hear him calling, perhaps to calm her, as he cut off the engine and drifted to intercept her. He brought her to shore wrapped in his outsize overalls. The cup of tea he put into her hand threatened to slip out of her grasp, and I ended up having to hold it for her. She drank from it, placid and uncomplaining. She did not look at me. She did not look at me the whole way home, as we sat together in the back of the retired lawyer's four-wheel drive. In bed, she turned her face to the wall and closed her eyes, asleep in a moment.

When finally she did look at me, the next morning, it was with eyes that were full of forgetting. She blinked at the sunlight - her eyes watering, then quickly closing again.

Kathleen left me the following spring, not wanting to sacrifice my warm body in winter. My new lover and I went for a holiday to Waiheke. One night, when we were walking her mother's dog, we found the body of a drowned fisherman on the beach. We ran screaming, while the dog stayed to nestle its nose into its prize. We yelled ourselves hoarse to get it away from there, momentarily forgetting, in our fluster, that the dog only obeyed commands in Maori. "Haere Atu! Haere Atu!" my lover screamed, hands cupped round her lovely mouth. We could not remember the precise command required and had to leave the dog with the body while we went for help.

I accompanied the police to the spot and watched as they pulled the fisherman from his moulding of sand. Water ran from the one tall angler's boot remaining to him. Sand had dried on his cheeks, and had formed a lid on one of his open eyes. After they'd put him in the ambulance and cruised quietly into the dark, without lights or siren, I inspected the man-shaped hole in the damp sand. There I found a sodden handkerchief, a nearly dissolved package of blue Zigzag cigarette papers and the label of a Steinlager bottle. Carefully, I wrapped the last two in the handkerchief, thinking they may be a cryptic message from Kath. I pocketed this damp knot and - trying hard to recall the Maori phrase for "Leave it!" - walked home to another beautiful lover.

Other Publications by City Media Production Services:
'The Night of Your Life - Sydney Gay & Lesbian Mardi Gras': A
photgraphic history of the Sydney Mardi Gras 1978-1993 in
paperback $19.95 and Limited Edition $50.

THERE IS ONLY ONE MARDI GRAS BOOK.

Also by City Media Production Services:
'Planet Rescue' - an extensive stationery range in 100% Australian
recycled papers reflecting the colours of the 'Outback'.